"While many have heard of AIM 1960s and 1970s, most probably warriors and their influence on Indigenous struggles for land and self-determination, then and now. These include the 1974 Ganienkeh land reclamation, which still exists today as sovereign Mohawk territory, the 1990 Oka Crisis, an armed standoff that revived the fighting spirit and warrior culture of Indigenous peoples across North America, and the Warrior Unity flag, a powerful symbol of Indigenous resistance today commonly seen at blockades and rallies. *The Mohawk Warrior Society: A Handbook on Sovereignty and Survival* tells this history in the words of the Mohawks themselves. Comprised of interviews with some of the key participants, as well as *The Warrior's Handbook* and *Rebuilding the Iroquois Confederacy*, both written by Louis Karoniaktajeh Hall, who also designed the Warrior/Unity flag. This book documents the important contributions Mohawk warriors have made to modern Indigenous resistance in North America".
—Gord Hill, Kwakwaka'wakw, author of *500 Years of Indigenous Resistance* and *The Antifa Comic Book*

"This clear and stimulating book had me on edge from beginning to end. No matter who we are, we can learn from these histories of the Iroquois Confederacy as related by its present-day members, lessons pertaining to non-hierarchical political organization and the care of the land. In the age of Black Lives Matter, this work makes the case for autonomous life-spaces free of US or Canadian state control".
—Michael Taussig, Class of 1933 Professor of Anthropology, Columbia University

"*The Mohawk Warrior Society: A Handbook on Sovereignty and Survival* is an excellent collection of stories about colonialism and resistance on Turtle Island—a must read for settler allies seeking to learn and unlearn the histories of colonial violence that structure our contemporary relations. In providing vital histories of state repression and Indigenous resilience, the teachings in this volume can inform all contemporary efforts working towards decolonialization".
—Jeffrey Monaghan, Criminology and Criminal Justice, Carleton University, coauthor of *Policing Indigenous Movements: Dissent and the Security State*

"I've been blessed, because I came to know the Unity Flag by seeing Oka on TV when I was young. When I got married they wrapped us with the flag, it has been a part of all the spiritual ceremonies that I went to, and it has been present at every blockade. Along with the Women's Warrior Flag, it is a symbol that's embedded in our spirit, and it's always been an inspiration. Louis Hall, Ganienkeh, and *The Warrior's Handbook* were way ahead of their time, back when people were just starting to fight back and fighting to get their land back. The intention of *The Warrior's Handbook* and Unity Flag was for all Indigenous nations throughout the hemisphere and the whole world to unite and, first and foremost, to fight. That's why this book is so important; it's something that Louis Hall has gifted to all Red nations."
—Kanahus Freedom Manuel, Indigenous land defender,
Secwepemc Women Warrior Society, Tiny House Warriors

"This is a compelling account of the political struggle for the return of Indigenous thought through the words of those Kaianerehkó:wa Mohawks affiliated with the original 1970s Warrior Society. It offers a trenchant and witty critique of settler colonialism together with a body of teachings aimed at reestablishing balance and harmony. It is for the Kanien'kehá:ka, the Indigenous peoples of Turtle Island and all people troubled by the state of our relations to each other and to the beings of the land that make us, as well as those who care for it."
—Eduardo Kohn, associate professor of anthropology at
McGill University and author of *How Forests Think*

The Mohawk Warrior Society

A Handbook on Sovereignty and Survival

Writings and artwork by Louis Karoniaktajeh Hall

Edited, compiled and annotated by Philippe
Blouin, Matt Peterson, Malek Rasamny
and Kahentinetha Rotiskarewake
in collaboration with the Louis Karoniaktajeh Hall Foundation

Coordinated by Philippe Blouin

BTL

The Mohawk Warrior Society: A Handbook on Sovereignty and Survival
Louis Karoniaktajeh Hall
Edited by Philippe Blouin, Matt Peterson, Malek Rasamny and Kahentinetha
Rotiskarewake
This edition © 2023 PM Press.

ISBN: 978-1-62963-941-3 (paperback)
ISBN: 978-1-62963-955-0 (ebook)
Library of Congress Control Number: 2021945133

Cover by John Yates / www.stealworks.com
Interior design by briandesign

10 9 8 7 6 5 4 3 2 1

PM Press
PO Box 23912
Oakland, CA 94623
www.pmpress.org
Printed in the USA.

Published in Canada in 2023 by
Between the Lines
401 Richmond Street West, Studio 281, Toronto, Ontario, M5V 3A8, Canada
1-800-718-7201
www.btlbooks.com

ISBN: 978-1-77113-601-3

Canadian Cataloguing in Publication information is available from Library and Archives
Canada.

Between the Lines acknowledges the financial support of the Government of Canada; the
Canada Council for the Arts; and the Government of Ontario through the Ontario Arts
Council and Ontario Creates.

Contents

This book is dedicated to all the *Rotihsken'rakéhte'* and their fellow travelers who have been upholding their responsibilities in accordance with the Kaianerehkó:wa before leaving this world in recent years.

Sakoietah James Gray, creator of the women's Warrior flag, designed in honor of his daughter, the late Iewaras Gray
Karoniatenien Mitch Gray, son of Sakoietah
Kakwirakeron Art Montour
Carl "Bo" Curotte
Akwiraienton Arthur "Sugar" Montour
Nikawenna:'a Harriet Boots
Billy "Redwing" Tayak
Jagwadeth Christopher Sandy
Kahentiio Lahache
Kawennaié:ri Janis Horn
Junior David
Dick Hill
and many others

We are an extension of the Earth. We are spirit. We are power.

PART I

An Introduction to Sovereignty and Survival

Editorial Committee

Ken' ní:tsi ionkhró:ri, ken' ní:tsi wakathontè:'on, ken' ní:tsi wakaterièn:tare.
"This is how it was told to me, this is what I have heard, and this is my understanding".

Writing down an oral tradition is a hazardous act which can require haphazard methods. Variations in traditional knowledge caused by the absence of an authoritative written source are ironed out and pinned down into a single narrative to be referenced in the future. Even the most righteous attempts to preserve endangered languages carry the risk of superimposing Western text-based understandings of language, where words are encased in neat boxes referring to definite notions and things, neglecting the ways in which context, history, tone and flow convey meaning. This means "salvaging" an oral tradition may represent the greatest threat to its integrity. Acknowledging this helps us understand why some opacity is often relied upon by holders of Indigenous knowledge: to preserve their traditions from external encroachment and to prevent their dissociation from all the relations and ways of living they enclose.

The tradition followed by the Mohawk warriors who lend their words to this book explicitly entails such cultural resistance. The people that European settlers named Mohawks call themselves the *Kanien'kehá:ka*, the *people of the land of flint*. As the keepers of the Eastern Door of the Rotinonhsión:ni Confederacy, which settlers called the Iroquois or the Six Nations, the Kanien'kehá:ka traditionally live on a territory stretching from the Mohawk River Valley to the Saint Lawrence River and from the Hudson River to the Finger Lakes region. There it meets the other Rotinonhsión:ni territories: the Oneida, the Onondaga, where grand councils convene, the Cayuga, the Tuscarora and the Seneca, who guard the confederacy's Western Door. The Rotinonhsión:ni Confederacy possesses a constitution that comes from precolonial times, the *Kaianerehkó:wa*, often translated as the *Great Law of Peace* or *Great Binding Law*, but more accurately rendered Great Good Footprints, or as the *Great Good Footprints*. When a calamity appears to threaten the Rotinonhsión:ni, the Kaianerehkó:wa instructs them to seek shelter under the Great Swamp Elm (*Onerahté:sons*, or *long leaves*),[1] and "when they shall find it, they shall assemble their heads together and lodge for a time between its roots". Following this protocol, when their language and culture were blatantly outlawed by colonial states, traditional Rotinonhsión:ni people retreated underground. Long refusing to record their thoughts and deeds in writing, they and their traditions were essentially nowhere to be seen. Yet when they did emerge in the historical record, it was in the form of some of the most defiant acts of resistance the North American colonial order has ever faced. Now that the calamity first unleashed against Indigenous peoples has come to threaten all life on Earth, the time has come to speak out.

Though Rotinonhsión:ni philosophy and ways of life are so intimately tied to their language that they simply cannot be translated into English, this book's editorial toolkit makes a novel attempt at the work of translation. By providing a glossary, timeline and background contextualization, we hope this collection will allow readers to better understand the oral testimonies, writings and paintings explaining the origin of the Warrior Society. Rather than shying away from translation, this book's interviews with four of its key members suggest that when the term "Mohawk Warrior Society" was adopted in the late 1960s, it was as the result of a cunning strategy to use the untranslatability of their language to their advantage. As early as 1724, French Jesuit Joseph-François Lafitau witnessed native speakers debating the meaning of *Rotisken'rakéhte*, the Mohawk word for *warriors*, suggesting that it must have been very old. The etymology proposed by Tekarontakeh in this book relates it to the medicine pouch containing the natal soil that Rotinonhsión:ni men receive after their coming of age ritual; in this definition, *Rotisken'rakéhte* translates into *they who carry the earth with them*. Despite differing definitions, what *Rotisken'rakéhte* refers to is unambiguous; it refers to the *council fire of the men*, whose gender role, modeled on the sun, is to provide warmth, light and protection both to the Earth and the women, who are modeled after the Earth. Concretely, this means that the Rotisken'rakéhte must assist and enforce the decisions made by the women's fire, notably in making sure that chiefs do not stray away from the Kaianerehkó:wa. The Rotisken'rakéhte, thus, traditionally act as the watchdogs of the Kaianerehkó:wa, at the behest of the women and at the expense of all instituted authorities. When a group of youngsters set out to rekindle the men's fire in the early 1970s, their respected elder Louis Karoniaktajeh Hall translated *Rotisken'rakéhte* into the *Mohawk Warrior Society*, a gesture consciously intended to evoke the idea of a secret paramilitary society, strategically provoking images and feelings of dread and fear in the mind of the powers that be.

For most non-Native people, the Mohawk Warrior Society immediately brings to mind the series of events that pushed it onto the world stage in 1990. In the spring of that year, land defenders set up camp at an ancestral burial site in the pines of Kanehsatà:ke to defend the land from developers from the adjacent French-Canadian town of Oka, who planned to use that land to expand a golf course. On July 11, Québec police forces raided that camp, and a police officer, Corporal Marcel Lemay, died in the firefight. To support their relatives, Mohawks from Kahnawà:ke blocked the Mercier Bridge crossing their territory, cutting off access to Montréal for eighty thousand commuters—who responded with violent anti-Mohawk riots. Lacking the firepower required to confront the warriors, some of whom had military experience from Vietnam, the Québec provincial police was replaced by more than four thousand soldiers from the Canadian Armed Forces, who immediately placed Mohawk territories under siege. It took seventy-eight days for the army's machine guns, tanks, choppers, jets, boats and allegedly its entire stock of barbed wire to force the warriors to eventually leave the pines. Virtually unfathomable to settler colonial society beforehand, traditional Kaianerehkó:wa people had given the world a glimpse of their existence and their capacity for resistance.[2]

Over the pines of Kanehsatà:ke flew a flag—a flag which has since been seen in almost all Indigenous struggles across the world, from the Zapatistas of Chiapas to the Wet'suwet'en on the West Coast. Displaying an Indigenous warrior wearing a single feather, circled by a sun against a bright red background, the "Unity flag" may have since become the single most famous symbol of Indigenous resistance. Yet to this day few know what it means and how it came to be. This book takes the longest route, with all the necessary detours, to tell its story. The flag's designer, Kahnawà:ke Mohawk Louis Karoniaktajeh Hall, also authored three crucial texts featured in this book—the *Ganienkeh Manifesto* (1974), the *Warrior's*

Handbook (1979) and *Rebuilding the Iroquois Confederacy* (1985). In addition to being a fiery polemicist and a prolific painter knowledgeable in history, philosophy and religion, Karoniaktajeh was a farmer, a butcher, a stone mason and an impressive bodybuilder. Until he passed away in December 1993, at the age of seventy-six, Karoniaktajeh dedicated his life to rebuilding his people's confederacy, originally intended to be extended to all nations as a formula for world peace.

Karoniaktajeh and the Mohawk Warrior Society fought and won several battles on the long path leading to the 1990 Oka Crisis. According to Atetonriatakon's testimony in this book, the first sign of the modern revival of the Rotihsken'rakéhte' was in 1968, with the blockade of the international border bridge that divides Akwesasne between the United States and Canada. Adopting the name "Mohawk Warrior Society" in the following years, the Rotihsken'rakéhte' gained traction and support throughout the 1970s, victoriously staging an armed reoccupation of Ganienkeh in New York State in 1974, obliging the Canadian government to fund their Indigenous schools and establishing a flourishing network of tax-free businesses to relinquish dependency on social welfare.[3] The funds that this allowed the warriors to raise contributed to the defense of their territories. In guarding them from external attacks, the Warrior Society was to reservations what the American Indian Movement (AIM) was to urban-based Indigenous peoples out west. The warriors also nurtured diplomatic relationships with the Black Panther Party, the Chicano Brown Berets and left-wing revolutionary groups all across North America and beyond, while simultaneously reaching out to the United Nations (UN) to defend their claims to Indigenous autonomy on a global stage.

For the contemporary Warrior Society, the Kaianerehkó:wa tradition they uphold has deep roots in precolonial history. Due in part to their crucial geographic position, nestled between the key watersheds connecting the Atlantic Ocean to the Great Lakes, the Rotinonhsión:ni played a central role as the largest Indigenous political, military and economic force the British and French colonial forces had to reckon with. European colonists were immediately fascinated by the elaborate matrilineal kinship system, consensual decision-making protocols and extensive diplomatic alliances of the Rotinonhsión:ni. Early travelers' accounts portrayed the Iroquois as living in an ideal primeval state where freedom and equality prevailed, an image that inspired the European Enlightenment's conceptualization of the state of nature. Eventually, the Sons of Liberty would don Mohawk costumes while throwing English tea into the Boston Harbor, while Benjamin Franklin would consult Rotinonhsión:ni elders when drafting the 1754 Albany Plan, which partly served as a blueprint for the Articles of Confederation (1770) and the US Constitution (1780).[4] As a living example of how a confederal system based on consensus and mutual liberty may indeed exist and thrive, it would seem that the Kaianereh'kó:wa tradition, once deemed savage, actually helped to provide the revolutionary inspiration that sparked the modern world.

There were certain differences, however, between the Kaianereh'kó:wa's intricate system of checks and balances and the ideas eventually picked up by modern democracies. For instance, the Kaianerehkó:wa vests the women with the exclusive role of appointing and deposing the *Rotiianérshon* (chiefs). Rather than being chiefs or leaders, whom the colonial mindset imagines as making decisions instead of their people, the Rotiianérshon are merely speakers; they have no coercive power, as their authority depends entirely on the consensus of the families they represent. The Kaianerehkó:wa is based on a concentric organization of council fires, or assemblies of matrilineal families, also referred to as clans. The very word for *family*, *Kahwá:tsire'*, refers to *a fire*, or literally the *gathering of all embers*, each person being an ember, an *Ó:tsire'*. When the matrilineal family reaches a consensus, their *Roiá:ner* (*chief*) brings their resolutions before the national council, and then before the *big fire*, the *Katsenhowá:nen*, of the confederacy. This way of organizing, bringing people to deliberate together until a consensus is reached before debating things at a higher level, has the effect of ensuring a straight line between political institutions and the people for whom they speak.

Most importantly, as the basis of Rotinonhsión:ni society, clan kinship is based on nature both as a symbol to aspire to and as the reality that humans live within. The three main Kanien'kehá:ka clans, whose interactions account for the decision-making dynamic in council, are modeled according to the habits and abilities of specific animals. The role of the Turtle Clan, *Ratiniáhton*, is to carefully consider the long-term continuity of the people and the Earth, which the Rotinonhsión:ni creation story recounts as being "on top of a turtle", *A'nowarà:ke*, also known as *Turtle Island*. Lacking fangs or claws, the turtle is slow, but it has to make quick decisions as to whether it has time to jump in the water or should pull its head, legs and tail into its shell; its role, therefore, involves careful decision-making. The word for the Wolf Clan, *Ronathahión:ni*, indicates that it is a *path-maker*, looking ahead as a scout or a sentinel, and in this capacity often being mindful of diplomatic relations with outsiders. As the wolf does not hibernate, it knows how to survive in all seasons, making it a perfect candidate for putting together the council's agenda. The resolutions decided upon are then handed over to the Bears, whose clan name, *Rotiskaré:wake*, refers to the *honeycomb* which bears are constantly looking for in the bush, climbing up trees and digging holes to do so. This suggests that the role of the Bear Clan is more analytical in nature, as they know the lay of the land and the possible obstacles that could be in the way. By bringing these perspectives together, Kanien'kehá:ka councils do not merely take nature as a metaphor for human life: they ground social life in the roles provided by nature, as humans are indeed part of that very nature upon which their survival depends.

To understand who the Kanien'kehá:ka are as a people, one must abandon the European model of the "nation" as a corporation-like body ruling over a territory and, rather, consider the people as belonging to their territory—in this case *Kanièn:ke*, the *land of flint*. Unlike the Western concept of sovereignty, which implies a legitimacy to own and rule over a land and all its human and non-human inhabitants, the Native sovereignty to which the present handbook refers is made up of both the freedom and the responsibility to live with the land and ensure the continuity of nature. This is evidenced by the fact that not only does every Roiá:ner have his own animal-based title, outlining his specific duties and responsibilities, but so does every single person, as babies receive unique names when they start showing their unique perspectives in the world. The coinciding freedom and responsibility vested in every individual's specific perspective accounts for the true meaning of sovereignty expressed in the word *Tewatatewenní:io*, meaning *we are all free/sovereign* or *we all carry ourselves*. Each person is responsible for society and nature and vice versa. Humans, nature and society are all inherently free, with each unique freedom being inseparable from its attendant responsibility.

When the natural freedom captured in Tewatatewenní:io is coupled with the notion of *Sha'tetionkwátte'*, meaning *we are equal in height*, one wonders if it is a mere coincidence that Iroquoian languages possess idiomatic expressions for the very two concepts in whose name modern democracy was allegedly established. One can imagine the tremendous influence of such Native conceptions on early European settlers used to living under the yoke of hierarchies based on divine right. However, settler colonial society did not return the favour. Its divide and rule tactics sowed discord within the confederacy, as some groups sided with the French, while others cast their lot with the English, or eventually the Americans— who ended up killing off and expelling most Rotinonhsión:ni people from their homelands. Colonial bodies of governance were gradually imposed on Rotinonhsión:ni territories, resulting in a complicated meshwork of overlapping colonial and traditional jurisdictions. As Indigenous peoples were subjugated into "domestic dependent nations" over the course of the nineteenth century, their traditional homelands were grabbed up by settlers and speculators. The remaining Native territories were divided into reservations, as lands "reserved" for their use, until assimilation policies, such as residential schools, would ensure the "vanishing race" disappeared for good. To control these reservations, band councils were imposed in Canada and tribal councils in the United States. Their chiefs would be elected following the majority-decision model of Western nation-states rather than the Native way based on consensus within and between clans. Thereafter, colonial governments would only recognize their own creations, the band and tribal councils, as legitimate interlocutors, in charge of administering the funds upon which Native peoples came to depend after having been forcibly deprived of their traditional means of subsistence.

Alongside these colonial governing bodies, a multitude of Rotinonhsión:ni longhouses continued to practice their traditional ways both publicly and underground, with several longhouses within the same community often proposing different interpretations of the Kaianerehkó:wa. This complex political landscape often baffled outside observers trying to make sense of the "authenticity" of Rotinonhsión:ni traditions. In particular, nineteenth-century anthropologists, such as Lewis Henry Morgan, found themselves at pains to distinguish the precolonial Kaianerehkó:wa from later cultural hybrids, particularly the 1799 Handsome Lake Code, a syncretic religion that inserted into Rotinonhsión:ni spirituality Christian notions of patriarchy, sin, confession and repentance. Yet as the Handsome Lake Code replaced the Kaianerehkó:wa in Seneca country and elsewhere, others maintained a firm resistance to the slightest sign of Christian influence by, for instance, continuously using the word *creation* instead of the *Creator*. It is from these staunchly traditional families that what came to be known as the "Mohawk Warrior Society" arose.

Much like his strategic translation of Rotihsken'rakéhte', Louis Karoniaktajeh Hall's words, which are the centerpiece of this book, must be understood, first and foremost, as defensive weapons in the psychological war waged against the minds of his people. It is in this capacity that he engaged his ancient traditions with modern means of representation, rivaling Western propaganda and advertising techniques with his bold and bright colors, provocative graphics and tongue-in-cheek punch lines. Relying on the natural law of survival and self-preservation, his texts are a spiritual call to resistance. They are not just meant to be read: they are handbooks, meant to be enacted, upheld, shouted and sung, just as his paintings and posters were to be hung, plastered and distributed from one corner of Turtle Island to the other. His words, thus, fulfill the same function as a War Dance, lifting the "fighting spirit" of his people, as a medicine for surviving a war of extermination. Keeping this in mind helps to make sense of Karoniaktajeh's use of humour, irony, mock epic poetry and self-made words and acronyms as part of his written medicine. It also helps explain why he attacks such ideas as the Bering Strait theory, less because of its peer-to-peer scientificity than because of its psychological effects in a context where colonial academics have often undermined the idea that Amerindian peoples naturally and fully belong to their land. Finally, it helps us understand the anger he harbors for organized religions, and for the Handsome Lake Code in particular, held responsible for taming the fighting spirit of his people into subservience.

Yet despite Karoniaktajeh's polemical stances, his work is actually full of very nuanced contradictions. He challenged tradition by supporting women bearing arms and engaging in military training, which was prohibited and discouraged by many traditional chiefs during his time. He staunchly upheld the Kaianerehkó:wa but mocked the taboo around reading it only in ceremonial settings, actively working with Kahentinetha and Ganyetahawi to establish a new version of his people's constitution in text and film formats before he passed away. In matters of economics, Karoniantakejeh argued for the re-establishment of the traditional cooperative economy of his people, attacking the selfish destructive nature of American capitalism but also recognizing the way communist governments systematically revert into autocracy and inequality. As he astutely put it, "It seems that no matter what type of 'ism' the people attach to their government the fascists take over". For him, the only remedy was for his people to revive and adapt their ancestral ways of living and thinking.

This book is both a compendium of oral tradition and a handbook for struggle. It sheds light on the cultural roots of the Mohawk Warrior Society in and on its own terms, shaped as they were in the 1970s by Louis Karionaktatieh Hall and voiced today by its survivors and fellow travelers. Highlighting their specific story as it was shaped mostly in Kahnawà:ke, Akwesasne and Ganienkeh, this book should not be taken as an exhaustive nor definitive representation of all warrior traditions present within Rotinonhsión:ni society. This is why this book opens with the customary Kanien'kehá:ka caveat: "This is how it was told to me, this is what I have heard, and this is my understanding." Even though the legacy of the Mohawk warriors for the overall movement for Native sovereignty can hardly be overstated, their story remains largely obscure to outsiders, as their underlying philosophy and background history have seldom made it into print. With its exclusive oral histories, archival documents, paintings, concept glossary, map with Indigenous place names and historical timeline, this book is intended to correct this state of affairs. Our hope is that this work may be a remedy to the lack of source material that has led many to present the Warrior Society as a band of rogue bandits, gangsters and the like. In their own words, rather than selling drugs, warriors arrested drug dealers and preserved their communities from their devastating effects. Rather than simply accruing capital for themselves, they shared it with struggling Indigenous peoples all across the continent, purchasing equipment for hospitals and sports teams.

Apart from appendices and the present introduction, external work on the manuscript has been limited to introducing explanatory footnotes and harmonizing the written form of Indigenous words. Amplifying the voices of the Rotihsken'rakéhte', whose powerful words speak for themselves, has been the main objective of this collaborative project from the start. Upholding the notion of alliance through separation conveyed by the *Teiohá:te* (Two Row Wampum), non-Indigenous editors for this project have focused on assisting and facilitating the transmission of this history to audiences who may have only learned about the Mohawk Warrior Society through defamatory news reports or objectifying academic research. We ourselves only discovered how many false conceptions were hanging in the air when we visited Mohawk reservations and spoke with some of the most insightful and profound thinkers we have met. The teachings we were exposed to concern not only the original peoples of Turtle Island but all human beings who struggle with the devastating effects of the war being waged on the natural world and traditional ways of living in harmony with it. As with the writings of Karionaktatieh, we hope this book will provide inspiration in the quest for true peace, both among ourselves and with the Earth we call home.

Notes

1   Refer to the "Skakwatakwen—Concept Glossary" section at the end of this volume for definitions of Indigenous concepts.

2   In Canada, the "Oka Crisis" had the effect of bringing Indigenous issues and policies of "reconciliation" to the forefront, in the hopes of preventing further bloodshed.

3   These tax-free businesses, including casinos, gas, tobacco and more recently cannabis dispensaries, led to accusations of smuggling and racketeering on the part of law enforcement. But what the governments of Canadian and United States consider smuggling, the Rotinonhsión:ni consider the movement of goods across their traditional territory, and what law enforcement considers racketeering is based on the presumption of Native peoples having to pay taxes as American or Canadian citizens, a designation the Rotinonhsión:ni have always fought to reject.

4   The Iroquois also participated in the Albany Conference of 1775 and the Continental Congress of 1776. The notion that individual colonies were allowed to retain their own constitutions while joining the United States bears much resemblance to the way in which Rotinonhsión:ni nations conserve their freedom in domestic matters, while allying with the confederacy.

PART II

An Oral History of the Warrior Society

—

This section gathers testimonies from some of the most prominent actors of the original Mohawk Warrior Society, recounting the origins and development of the revival of this traditional organization in the 1960s through the 1990s. These edited transcripts from interviews conducted between 2015 and 2021 with warriors Tekarontakeh, Kakwirakeron, Kanasaraken and Ateronhiatakon share the untold story of how the Mohawk Warrior Society came to be one of the most daunting Indigenous resistance groups in the Americas, whose daring actions—land reoccupations, armed self-defence, economy building, etc.—would inspire generations to come and compel colonial states to reckon with the social force and political weight of Indigenous sovereignty.

Tekarontakeh Interview

Tekarontakeh Paul Delaronde is a Kanien'kehá:ka from the Wolf Clan. He was raised speaking his native language by traditional grandparents from Kahnawà:ke, who had been part of an effort during the 1950s to re-establish an autonomous traditional community in the Mohawk River Valley, his people's original homeland. These childhood experiences helped Tekarontakeh develop the crucial knowledge and understanding of his people's traditional ways, which he inherited from his elders. His profound attachment to Indigenous independence brought him into various confrontations with colonial authorities at an early age. He played a leading role in rekindling the fire of the Rotihsken'rakéhte' (Mohawk Warrior Society) in the early 1970s. Since then, Tekarontakeh has taken part in virtually all the major struggles of the Rotihsken'rakéhte' up until the 1990s. Today, he travels throughout Rotinonhsión:ni (Iroquois) territory and beyond, imparting some of the ancestral wisdom that he received directly from his grandparents and elders. Tekarontakeh's fluency in his native language, his intimate knowledge of the Kaianerehkó:wa (Great Peace) and his vast personal experience building Mohawk autonomy in the late twentieth century make him an invaluable resource in better comprehending both the history of his people and the uniqueness and depth of their traditional political philosophy and worldview.

The Rotihsken'rakéhte' and the Kaianerehkó:wa

There was no such thing as a Warrior Society in our past or in terms of how we lived. The men were called Rotihsken'rakéhte', and they had a responsibility modeled after the sun. The sun helps support our mother, the Earth, bringing forth life. The sun is there to give warmth and protection so that the young ones can grow and life can continue. Not just for the humans, but for all the creatures of life. We follow what creation showed us, which we call *Sha'oié:ra*. Some people say *Sha'oié:ra* means *natural*, but not how the white man understands it. When we say *Sha'oié:ra*, it means the *direction creation goes*. We always follow the examples of creation, because it has shown us from the beginning of time that it continues to exist and goes on, bringing forth life. It is a cycle set forth by creation, where there is always a renewal of life. Through these cycles, we humans perceive the everlasting continuation of life itself. So we say that we travel in the direction of the creation: Sha'oié:ra is a natural way, the way of creation.

As men, our responsibility is to be like the sun, to reinforce what the mothers tell the children. With our light, we help to educate the children. We help them to see, and we point things out to them. Whether we are a father, an uncle, an older brother or a grandfather, it is our responsibility to give children the best education for life. I should not say "education", because it's the "knowledge of life". I remember the first day I was going to school my grandfather said to me *Tóhsa sathón:tat naiesa'nikonhráhkhwa*. I was just a little kid then, and I didn't know what it meant, but I learned what it meant: *don't allow them to take your protection*, which is your mind. We call the mind *O'nikòn:ra'*, which literally means *that which takes care of you*; and we say *Sa'nikòn:rare*, meaning *it watches over you, it takes care of you, it is cautious of you*. If you exercise and use your mind, it will help you and protect you. You should not let somebody else use your mind: creation gave it to you; it is yours to use.

In our language, the word that translates into *warrior, Rotihsken'rakéhte'*, means, *they who carry the Earth with them*.[1] When a boy reaches a certain age, and his voice starts changing, his female relatives who took care of him as a child pass him over to his uncles, and he undergoes his rite of passage ceremony. He has to fast for four days and nights, and when he is done his uncles ask him what he learned from his experience, if there is an idea or a vision that stood out in his mind while he was fasting. He might have seen a hawk or a bear come to him, something that will become his symbol, his totem. Then one of his female relatives makes a medicine pouch for him, where she puts three articles: something that symbolizes the vision he had when he was fasting, his umbilical cord, which his female relatives kept and dried when he was born, and a handful of soil from his mother, the Earth. From then on, he will hang his medicine bag on his neck or his waist to keep his mother close to him and to remind him of his duties and responsibilities to his family, to the people and to the land. The women do not carry a medicine bag, because they are already one with the Earth, as *Ka'nisténhsera'*, or *life-givers*. But the role model for the men is the sun, our eldest brother. We are the supporters of the women, and we carry the Earth with us, just like the sun carries the vision of the Earth when it passes through the sky.

When a man fails to take responsibility for his relatives, we say *Wahshakotewén:tehte*, meaning *he leaves them in the dark*. It refers to the first glimmer of light in the morning, the twilight. Since the men's role model is the sun, their responsibility to their family is the same as the responsibility of the sun to the Earth. The Earth will produce life, and she will do her best to protect and raise that life, but she needs the support of the sun. So when we say *Wahshakotewén:tehte*, it means that he has prevented the sunlight's warmth, light, protection and reinforcement from reaching the Earth and his family. The women are rooted in the Earth. When the women dance, they shuffle their feet without leaving the ground. Whereas when the men dance, their feet leave the ground, because they are not connected to the Earth in the same way as the women. As I said, the men are like the sun. One day the sun is shining, and another day the sun is not shining. So the men's feet go back and forth, like the sun shining upon the Earth.

Today, people say they carry out the ceremonies, but they are not ceremonies of worship: they are festivals for the people to recall our history and to remind us of what we have learned. We enjoyed peace at different times of our history, but the peace was often broken, because human beings tend to develop amnesia; they forget about the things that make life suitable. The first time in our history that we can remember the peace being broken, our people came up with a festival called the *Atón:wa*. It was to teach the people to start respecting each other and appreciate what each person does and how we contribute to our collective well-being. Notably, this ceremony reminded the people that they need to love each other and work together and reaffirm the peace among themselves, both as individuals and as a people. So our people did this, but we moved away from this peace in time. We started fighting, and the wars began once again.

So our people came up with another ceremony to complement the first one. This one was called *Kanenhó:ron*, or the *Seed Festival*. It consists of a drum dance and a thanksgiving address to all elements of creation that provide role models for human life. The Kanenhó:ron reminded the people of the first ceremony, about how people had to get along and how things survived because we worked in harmony. This ceremony placed nature as our example to help us maintain the peace which we were instructed to uphold in the first ceremony. It taught us that the Earth and our women are the same, and that the men are like the sun. The thunders and the winds are like our grandfathers; they bring the rain, constantly renewing life for us and constantly showing us, reminding us and teaching us. The moon, she is like our grandmother with all her wisdom. She is the one who determines how the children will be born, she is the one who watches and manages the cycle of the women each month, and she is the one who tells us what seeds to put in the ground and when. Then there are our immediate cousins, the waters, who support us every day. Then we have our distant cousins, the stars, who are always there to guide us and to remind us of our ways. The Kanenhó:ron showed the people how all creation sustains us, how all these things come at different times, at the correct times, and how they all work together. That is why we refer to the strawberries, the blueberries, the acorns, the pecans and all the foods that grow as our sisters. We call the foods that we cultivate our *younger* sisters: the corn, the beans and the squash in all their different varieties. We have to cultivate them to help them become equal to the strawberries, the *older* sister, who already knows how to take care of herself. That was pointed out to our people, and it brought them back together.

Then a third time, yet again, things got bad. The *Kaientowá:nen* was created to remind us that to have the things we want, we must work for them. Things do not just happen; we must make them happen. For things to work, we must *make* them work! The *Kaientowá:nen* is known as *the peach stone/bowl game*, but it is not a game; it has no winners or losers. The Kaientowá:nen is a time when we come together and enjoy ourselves, and we play this game, and we put everything we have into it. The idea is that we must give the best of ourselves to benefit. It was meant to tell us that we cannot expect to sit under a tree and think creation will feed us and do everything for us; we are responsible. If your family is hungry, you have to go out there and work and ensure your family has what it needs. So everybody has some form of responsibility, and all of us have the responsibility to pass this knowledge on to our children to make sure that they have a good life. The Kaientowá:nen reminds us that the Earth has provided everything we need to live. The world is perfect. But we have to work with all these things that she provided for us. If things do not go as expected, we have to learn from our experience.

However, as generations went by, our people started fighting again. This last time is when Dekanawida, Hiawatha and Jigonhsasee unified the Rotinonhsión:ni Confederacy and re-empowered the women, according to the story. They brought us the *Ostowa'kó:wa*, the *Great Feather Dance*, to remind us that the first, second and third festivals come together. Something was needed to *bind* together the three principles from each festival—peace among the people, harmony through the living example of nature and giving the best of ourselves—so that these principles could never be separated again. They come together in the same way that life cannot continue if the sun stops shining or the rain stops pouring. The Ostowa'kó:wa bound these principles by establishing a formula for people to resolve their differences within longhouse council, which became our constitution, the Kaianerehkó:wa. This is why sometimes, in English, they translate the *Kaianerehkó:wa* as the *Great Binding Law*. But it has nothing to do with "law", it refers to binding the principles of life. In a literal sense, it means something closer to the *footprints for the great good*.

Today, some people have been taught to believe that the physical building of the longhouse is sacred. However, it has never been about the physical building of the longhouse. We use the word *longhouse* symbolically. The length of the longhouse extends from where the sun rises to where the sun sets. The Earth is its floor, the four directions are its walls, the sky is its ceiling. The longhouse buildings are just there to keep us out of the cold, rain and snow! The longhouse became the symbol of our confederacy when forty-nine families came together to accept the Kaianerehkó:wa. The British referred to us as the "Five Nations", and the French referred to us as the "Iroquois". However, we have always referred to ourselves as the *Rotinonhsión:ni*, the *people of the longhouse*.

Following the Kaianerehkó:wa, the longhouse would have three sides. Two sides would debate the issues, while the third side would sit and listen. Whenever the two sides could not "come to one mind", the third side of the house would break the deadlock. Nevertheless, there had to be a consensus. So when a decision is made, the tiebreaker does not rule until all our minds have come to accept the decision.[2] Otherwise, you would have a majority ruling a minority, which means a divided house. Our people would not allow for that division to happen, so if they could not come to a decision, they would tell everyone to go home, sleep on it and address it again at a later date, after they would have acquired more information. That does not mean that we will all think the same, only that we will arrive at something we can all accept. We say *Tentewatate'nikonhrí:sake*, meaning *we will search within each other's minds for the truth*. Everyone has something specific to bring to the discussion, and when we feel that we have come to an agreement, we still have to "stir the ashes" to find out what everybody thinks. This is how consensus is achieved in our society. This method of deliberation was intended to be extended to all Native peoples. And when the Europeans came, this formula was extended to them too. The Dutch, Germans, French, British and Americans—it was extended to all.

Who We Are

Native people always identify themselves by the land on which they live. For instance, the Kanien'kehá:ka are not Kanien'kehá:ka people. As we inhabit *Kanièn:ke*, the *land of flint*, we are *Kanien'kehá:ka*, the *people of the land of flint*. Next to us are the *Oneida*, who refer to themselves as the *Onyota'a:ká*, the *people of the standing stone*. Then, there are the *Onondaga*, or *Onöňda'gaga'*, the *people of the land of hills*, and the *Cayuga*, the *Gayogohó:nǫ'* the *people of the marshlands or swamplands*. Finally, the *Onöndowa'ga:'*, also called the *Seneca*, are the *people of the big hills* or *mountains*. We always refer to ourselves by the land we inhabit. We can go to any part of the land to hunt, fish and gather medicines to support our family, and nobody in the other territories can keep us from doing it, because they do not own the land. They do not own the animals. They do not own the fish. They do not own the trees. They do not own anything. All the peoples in the Western Hemisphere looked at the land as our mother. She is *one* mother: the mother of us all. Just because we speak different languages or have different ceremonies and cultures does not mean that she is no longer our mother. That is why we never had borders. When the white man came here to the Americas, he was amazed that we had no standing armies to protect our territories. The idea of territories and borders came to us from across the ocean. They said that the Mohawks, Oneidas and Algonquins were separate nations, but that is not the way we think. The land is our mother. We cannot own our mother; we merely have use of her. That is why land could never be sold. We could never give our mother away or cut her into pieces.

We are Kanien'kehá:ka, but, more than that, we are *Onkwehón:we*. We use that word for all Native peoples, but it does not exactly mean *original people* or *real people*. It means something closer to the *people of the original way*, the *way of forever* or *the way of creation*. *Ón:kwe* means the *people*, and *ón:we* means *forever*, in the sense that creation is forever.[3] As we were put here originally, we would always maintain the original ways. This had always been our way, but, when the Europeans came, they brought and instilled new ways among our people. The Europeans brought their religions, turning us into a people of faith and, thus, putting our fate in someone else's hands. They worked to find ways in which we would not resist, defend or protect ourselves but only comply instead. This happened to our people throughout Turtle Island for generations,[4] although there were always families that never relinquished their knowledge and their ways. Many of these families had to go underground to preserve that knowledge.

The Roots of Resistance

By the turn of the century, many people could no longer practice their traditional ways here in Kahnawà:ke. We lost our songs, dances and ceremonies. Before 1924, they raided our ceremonies like some drug bust.[5] My grandmother would tell me that if Christians in the community heard them practicing, they would call the Royal Canadian Mounted Police (RCMP), who would come to beat people up and arrest them for carrying out their traditional thanksgivings. If we were going to express our thanks, they wanted it to be in the village, in the church, using the white man's God to show our thanks. But we knew that was not our way, so we continued underground, hidden in the woods. After 1924, the colonial powers must have thought we had finally lost our traditions, so they stopped the raids. At that time, most of us did not know our traditional songs and dances anymore, so we turned to our brothers and sisters in the other territories and gathered all the pieces to put the puzzle back together. Our brothers and sisters from the other Mohawk communities helped us to regain our traditions and re-establish the Kaianerehkó:wa, and in 1928 a new Kaianerehkó:wa longhouse was built in Kahnawà:ke.[6]

As a kid, I used to hear old-timers talking about what they went through. I was just a little guy at that time, but I listened diligently. The moccasin telegraph was better back then than it is today.[7] We always knew what was happening, because our people would constantly carry news across our communities. That is how I learned about how our ways were revived in Ohswé:ken in the 1950s.[8] I knew some revivers like Lawrence Nanticoke, Elwood Green, Coleman Powless and Dick Hill when I was young.[9] They were trying to revive the Rotihsken'rakéhte' so the men could organize themselves and fulfill their duties and responsibilities. That is the first time I remember the Rotihsken'rakéhte' being revived in modern times. The RCMP frequently attacked traditional people from Ohswé:ken back then. They were beaten up and thrown in jail, because they had tried to take back the Council House and place the rightful government of our people back in power.[10] In those days, the Canadian government did not fear hurting or even killing Native people, so they just came in and beat us up whenever they wanted to.

At that time, the Saint Lawrence Seaway was being built in Kahnawà:ke.[11] It was catastrophic, because it cut us off from the Saint Lawrence River, where we fished and boated freely. The seaway ended all agriculture and farming on our land, and they have never been restored. Before the seaway, there were no fences in our community. All the animals, cows and sheep, ran freely. The seaway put an end to this way of life. In the 1950s, Kahnawà:ke was almost entirely controlled by the Church, making resistance against the seaway non-existent or very weak. Only a few families tried to stop it, and my family was one of them. My grandparents' home was directly in the way of the canal they were trying to build. At one point, the Army Corps of Engineers were ready to use dynamite to get them out of their farmhouse. Other family members convinced them to leave, and the Army Corps blew the place up as soon as they left the house. It had already been set up to blow while my grandparents were still in the house! My grandfather, Louis Diabo,[12] was one of the real activists back then. He was a longhouse chief, a Roiá:ner.

Louis Diabo and five others went to Ottawa to protest the seaway. The minister asked them, "Why are you the only ones objecting to this?" My grandfather said, "No, we are not. We have been having meetings in our community, and everybody is against this". The minister pulled out a book and showed him all the names of people of Kahnawà:ke who were supposedly ready to sell their lands to make way for the seaway. My grandfather got upset with those who did that and said, "I do not want to live among traitors and liars". So he packed up our family and went to other communities to ask who would join him in starting a new life away from those backstabbers. Few people were willing to take the initiative. There were two families from Akwesasne, our family here in Kahnawà:ke and a few others from different places who ended up going along, and that is how a small group took over some land in the Mohawk River Valley in the late 1950s.[13] I was about five years old at the time.

We moved near Fonda, New York, right on the Schoharie River. We built homes and a longhouse and started farming. The men in our community continued to be ironworkers, laborers and part-time workers in nearby towns. We did not have any government funding; we had nothing. My grandfather knew that it would be useless to make a land claim, so we just went in and occupied the land. We stayed there for about a year before we were taken to court. Most people who came there only spoke our language; only a few could speak English. We did not want to take it to court, but we were dragged there, and the judge decided to evict us.

From there, we went to Onondaga, where we stayed for a year. My grandfather did not want to come back to Kahnawà:ke, but the family encouraged my grandparents to come home. Finally, after much coaxing, we came back. Nevertheless, we continued our fight to revive and teach people who we are. My family was always fighting against the Indian Act system imposed upon our people,[14] and we continued to push for our language to remain strong. We were able to get help from our friends in Onondaga and Ohswé:ken to get our songs and dances back. My brother, cousins and I practiced singing and dancing every day, thus, reviving our songs and dances in Kahnawà:ke. Our generation got a lot of encouragement and teachings from home. Growing up and being raised by my grandparents, we heard a lot of older people talk about things from a long time ago. All of this was explained to us in our language, which we learned. We were always at the longhouse when we were teenagers, listening to the council and grand council discussions. Our grandparents took us to every meeting in Ohswé:ken, Tyendinaga, Onondaga or any other place that hosted an important meeting. We sat and listened as well as children could listen, and we learned a lot. We heard about our rights as humans, as Onkwehón:we, about our land and about the political system, language, culture and religion that were forced upon us.

One thing the older generation would never do was to tell us what to do. They shared with us all their knowledge, all their experiences, and they left it up to the younger generation to make of that knowledge what we could. So us younger ones, we listened to the old-timers telling us that this is our home, that we have responsibilities, that we have our rights. Being fifteen or sixteen years old, we did not have the diplomatic experiences that the old-timers had. They used to say, "Let's send a letter to Albany, send a letter to Washington, send a letter to Ottawa". That's what they used to do. They had paper tigers being sent out there, but the paper tigers had no teeth. We were the first generation to get really physical.

Reviving the Rotihsken'rakéhte'

In the past, if somebody needed help building a house, barn or whatever, the singing society would announce that assistance was needed for a house building, farm raising or big haying day. There, they would sing for everybody while the people worked and celebrated; people would come to hear them at the particular event where they were singing. People would bring lumber, nails, tools, windows, doors and help build. Then they would have a big meal, and the singers would sing, and everybody would dance and enjoy themselves. The singing societies were well known for doing that. Sometimes there would be several different singing societies in attendance. One group would have their set of songs, another would have their own, and they would share songs. The little kids would learn verses from the different songs, and eventually they would create their own singing group.

By the end of the 1960s, we had formed a singing society, just a few of us getting together to sing. Then we decided, "Why don't we rekindle the Rotihsken'rakéhte'?" So we went to the council in Kahnawà:ke and asked the *Rotiianérshon* (chiefs) if they would ratify us, sanction us to become, once again, the Rotihsken'rakéhte'. The Rotiianérshon said, "No", and when we asked, "Why not?" they said, "We don't have the authority. Creation gives you authority; you already have it. The authority is in the Kaianerehkó:wa. It's your responsibility, your duty, to do this. You don't need our 'okay'". So we did it; we rekindled our fire as "the men's fire". We started traveling to the other communities and discussed rekindling the local fires and rebuilding our people. The momentum just kept growing and growing. There were only seven of us at the time. We asked Karoniaktajeh, Louis Hall, the artist who made a crest for our singing society, to create a new one for the Rotihsken'rakéhte'. What he did was beautiful, so beautiful that it became the crest on our Unity flag, the one we use today.

Louis Hall was not a longhouse person at the beginning. He was initially a very devout Catholic on his way to joining the priesthood. One day, he came across some Bible material that caused him to question his beliefs. He started looking into it more until he uncovered many contradictions in the Christian teachings. He used to argue with the longhouse people while promoting Christianity, and then one day he became interested in finding out more about the Kaianerehkó:wa. There were many intelligent men in Louis Hall's generation, like Frank Natawe, Roy Montour and Stanley Myiow. They were all fluent speakers of our language and English, and Frank could speak French. They would sit at their beer table and discuss the Kaianerehkó:wa. Then they started showing up at the longhouse. They would listen, observe and watch and were reinstated into the confederacy at the longhouse. It was a tremendous boost for the people of the longhouse when that happened. These men could write, speak and teach, and they were quick learners. They were knowledgeable in history—not just our history but also world history and Christian history. I sat in Louis Hall's house when different cardinals or bishops would come from Montréal and try to debate him. I saw him sit down with Presbyterians, Methodists, Lutherans. Nobody could beat him in a debate; it was crazy! They would all walk out with their tails between their legs, because they could not keep up with him; he knew more about their religion than they did.

When he gave us our crest, Karoniaktajeh explained some things to us about psychological warfare. He told us stories about the battle of the Plains of Abraham, near Québec City, when the French were defeated.[15] It was not the British who defeated them; it was the Iroquois. Actually, the French defeated themselves. All those young soldiers growing up in France had always been told that the Iroquois were "devil people". Now, they were young soldiers sent over here, and they had never seen any Iroquois; they had only imagined them in fear from what had been taught to them. During that battle, the French outnumbered the British, but they had no idea that hundreds of Iroquois warriors were at the British garrison. They came marching at each other, as soldiers did back then, and fired the first volley of bullets; but suddenly the British lines opened up, and out came hundreds of Iroquois warriors, screaming their war cries as they ran towards these French soldiers. The French soldiers froze; the devils themselves were coming at them. They were so afraid that they dropped their guns, and our people just overran them. The French defeated themselves by brainwashing their children to believe our ancestors were devils and horrible creatures.

Karoniaktajeh told us these stories to build up our spirit. He would say, "You call yourselves Rotihsken'rakéhte', and that's fine, but what if you called yourselves the Warrior Society? You know the white man has brainwashed himself into believing that every Indian is a fighting machine.

You can use the weapons you have in your arsenal, your psychological weapons". We said, "Okay", and we wrote "Rotihsken'rakéhte'" on top of the crest and "Warrior Society" underneath it. We took it to the printer, who told us, "You know, if you print seven it's almost the same price as getting 250. For a little extra you could print 250 of them outright". We thought, "Jeez, I guess we'll have the extra, in case we have more people interested in joining us". So we took 250 of them. When we got home that night our mothers sewed them onto our jackets for us. Soon we were walking around town with those jackets, and all the young people liked them. "Can I get one of those?" So we gave all 250 of our crests away to everybody. Now all these young guys were walking around with this crest on their jacket saying "Rotihsken'rakéhte' Warrior Society". Suddenly, the police saw a couple of hundred Indians boldly stating they were part of a Warrior Society! That put some real fear into them. When we went to other territories, we always had our crests on our jackets. We put them on denim jackets, leather jackets, some had brown leather jackets with a fringe. Whatever you had as an everyday jacket, you just sewed that emblem right on.

We began wearing that Warrior Society crest around 1969 or 1970, right after the Akwesasne International Bridge blockade in 1968.[16] At that time, we were already discussing actions we could take, but we had not yet put our council together. When the blockade was going to happen, three of us left Kahnawà:ke. At the time, we had no car, so we walked to Akwesasne, sixty miles away, to be a part of it and defend the rights of our people. It was the coldest time of the year, it was freezing, and it took us a full sixteen and a half hours to jog to Akwesasne. That was how committed we were! They had the blockade already organized in Akwesasne. We got there, and Kahentinetha showed up with her brother Frank. Afterwards, they charged me with assault and battery of forty police officers. I was fifteen years old! If you had seen me at that time, I was maybe five feet tall and must have weighed ninety pounds, and they charged me with assaulting them! All the charges were dropped eventually. If you ever see the documentary movie *You Are on Indian Land*, you see a station wagon that keeps blocking the bridge; that was me.[17] I kept blocking that bridge.

There was resistance! When the sixties came along, the hippie movement brought what we were doing to the world's attention. At that time, the American upper- and middle-class young people were unhappy with life, so they had Woodstock, San Francisco, all that stuff going on. The guys coming back from Vietnam did not like what was happening out there. At first, we did not really feel that we were part of it, but when the Civil Rights Movement started, and the African American people stood up, it felt like the Motown train was coming through Native communities. We jumped on that train, sharing our stories with every young non-Native person who wanted to listen. We talked about ecology and the destruction of our lands. Suddenly, there was this new thing that became the environmental movement. Native people were printing posters of Sitting Bull saying, "When the last tree has been cut down, the last fish caught, the last river poisoned, only then will we realize that one cannot eat money". It was finally a time where we could come out and speak and feel there would be an audience willing to listen!

High School Sit-In

When I was in high school, we had a sit-in.[18] We had been asking for our own high school in Kahnawà:ke for years, but the government would not give it to us. Kids from Kahnawà:ke were bused to the Howard S. Billings Regional High School in Châteauguay, the settler town next to Kahnawà:ke. For us to go there, the Department of Indian Affairs had to pay extra money. Once schools got their money at the end of October, they started kicking out Native children left and right for any little reason. Many of the kids were experiencing problems at Billings. However, I did not experience any issues at all. I was the only kid going to that school that did not have to follow a dress code, that did not have to take history or do what everybody else had to do, because I stood up for myself. When I was told that I had to dress according to the school policy, I said, "No. It's just a policy. The law says that you have to give me an education, and law supersedes your policy". They looked at me and said, "What the hell kind of a kid is this? He's talking law to us!" The school staff was not even familiar with what I was saying. They were in education, not in law. Here I was rattling all kinds of stuff out at them. I had learned from the best: Louis Hall, Peter Diome, Frank Natawe.[19] They were very wise men and always said, "You'll never get anywhere if you don't assert your sovereignty". So I asserted my sovereignty in everything I did. When the other kids had problems, I was home doing my homework. When the other kids' parents asked me why I did not have problems at school, I told them it was because I asserted my sovereignty. Half of them didn't even know what that meant. They wanted me to help them get their kid back to school. I said, "Tomorrow you should accompany your kids to school; go to the office and talk to the principal about getting your kids back in. I'll take care of the rest". The following day, I went to all the bus stops to tell all the kids what was happening. I said to the school staff we would refuse to go to class if they didn't allow the kids back in. We would have a sit-in.

The sit-in lasted three days, and I told the parents to have spokesmen to represent these students. I did not want to be their spokesman, so five other kids were selected. When the head of the Châteauguay school board showed up with the principal, vice principal and everybody else, the school committee from Kahnawà:ke was there to support us. I had brought a bag of rattles and drums to sing while we were having our sit-in. Suddenly we realized that most of the parents and the school board were backing down. They were intimidated by our people. It was then that some of the parents at the back came over and said, "You better come up. They're letting our kids have it. You got to help us". I went over to see what was going on. All I heard was that principal yelling, "And what are your demands?" I was standing on the stairs, and one of the things Louis Hall always told me is "always be on a higher level than them". Here I was on a higher level, talking down to them, saying, "I will tell you what our demands are: we want our own vice principal, our own guidance counselor, our own language and culture teacher, our own language and culture in our school and our own Indian student council". They were all listening and said, "There are no Natives available who would be qualified enough to be a vice principal. The qualified one is Eddie Cross, and he is already the principal at the school in Kahnawà:ke. There is nobody qualified enough to be a guidance counselor either". I said, "Do not tell us who is qualified! We will tell you who is qualified! You have five counselors here who cannot seem to deal with any of our issues". He asked me who I had in mind. In the corner of my eye there was Clifford Diabo. I could see his leather jacket. I grabbed him and said, "This is our guidance counselor!" So he became our first guidance counselor. We got four out of our five demands. The only one we did not get was an Indian vice principal.

The newspapers, the *Montreal Gazette*, the *Star*, the television, all the media covered the story. When the band council showed up, Ron Kirby tried to talk to us,[20] but we did not even want to listen to what he had to say. You see, there was no master plan at that time, we just did whatever was necessary. After that, people in the community thanked me. However, I cannot take credit for what happened, because I just happened to be there, and I am glad to have people who coached me: my grandparents and the elders; I credit them for passing it on. All the kids I was going to school with did not feel any different from me; they just did not have teachers at their homes the way I did.

Longhouse Revival and Handsome Lake

By that time, still a teenager, I was already part of the Rotihsken'rakéhte'. We went all around the confederacy, talking to others. Everybody started setting their councils back up. I started in Akwesasne, Kanehsatà:ke and then met up with the Oneida, the Tuscarora; I traveled all over. At that time, the Six Nations Confederacy did not know how to deal with us, because they couldn't come out openly and just tell us we don't know what we're doing. At some point, we asked them for a recital of the Kaianerehkó:wa. They answered, "But it has not been recited in two hundred years!" So we said, "Well, exactly! Don't you think it's time to recite it?" The first modern recitation of the Great Law was held around 1970 in Ohswé:ken. However, when we went there for the ten-day recital, we only heard religion for ten days. What they were reciting was the Handsome Lake Code.[21] We got into a big war of words over there. Furthermore, Mohawks were constantly being condemned, because Mohawks did not follow the Handsome Lake Code. We were Kaianerehkó:wa people. George Washington and Thomas Jefferson were happy with Handsome Lake. They did not have to come in to destroy us anymore; we would destroy ourselves with this new religion. Then the Americans could take the example of Iroquois and draw inspiration from the Kaianerehkó:wa and their constitution.

The Handsome Lake religion kept pushing on our people to believe that we do not need our knowledge, that all we need is faith. We are not superstitious people, regardless of how Hollywood, the history books and everybody else portrays us. We are very realistic people. When we talk about what we believe in, we call it *Karihwí:io, the way of reality*. It comes from *Orihwí:io,* which means *something that is definite and unquestionable*. We follow the way of reality. However, when we talk about the religions that came from across the ocean, we call them *Karihwiiohstónhtshera',* a *man-made reality,* because it's only a reality in your mind, not in the real world. By contrast, Karihwí:io is just what is, what is there. There is no question that there is water. There is no question that there is air. There is no question that the trees exist, and that the grass grows when the rain falls. There is no question; it speaks for itself.

When we say *Tewatatewenní:io*, meaning *we are all free*, or *we are all sovereign*, what we mean is that freedom is a natural reality. *Tewatatewenní:io* comes from *Tsi ní:io(ht)*, which means *the way it is*. We are, thus, *people of the way it is*; we follow the way of creation, the way of nature. Nature is free, and since we are a part of it, we are also free. We cannot control nature; we have to go its way. So Tewatatewenní:io means that we are people who follow the way of nature, which is based on freedom. Nobody has the right to tell us that we cannot be, just as no one can tell the sun to stop shining or the wind to stop blowing. We go by what nature has prescribed for us, not by what a man has to say. Creation has given us the ability to take care of ourselves and of those who are important to us: our families, our people and all our relations on this land with us. Because they are all our relations, we are all connected. There is not a single thing on this Earth that is not connected. This explains why when we struggle to be who we are, to maintain who we are, we are not just doing it for us as the Kanien'kehá:ka. We do it for all of creation, because, as the older people always told us, we will never find peace if those around us are not at peace. The Kaianerehkó:wa tells us this.

The Handsome Lake Code turned the Kaianerehkó:wa into a religion. It turned creation into the Creator, into a man sitting somewhere above the clouds. However, when we talk about power in our language, we refer to the *Ka'nisténhsera'*, the *life-givers*, meaning our women, our mothers. How can we credit a life-giver that we do not know, something that we have never seen, something that is not even among us, when we know very well where life comes from? We know who brings us forth, raises us, teaches us and loves us: our mothers. And their power comes from the Earth. We are all connected to that power, because we all come from that life-giver. Men are involved with the creation, but the foundation of life is the woman.

Just like it tried to get rid of the Rotihsken'rakéhte', the men's fire, the Handsome Lake Code tried to get rid of the women's fire. It turned clan mothers and the so-called chiefs into religious leaders. They have a special group they call *faithkeepers*. They say the Handsome Lake Code came from "the four beings coming from heaven". Where the hell does that come out of? Christianity! Those are four archangels. They let men do wrong; all men have to do is repent at a Handsome Lake ceremony, and the Creator will forgive them all their sins. But not the women! They will go to hell and will have to pay for all their sins. Handsome Lake deprived the Ka'nisténhsera', the women, of all their power. He killed all the most powerful women in his witch-hunts.

Here in Kahnawà:ke and Akwesasne, we already knew Christianity, because both territories were once Jesuit missions. So Mohawks had no reason to accept the Handsome Lake Code. When there was just one longhouse in Kahnawà:ke, it followed the Kaianerehkó:wa. When they brought the code to us, we told them, "We fought hard to get rid of all this stuff; we fought hard to get rid of Christianity, and now you want to bring it all back". Kawisaienton, Karionwakeron and Onenhariio revived the longhouse in Kahnawà:ke at the beginning of the twentieth century.[22] Then there were others like my grandfather Louis Diabo who fought hard to bring the traditions and the Kaianerehkó:wa back. They knew what religion was and would not accept the Handsome Lake Code. Much work had to be done to revive our old ways. Despite the Church's efforts, our people still maintained the clan system and governed ourselves according to it. Even though we were Christians, that was still the only system we knew. When the government pushed to enforce the Indian Act on us in the 1920s, things started to change. Slowly the money started coming in, and then the corruption began.

Previously, each clan lived in different areas of the community: Bears, Turtles and Wolves. In our system, when a man marries a woman he moves to her territory. Their children grow up with her clan. Canada took that away from the mothers when they allotted land to men under the Indian Act. The women had to leave and raise their children in a place where they could not carry on the duties and responsibilities of that family anymore. That is why there is so much confusion in this community today. People forgot which clan they come from, but now we are trying to revive these things again, despite all the agents all over our territories whose job is to keep us divided, keep us fighting with each other and keep us at odds with one another. This makes it hard not only for us but also for the Ojibwa, the Chippewa, the Cree, for everybody. The same tactic has been used all around the world: divide and conquer. Separate people from the old structure, so they do not know who they are anymore. They have been very successful at it up to now.

The Rotihsken'rakéhte' was revived to defend these things, to defend us. We had warrior gatherings to talk about what we could, and we seemed to accomplish a lot more when we had no money. Since the money started coming, with millions and millions of dollars being poured into our community to keep us calm since the 1990 Oka Crisis, we cannot get a damn thing done. Money is taking away the minds of our people. We treat our children like our property rather than our responsibility. Our people forgot their history. When a white priest called Dave Blanchard was brought here to teach the history of Kahnawà:ke, I listened and realized that he was wrong in a lot of what he said,[23] so I had to correct him. He asked me, "Where did you read that?" I said, "I didn't read it, the old people told me!" I had people coming to my home when I was a young boy, and I listened to them, and they all spoke the language. They talked about Chief Joseph, when the Americans were trying to stop him from coming to Canada to seek sanctuary with Sitting Bull.[24] They had lived those times, so I heard these stories firsthand. A lot of our history was not recorded. The thing is that our language does not change, so our history does not change. They always try to give you the impression that oral tradition changes as time goes on. No, it does not! It is all in the language. The history is in the language, and the language does not change. It is only changing now. In fact, it is not so much the language that is changing but the minds of our people. They have white minds speaking our language! The words no longer mean what they say. Look at our word for *it's raining*, *Iokennó:ron*. What it actually says is that when the water is falling from the sky, *you can see that it is precious*. It's telling you that when that water falls from the sky and hits this earth, it will quench the thirst of all the plants, the animals, the insects and the birds, that it will refill the rivers, streams and even the underground streams. What it says is that it is plain to see that it's precious, because it will help life to continue. But when you say "it's raining" in English, people think, "Oh, there goes my golf game, there goes my sun tan, my hairdo", and so on. That's the difference between really understanding our language or understanding it through English.

Occupation of Indian Affairs Building

Language has always been important. We may not have books, but we have an oral tradition. That oral tradition is very visual, because our language is a descriptive language. It's a live language; as a person talks you can see in your mind all the images brought about by that word, and then you realize what it really means. I was lucky enough to have grown up in a home where English was forbidden. Most of the teaching was at the longhouse and in our homes when I was young. That changed in 1972, when a mother refused to send her son to school outside, as she felt he was too young to be exposed to drugs and other things. She went to other homes, talked to other parents and began the Indian Way School in Kahnawà:ke.[25] The parents of these young people initiated it. It started with three children. Once the word went around that we were starting our school, we soon had forty students! Now, we had to help to support the school. The longhouse stepped up to the plate and said it was our duty as longhouse people to support what our mothers and children needed. In 1972, when the time came to get some funding, some of us Rotihsken'rakéhte' accompanied some women to Ottawa, and we occupied the Indian Affairs building for two days. When eight of us went to Ottawa for the occupation, we had no idea that the Bureau of Indian Affairs (BIA) was also being occupied in Washington.[26] My father was down in Washington with my cousin Jimmy Deer and a few others. They were all part of the Trail of Broken Treaties, but we had issues at home that still needed to be dealt with, so we went to Ottawa. While we were occupying, one guy in our group called home. He came back saying, "Hey you guys. They just took over the BIA in Washington!" We asked, "Who!?", and he said, "The longest walk! Five thousand of them took over the BIA!"

When the government people came back to the hotel, they brought the Ottawa chief of police, who immediately got scolded. We asked him what the hell he was doing there and told him that he had nothing to do with us, and that he had to get the hell out of there! So he left. We were not diplomats. The others still tried to stonewall us, so finally my friend Alan Cross said, "Listen, either you do what we're asking, or else in twenty-four hours we'll have five thousand Indians in here. We'll take over all these Indian Affairs buildings and take over Ottawa!" They kind of laughed. Then Alan Cross said, "If you don't believe us, call your counterparts in Washington and find out what's going on over there". So John Ciaccia asked one of his associates to make a call and find out what the hell this was about.[27] The assistant came back in and whispered in John's ear, "Well, John, it seems like five thousand Indians just took over the BIA in Washington". Suddenly they realized how serious this was. At that point, they ended up telling us they would give us the tuition and everything else. So we left with all these promises, but they reneged on them.

When we came back a second time, there were at least fifty of us, most of whom were not the diplomatic type. I went to the bars and started talking to the guys, telling them how Indian Affairs reneged on their promises. They showed up at the longhouse the following day in carloads, and we went back to Ottawa. Those were the biggest guys in Kahnawà:ke, and not the diplomatic type. They knew their responsibility, and they knew force would be used against them. So we went in and took over Indian Affairs again, occupying a big conference room. We said, "We came here to make sure you fulfill your promise. We don't want your Indian Affairs money. We want our money from our trust fund".[28] They tried to tell us there were no more trust funds, that it was all put into consolidated funds. We said, "Bullshit, it's still there as far as we're concerned!"

Their first response was to call in the Ottawa riot squad to come and take us out. They came up the elevators, the door opened, and we saw them. As soon as the boys saw all the shields, helmets and clubs, they screamed. They flipped the tables and chairs. Somebody broke off the legs from tables and the chairs and said, "Come on! Let's go!" All of a sudden, the riot squad backed down the stairs. The assistant deputy minister of Indian Affairs John Ciaccia had already quit, because we drove him crazy. There was no way Ciaccia could get the Indians to understand that they had to follow those rules. We were not there to follow rules. We were there to get the tuition for our children and to have permanent teachers and the materials they badly needed. They got Irvin Goodleaf,[29] the assistant minister, who is married to my father's sister, to come in and deal with us. They figured out they might as well fight fire with fire, Mohawks against Mohawks. However, he came there knowing that he better treat us right or at the next wedding he would get the beating of his life. So he came over directly to my father and uncles and started talking with them. "Listen, go to the hotel, he said. The dinner is on us. You guys order whatever you want. I'll come back and see you over there". "Okay", said my father, "but you better get it done". In other words: "You got to come home!" So he came back to the hotel and said, "Okay, you're going to get the tuition, you're going to also get a school bus,[30] and they're going to give you money for the building". We needed that new building, because we had been using the cookhouse of the longhouse until that time. In the end, we got our school, our school bus and the tuition for our kids in this school, which is still operating today.

Kahnawà:ke Evictions

The following year, in 1973, non-Natives were evicted from Kahnawà:ke.[31] This happened because for many generations different non-Natives would come to this community. At that time, there were 2,900 non-Natives living in this community, compared to about 5,000 Natives. We have a story about non-Natives. In 1704, our people had purchased a Russian church bell from a foundry in Moscow, where they used to make the bells. It was being delivered on a ship, and on the way the ship was attacked by Americans, who took our bell and brought it to Deerfield, Massachusetts. They went there to get our bell back. I assume the British or French had a beef with these people, because they wanted to attack them. They asked us if we would join them. "By the way", they said, "your bell is down there". "Our bell? Yeah! We were waiting for our bell!" So our people joined them, and there was a fight. It was called the Deerfield Massacre.[32] Obviously, when there's two white guys fighting and killing each other, it's never called a massacre. We got our bell back, yet we lost some of our warriors in the process. It was always our way in history that when we lost a relative, we replaced that life. Usually, we would take children and bring them back to replace the life we lost. A girl called Eunice Williams was brought from Deerfield at the time. She was raised in Kahnawà:ke, and she married here and still has descendants here today, the Williams family. They say that the actor Steven Seagal is a descendant of Eunice Williams.

We have another story, which is about the French, at the time when they were having their revolution. Their people were guillotining the royalty, chopping their heads off, trying to wipe out all the blue bloods. King Louis XVI had two grandsons, who were twins. He knew that if the common people got hold of them, they were going to kill them, so he put them on a ship to North America with their governess to get them away from those killers. On the way, an enemy ship attacked, and the French ship got blown up pretty badly. One of the twins died, but the governess and the other one survived, and they put them on a ship and brought them to Whitehall, near Albany, New York. That's the home of what they call the American Navy, not far from Ticonderoga. At that time, people from Kahnawà:ke took their furs to trade down there. A Mohawk was there selling furs when the governess showed up. The Native people were known to be good to all children, no matter their color. The governess knew that eventually some commoners from France would come over to hunt them down. So she left the boy with this Mohawk man and asked, "Could you watch this boy for now? I've got some things to buy, and he's giving me a hard time". The old man said, "Yeah, go ahead and leave him". So he stayed with the boy, and he waited for days, but this woman never came back. He wanted to go home, but he didn't want to abandon the boy, so he brought him back to Kahnawà:ke. The following spring, after he had trapped, he brought the boy back with his furs to Albany. He thought that he would run into this woman again. He inquired about her, but nobody had heard about her. So finally he just kept the boy and raised him here in Kahnawà:ke. The boy married here, and some say that certain of our family names come from the grandson of the French dauphin: Diabo, Delisle, Montour, Jacobs and Williams. When his children were grown, he left Kahnawà:ke and moved to Akwesasne. He built his house a couple hundred feet from the water. It's an A-frame house, with a roof that almost touches the ground. It's still there, with a plaque that says it's the home of the missing dauphin.[33]

Our people always took care of non-Natives; they took in blacksmiths and bakers and all, but at some point, there were too many people coming in. They were living in homes that our people could otherwise use. All our young families were forced to move to Lachine, to Châteauguay or elsewhere. At that time, the government allocated a half-acre of land to each man of a certain age to build his home and raise his family. Yet the lands were now being given to non-Natives.[34] Grants that helped people build their homes were now given to non-Natives. Meanwhile, the young Native families all had to leave. My uncle, a war chief at the time, took action. Near his place, a French guy was clearing the land. My uncle went over to him. He was just curious to know who was moving in. He asked the guy, "Who are you working for?" The French guy answered, "I'm not working for anybody". My uncle asked, "Whose land is this? You're clearing the land. You got to be working for somebody from here". He answered, "Nah, this is my land. I'm building my home". My uncle asked, "Are you Native? Are you a Mohawk?" He said, "No, but I have a band number". So my uncle said, "That doesn't matter. If you're not Onkwehón:we, you don't have any right to build a home here". My uncle got angry, because the guy said he had received a grant, a band number and a plot of land, and now he could build here. My uncle took it to the longhouse and told them about it, asking them, "How many of our young families can't come home because these guys are taking up the land? They're taking the grant money, just because they've got a number".

So the people had meetings about it. We had already formed the Rotihsken'rakéhte', and often when we found out somebody was gathering hay or wood or building a barn or a house, we would all go there and help. Then one day we were gathering hay for the fall cutting, and when we finished, late in the afternoon, we passed by the longhouse and saw all the cars there. We stopped in to ask what was going on. There was no ceremony scheduled, so it had to be a meeting. My uncle came out. I asked him what was going on. He just said, "People want to know if the warriors are ready to back us up". "Back you up for what?" "Well the people had a long meeting, because they feel that it's time that all the white people who are here leave. Are you ready to back us up?" I said, "Well, you're the war chief, you tell us!" He answered, "Yeah, I'm the war chief, but you've got all the warriors". "Well", I said, "they're here, ask them. I don't speak for them!" He was saying that I had all the warriors, because I hung out with them, and I was their age. I was always talking to them, and I passed on to them all the things I had learned from the old people, my grandparents, Louis Hall and others. So my uncle had the impression that I controlled the warriors. He asked them, and they decided that if that's what the people decided, that's what they would do. They made the notices, and we delivered them to the non-Native families, giving them thirty days to leave. If anybody needed more than thirty days, they had to come see the council and give their reason why they needed more time. Some got an extra thirty days, and we gave some farmers an extra year or even more to get their harvest and find a new farm. Most of the non-Native people understood. They thanked us for letting them stay as long as we did. Some of them had stayed here for three generations, and they were grateful for it. However, the band council was not grateful, just because they were not in charge of the campaign.

Most of the non-Natives left, except for a few holdouts. They stayed because the band council told them that they were not required to leave, and that they would get police protection. When the Rotihsken'rakéhte' started to go around giving eviction notices, the local police did not want to be part of this. They stood back and did nothing; the police were outmanned. They knew they had to continue to live here and were careful not to antagonize us. Then Chief Ronald Kirby and Jean Chrétien tried to send in the army.[35] The federal government preferred to use the federal police (RCMP), but Kahnawà:ke was out of their jurisdiction. Many did not understand what that meant. Kahnawà:ke is not a reservation. It still is not a reservation. It's still under the title of the Iroquois Confederacy. They went to the provincial police (SQ), which were more than happy to step in, as they tend to consider everything within the borders of Québec as theirs. They came in with the riot squad, but they would not attack us right away. They waited until the evening, when most of us went home for supper, and there were only maybe five of us left behind. Then about forty of them moved in with their clubs and shields. The five of us ended up fighting like hell with them. We were overpowered, but we put up a good fight!

I was the only one who got away, with two broken ribs. Back at my father's house, the phone rang. It was the local chief of police, calling my father and asking him, "Can you come down here and do something? They're going to tear this place apart! All those warriors are here!" Junior Jacobs was at my father's place, so I asked him to give me a ride. Junior dropped me off and went to Louis Hall's place. As soon as I got out of the car, all the guys were already there ready for action. We started turning over those police cars. By then the police were exiting, throwing tear gas at us, trying to blind us so they could get away. I don't know how they all managed to squeeze into a couple of cars, like those clowns at the circus all climbing up in a tiny car! We got about six of their vehicles, and we just flipped them on their roofs and everything. It was unreal.

Then all the warriors went to the band council office. Ronald Kirby was hiding in another guy's house, next to the police station. All the young people started throwing rocks into the band council's windows. None of us had weapons initially, but when the police took off they left their clubs and helmets behind, so we helped ourselves. When they came marching back, hours later, they all carried guns like soldiers. In those days, nobody had automatic weapons. We had .22s, shotguns and rifles for hunting. When we saw them coming at us with guns, we knew that they would want to use them. Everybody ran home and got their rifles. Since we knew that they would come after the longhouse people, we dug our bunkers and prepared to hold out right there. We had no idea what they were going to send against us.

By that time, other Native people were flocking in from everywhere in North America to Kahnawà:ke. They came from Oklahoma, California, Cree Country, everywhere. The police blocked the roads. They wanted to catch people coming fifty miles away, but our supporters managed to come in anyway. Now we had a siege, and the SQ would no longer attack us, because they knew we had the manpower. They knew we had guns, and that we were ready to go all out. So they started terrorizing people in the community. When police came into the territory, they did not ask, "Are you a good Indian?" You were an Indian, so they would beat you up, that's all. They would also abuse women. People came to us, saying, "Something has got to be done. They've got to be stopped. They're abusing people, beating up the kids and everybody", so we decided to put four men into a vehicle and started driving around. Every time we would see the SQ, we went after them. They would start flying over the bridge or speeding towards Châteauguay or Saint-Isidore. They act tough when they beat up defenseless people, but now they were up against the Rotihsken'rakéhte' who would not take a back seat. We went after them, chased them, and, boy, they were scared!

Finally, they came back and asked for a meeting. They sent in this sergeant, a couple of lieutenants and low-level cops. We said, "Well, okay, we'll have a meeting at the longhouse". They came to the council, and all the people were there. The cops started talking about their position and asking questions to the council. We were watching this, listening. We took my twelve-year-old nephew outside, and we said, "Listen, when they finish, we want you to tell them this". We told him what to say, something short but eloquent. When they finished, he was sitting next to the Rotiianérshon. He got up and said, "I can't give you a response to your questions, because I don't have the authority. I'll have to take this back to my superiors. When I have the answers from my superiors, I will let you know". He turned around and walked out. Those cops were so insulted, they got up and said, "This is an insult! It's unacceptable!" We said, "Listen, you're the ones insulting us! You have no power either, you're just a bunch of messenger boys. The police sent us a messenger boy, so we sent you a messenger boy in return! Go back and get people who can make a real decision, and then come back here!" They left, very annoyed with us!

They did send back some higher officials, who told us, "We want your men to turn in your weapons, and we want all these American Indian Movement (AIM) guys and Native people who don't belong here to go back home where they came from". We listened and answered, "First of all, we're not turning in anything to you. Do you want us to pull out our teeth and be defenseless? No, that's not going to happen. Furthermore, all our brothers and sisters from other territories are our guests. You, on the other hand, are not. So don't tell us when our guests will have to leave. You have to leave! Our guests will leave when they are ready, on their own accord. Until then, there's nothing further to talk about". That was the end, and they left. They filed all kinds of charges against us, and in the end they got nothing. Suddenly, all our young people started moving back home, into all the houses that became available. The whites left, and all the Mohawk families living across the bridge in Montréal came back. Later on, I would run into some people who had been against what we were doing, who said, "Let me shake your hand. If it wasn't for you I wouldn't have a house here in Kahnawà:ke today". Inside, you just want to tell them to get lost, but you also understand them. They had been conditioned to oppose anything the longhouse did, but they were grateful to have a home, and they knew that without the longhouse they would never have gotten a home here.

Nowadays, the band council is pushing for the eviction of mixed couples, just another tactic to divide our people. People ask me, "Aren't you the one who led those evictions back in 1973?" They automatically figure that I would support them. I tell them, "No, when we dealt with these issues, it was with those families who were undisputedly white". We did not bother with mixed marriages. That was not our mandate. It had nothing to do with the longhouse people. They keep trying to drag the longhouse people into this fight, but we keep saying, "No! We see what you're doing. You're just trying to use us!" Every individual has the right to express their own opinion, but they should do it as individuals, and not claim to be representing the traditional people.

In 1985, Bill C-31 made things even more complicated.[36] There was a clash of minds, cultures and ways. Now, people who had married outside were allowed to come back with their families, because they were granted Native status, but their background was different. These people returned, and suddenly they held all the positions in the community. They are the ones in the police forces today, taking bureaucratic positions, while everyday people who have always lived here are seen as the lower class. These new people came back, bringing their so-called "progressive ways" into our community, taking the jobs, slowly bringing in the municipalization program, which would turn our territory into just another municipality. People barely realize that this is going on now. The only difference between a reservation or municipality now is that we don't pay school or property taxes.

Ganienkeh

The Rotihsken'rakéhte' grew a lot, rapidly. More and more guys were saying, "This is what we've been waiting for. We're tired of talking; we want action, and we want results!" They were not looking for a war. They just wanted to do something. Instead of just saying, "Gee, I'd like to build a shed there" year after year, finally you get tired of talking about it, and you get out there and build it. What we wanted to rebuild was the confederacy. That's when we took over Moss Lake.[37] Many people think that going back into the mountains and taking the land back was a new idea, but there was nothing new about it. As I said, back in the 1950s, my family tried to establish a new community in a part of our ancestral homeland. After the evictions, there was a great division among the people of our community. There were people who supported the evictions and people who did not. They were at odds with each other, and it was a very volatile situation. The people of the longhouse never intended to fight with their people. The Kaianerehkó:wa says that we should never spill each other's blood, no matter what. Either you go to council to discuss these things, or else you might be better off separating from each other for now and taking time to heal. To avoid a civil war in our community, we decided to leave and avoid that fight with people here. If we had to fight, we would fight our real enemy: the government.

The Rotihsken'rakéhte' started to plan the occupation of Moss Lake. We approached the council and the people to tell them what we wanted to do. We got the support of the people of the council in Kahnawà:ke. Then our delegation went to Akwesasne. A meeting had been called for all the Mohawks. They came from Kanehsatà:ke, Tyendinaga and Kahnawà:ke to Akwesasne, the most central of all the communities. The project was put to everybody, and it got real strong support. Everybody said, "It's about time!" The council advised us to take it to the grand council of the confederacy and offered to accompany us. The grand council also supported the project, but they were unable to sanction it. They wanted to know where the occupation would take place first. We said that for security reasons we could not disclose that information, but that it would be on Mohawk territory. They said, "Well, until we know for sure, we won't be able to sanction it". We had to accept that. We knew that there were always informants. If we let people know where we were going, they would be ready for it and try to stop us. One man insisted on knowing where we were planning on building our community. "I have a right to know", he said. So we told him, "All right. We're going to take land in Vermont!" Two days later, it was on the news. Vermont had put 250 extra state police and border patrols to watch the Vermont border. Now all the grand council people believed it would be in Vermont, and they could not sanction the move, because it would have been on Wabanaki territory. However, that camp near Moss Lake in the Adirondack, where we were heading in reality, was Mohawk land.

On May 13, 1974, we took it over and called it *Ganienkeh*, meaning the *land of the flint*. At that moment, it became public knowledge where that land was. When searching for the land we would take, we did not consider private land. Our fight was not with private citizens; it was with the American government. We looked for any land that belonged to the state and the government. Finally, we settled on an abandoned girls' camp where the Rockefellers, the Kennedys and all those kinds of families used to go. They had closed it down, and then it was given to the state as parkland. It was 612 acres. We took it, but not because we thought it was the ideal place to start a new life. It had water, much forest, and there was only one way in and one way out. We took it because it was *defensible*. We knew that our fighting tactics would require using the forest. We also know that they could not cut off our water supply, since we had the lake. So we took it over.

In the beginning, we got no opposition. The locals thought it was great, since it would help tourism to have a bunch of Indians doing Indian dances and selling souvenirs. When they came and talked to us about it, we explained to them that we come from different walks of life. We are iron workers, farmers, school teachers, carpenters, but not a single one of us here comes from Hollywood. We are not performers, nor will we dance or perform for anyone. If you want to buy crafts, we can make some as a side thing, but we are not going to sing and dance for anybody. We told them we were there because we wanted to create a life and a future for our children. Our main objective was agriculture, the same way our people lived in the past. Then they changed their minds: "Oh! We don't need that here!" From then on, they went against what we were doing. They started to scare us by shooting at us. They shot at us sixteen times before we ever retaliated. We tried to inform the US government, the state of New York, the local townships, but nobody gave a damn.

Militias were already in the area. They called themselves the "Big Moose people". There was the John Birch Society, the Minutemen, all kinds of redneck groups.[38] They were recruiting people from all over New Hampshire and Massachusetts. They had meetings up at the Big Moose Inn.[39] After they shot at us sixteen times, our people decided it was enough. We decided that the next time they shot at us, we would return fire, shoot at their tires, stop them, detain them and call the cops to take away those goddamn troublemakers. One time, one of the cars that shot at us was fired back at. When bullets stray and ricochet you have no control. The ballistic reports at the time showed that the spare tire in the trunk was hit and a piece of the .22 caliber bullet that was fired broke off and hit a young girl who was sitting in the back. Her father, mother and uncle all had their kids in the car when they passed and shot at our community in the dark. Nobody knew there were kids in the car. Another time some hoodlums attacked us and a bullet ricocheted and hit one of them. Nobody was killed, but they did need medical attention.

The state police came with the federal government, stating that they had warrants and had to arrest somebody and press charges. Some guys wanted to turn themselves in to avoid our people being attacked. Our people said, "No! Nobody! Either it's none of us, or it's all of us. If they want this resolved, they have to do it in accordance with the Two Row Wampum agreement".[40] It had to be dealt with nation to nation in a diplomatic way. Ford was the president of the United States at the time. They knew that there was no way that we would just give in. We had much support from the World Council of Churches, the National Council of Churches, the State Council of Churches and many different dioceses. We also had a lot of support from countries worldwide: Italy, Finland, Sweden, Germany and Egypt. The day we moved into Moss Lake, we sent guys to the United Nations, in New York. They gave a package to every consulate in the UN telling them about our move.[41] Our manifesto outlined the history of who we are.[42] We put it on an international level from the start, so the United States could not blackout what was going on, keep it isolated and allow a mass murder to happen, as they did at Wounded Knee.[43] The governor did not want to end up like Rockefeller with Attica.[44] He knew that he had to be more diplomatic. President Ford did not want to come across as a killer, so he appointed Forrest Gerard, the deputy minister of the Bureau of Indian Affairs, to resolve the situation.[45] The agreement said that either the president or somebody specially appointed by him would look into the matter and see that the peace was kept. That was the first time in over two hundred years that the United States followed the Two Row Wampum. We made that happen. President Ford admitted that the Two Row Wampum was still in effect, and that the Indigenous canoe was independent from the settlers' ship. Nobody has followed it since, in any case. At that time, before the agreement was completed, the United States had to provide compensation for what had been done to us, for all the violent attacks we had been subjected to ever since we set up our encampment at Moss Lake. That is what the treaties say: if they, meaning the outside authorities, ever find that their people are in the wrong, they have to deal with them. If the people did something wrong, if the local people had been attacking us, it was only because the federal, state and local governments did nothing to stop them. They encouraged these people to feel that they had the freedom to shoot at Indians. They never compensated Ganienkeh for what happened, but the fact that they had to follow the Two Row Wampum meant a lot more, because a precedent was established.

Relocation

After three years of being in those mountains under siege, finally we said, "Okay, we've accomplished what we set out to do". At first, we had taken over 612 acres, and when we left we had 1200 acres. We kept taking more and more land, and nobody could stop us. However, we realized that our project would not work there, because it was in the middle of the snow belt. It had an abridged growing season, and acid rain was starting to kill the trees and poison the lake. We told the government we planned to move to another part of our land. We were not relinquishing our claim to anything. Just because we are not occupying the land does not mean that it is no longer our people's homeland. We decided we would move up closer to Kahnawà:ke, at Miner Lake.[46]

The state tried to negotiate with us. They were trying to get us to settle on land that did not belong to the Mohawks, as the Oneidas traditionally claimed it. We told the Oneidas about the land that had been offered to us as a replacement for Moss Lake, letting them know that there was land available there to move to if they would like to. The state said, "It's the only land available. We fed all our information into our computer. That's what it gave us". Louis Hall replied, "Well maybe if you let us feed *our* information into the computer, it would tell you there are nine million acres of uninhabited Mohawk land". In the end, we just told them that we were moving one way or another. "You can cooperate with us, but if you don't, we're moving anyway. If you want to fight us, go ahead, let's fight; it's nothing to us!" We ended up taking over Schuyler Falls and Miner Lake. We told them afterwards that we would continue to acquire lands, and that they would automatically fall into the jurisdiction of the Territory of Ganienkeh, the Mohawk Nation and the Iroquois Confederacy. That was our objective: to enlarge the domain of the Mohawk people and the Iroquois Confederacy.

There were a lot of meetings and negotiations. Finally, the state offered to help us with finances. They said they would give us money and provide us with trailers. We said, "No, the only thing we want from you is to leave us the hell alone!" We took on the renovation of all the old buildings. We pulled out all the nails and everything, and we just got help from everyday American people. I remember some guy who had a tractor trailer. He came and offered it to us, drove it in, and we loaded all our lumber on it. Then he drove it all up to Altona for us, where we unloaded all of it and recycled the lumber to build our first homes!

The Rotihsken'rakéhte' and AIM

There were so many events in that short period, from 1970 to 1980. The so-called Oka Crisis in 1990 was one result of all those things that had happened during that period: Wounded Knee, Moss Lake and Fort Kanasaraken in 1979, when we drove the police force out of Akwesasne.[47] The people here always heard about these things. They knew we were from this community and were key players in all the events. When Akwesasne sent out a cry for help in 1979, many people who had never really been involved suddenly joined us. As a people, we look out for each other. Back in the 1970s, when the James Bay project was going on, the Crees came here and asked us to protest in Montréal.[48] A few of us attended; we carried a big drum, sang and led the procession against Hydro Québec. We have always been willing to help our people across North America. Many started to look at Kahnawà:ke as a community that will always defend itself and take a stand.

The Rotihsken'rakéhte' had duties. We never initiated the conflicts. The only thing we initiated was going back to the mountains and taking over Moss Lake, which we called Ganienkeh. However, we did not do it on our own. We went to all the people and our local council, and then to the national meeting of the Mohawks, then to the grand council of the Iroquois Confederacy. We had the support of everyone. We also contacted Native people from right across North Turtle Island, and everybody was supportive. Only then did we make our move. Moss Lake was the only time the Rotihsken'rakéhte' ever initiated anything on their own. Everything else, such as the evictions, had been decided by the people. They asked us if we would support it, and we said, "If this is what you people decide, we support what you decide".

If you compare the Rotihsken'rakéhte' to the American Indian Movement (AIM), you will see that we were more oriented towards building the community. AIM was an organization and was not representing itself as a people. They did not have a constitution as we had. The people of Ganienkeh got along very well with AIM, whether we agreed with their philosophy or not. AIM was very respectful of Ganienkeh, because we took action and accomplished a lot, whereas the rest of the Iroquois Confederacy was doing nothing. The people of AIM were also action people. They were at Wounded Knee just before we took over Ganienkeh, and they knew many of us from being in Wounded Knee. Vernon Bellecourt had that respect for us, and Dennis Banks too.[49] We did not always agree with them, but our respect was mutual. AIM was trying to become part of the UN as a non-governmental organization (NGO), but we did not want any part of NGO status. We wanted to be recognized as a people.

When we visited the UN, we reminded them that the constitution of the Iroquois Confederacy, the Kaianerehkó:wa, was the cornerstone of world peace. Our confederacy was the first example of a league of nations on the planet. People like Tecumseh and Pontiac were part of confederations.[50] The Algonquins had their own confederacy.[51] For thousands of years, there were many confederations here in the Americas. Historically, we all had alliances of some kind with other nations. The Iroquois stood out because of our constitution, the Kaianerehkó:wa, but we were not different from other confederacies of Native peoples. The fact that we had this constitution encouraged us as the Rotihsken'rakéhte' to take a different route. We did not impose the Kaianerehkó:wa on anyone. The only thing we did was to encourage other nations to stop fighting and stop the wars! There is no reason people should lose their fathers, husbands, children or other loved ones because of war. Everyone has a right to live.

Financing and Solidarity

By 1986, a large cigarette trade had started on the south side of the imaginary line. In the US, Native peoples also had casinos and gas stations, but nothing was happening in the north. We were always talking about developing an economy, but we lacked the resources to do it. We said, "Well this business does not seem to be so hard! Why don't we start generating an income to help our people? With that money we could build a flea market, acquire some land, buy farm equipment and all sorts of things". So we started selling cigarettes from the back of a pick-up truck in Kahnawà:ke. That was the beginning of our new economy. The cigarette trade helped fund the building of the bingo hall. We were able to support the hospital by purchasing a new heart machine. We bought trays and utensils for the inpatient elders. We helped finance various sports and activities in the community. We even bought a new Zamboni for the arena.

At first, some people did not want to take our money. They said, "Oh! It's blood money!" But we were not the mafia going around breaking legs to make money. Most of the people who criticized us back then got rich from the businesses we started. The band council, the police force, they all ended up getting their share in some business. Meanwhile, the people who started the business are no longer part of it. Growing the business from scratch was not about a few individuals getting rich off it. That was not why we started selling cigarettes in the first place. We wanted to build financial self-sufficiency as a community, not get rich. We helped our brothers and sisters from other territories, from British Columbia and across the prairies, when they needed it. At that time, we also bought grain and hay during the drought in Western Canada. Canada subsidized the white farmers and ranchers, but nobody subsidized the Natives. Since there was no drought here, we transported it by rail to Saskatchewan, to Chief Louis Taypotat.[52] He was a rancher and a farmer himself, and was chief of the council there. He knew who needed help, so we left it in his hands to hand out as needed. Also, when the women of British Columbia needed help with drug issues their children were experiencing, we helped out. These mothers established summer camps for their youth, which we financed. Their four-week camp sessions helped those mothers establish stronger and healthier relationships with their children. We also financed sports teams, including Vancouver's North Shore lacrosse team. We did many good things in the 1980s and 1990s.

They called us when the Québec environmental police raided the Mi'kmaq people's territories over the salmon issue.[53] We immediately told the Québec government that if the abuse of those people did not stop, then we would take whatever action we had to to stop them. Québec did not want the Mohawks to get into this fight. We often sent delegations of Rotihsken'rakéhte' to help with other Native struggles. When the "Oka Crisis" was going on in 1990, some of our people were dispatched over there, but we shut down the bridge, roads and passes as a community. Later, the Oneidas in Ontario took action on their own. They had all this infrastructure passing through their community, power lines, Highway 401, so they could easily disrupt everything. Canada started panicking when it understood what all the other Native peoples and their allies could do. They know there is no way to control us. They had no foresight when they put a bridge, a canal, railroads and power lines on our land. They cannot babysit all that stuff! Every single one of our communities is full of infrastructure. The invaders made themselves vulnerable, and they consistently underestimated us. They thought, "Oh! There are only a hundred people there, and they are finished". But we are everywhere! It only takes one person to cause significant infrastructure damage. We could go in any direction within a two hundred–mile radius of their precious infrastructure and find something to destroy in any Native territory.

We went to New Brunswick for the fishing fight.[54] We have been to Maine and Washington State as well. I was with Mike Chosa and his people when they took over that park in Chicago.[55] We have been all over Turtle Island, and people are always happy when a Mohawk shows up, because we bring the Kaianerehkó:wa with us. It encourages people to know that they have a family if somebody does something wrong to their people. There was also Kanonhstá:ton, in Caledonia, next to Ohswé:ken.[56] Our guys were up there all that time and brought the knowledge back to that community about the Kaianerehkó:wa, which helped to re-empower the women. Today, the women up there are very powerful! Back in the 1920s, it was people from there who came here and reintroduced the Kaianerehkó:wa to us, and almost a hundred years later we are the ones going up there to bring it back to them. There is always someone retaining the traditions and keeping the people strong. A reporter interviewed me for the *Tekawennake* newspaper in Ohswé:ken and asked me many questions about the Kaianerehkó:wa. She asked, "Where did you learn all this stuff?" I said, "From here!" She said, "From here? I've lived here all my life, and I never heard this stuff!" I explained to her how the Kaianerehkó:wa people had to go underground for a long time. They did not have to go underground out there in Ohswé:ken, because it was established by Joseph Brant, who was a Loyalist close to the Anglican Church. They did not come under pressure the same way we did. They were able to maintain the songs, ceremonies and dances. They brought back the Kaianerehkó:wa to us in the 1920s and helped us re-establish our longhouses, our councils and our way of performing condolences. Often people take for granted that somebody else will be there carrying on these things. Everybody is waiting for somebody else to carry forth this knowledge, but it has to be done.

When we visited other communities to assist them in their struggles, we brought our experience and knowledge to the land defenders. We never told them what to do. We explained what we did in the past, what worked and what did not. They asked us to set up a communication center, because we had vast experience; this is how we helped get the word out. The people are really grateful for what we did. It is our job, duty and responsibility to keep the Kaianerehkó:wa alive. I don't believe my job is to be a title holder. My job is to help to keep our way of life, to be a reminder rather than a teacher, to help to remind our people that nothing is lost. The only thing that's lost with many of our people is our memory.

What It Means to Be a Warrior

I was twenty years old when I started experiencing fear. I was a warrior according to what my understanding of a warrior was. We were getting ready to fight with the SQ and the army, if necessary, up in Kahnawà:ke, and I was more than ready. From what I remember, there was not an ounce of fear in me as I walked into the cookhouse. There I saw my father and my uncles, men I looked up to all my life as being fearless. I saw them, and they were puking. They were sitting there like they were going to die, and I asked my grandmother what was wrong with them. She said that they were afraid. I kind of laughed, because in my mind these guys had no fear. Then she said, "They're not afraid of fighting. They're afraid that if they go off to fight, and if they don't return, nobody will take care of their families". That's when it hit me. I was a single guy, I had no children, I had nobody to be concerned about but myself, and I thought I was being responsible, but I did not know what responsibility really was, because I had nobody who depended upon me. If I was gone, no child would starve, no woman would be husbandless. That is when I learned what fear is. It has nothing to do with the fighting; it is about the responsibility that the decisions you make may affect the lives of others.

A lot of people today want to call themselves warriors, but they don't know what a warrior is. They think that being a warrior is wearing a tattoo or a jacket with the Unity flag on their back. They think that it's about carrying an AK-47, putting a mask and camouflage on. They think that is what makes them a warrior, but that has nothing to do with it. Being a warrior is about taking responsibility for your family and for the Earth. When people say, "I'm ready to die!" my reaction is that we don't need you in that case; dead men don't accomplish anything. We need men who want to live, because they are the ones who are ready to take responsibility. They are the ones who are willing to help with the survival of our people. Any idiot can die, but to live is a big responsibility.

Notes

1   The meaning of *Rotihsken'rakéhte'* is discussed more thoroughly in the "Skakwatakwen—Concept Glossary" section at the end of this volume.

2   In confederacy grand councils, the three sides of the longhouse are: the "elder brothers" (Mohawk, Seneca), the "younger Brothers" (Cayuga, Oneida, Tuscarora) and the "firekeepers" (Onondaga), who are the tiebreakers, resolving deadlocks between the two other parties, all the while ensuring the consensus of everyone.

3   This meaning of *Onkwehón:we* as *people of the original way* is close to the ethnonyms used by several Indigenous peoples across the planet, for example, Anishinaabe (Algonquin), Innu (Montagnais), Deniize (Wet'suwet'en), Dene, Tiwi (Australian Tunuvivi), Ju/'hoansi (South African IKung), Runa Kuna (Ecuadorian Achuar), etc.

4   For an explanation of A'nowarà:ke, or Turtle Island, see the glossary. As Tekarontakeh says, "Our ancestors knew that this land had the shape of a turtle, because they were free to travel across it. There were no borders".

5   See Timeline, "1924 Raid on Ohswé:ken".

6   See Timeline, "1928 Kahnawà:ke longhouse".

7   The moccasin telegraph refers to the networks of Indigenous "runners" sharing information between communities.

8   Ohswé:ken, also called Six Nations of the Grand River or just "Six Nations", is the single largest reservation in Canada, with close to thirteen thousand inhabitants coming from all nations of the confederacy, along with people from other nations, such as the Anishinaabe. It was established near Brantford, Ontario, in 1784; see Timeline, "1784 Haldimand Proclamation".

9   Hadocsay Lawrence Nanticoke (1921–2008); Elwood Green (1936–1998); Coleman Powless (1929–1983); Dick Hill (1949–2014).

10   See Timeline, "1959 Ohswé:ken Raid".

11   See Timeline, "1959 Saint Lawrence Seaway".

12   Tekarontakeh's grandfather, Ahnionken Louis Diabo (1877–1957), became internationally famous after resisting the seaway construction while the area around his house was being devastated by excavation work and dynamiting; see Timeline, "1959 Saint Lawrence Seaway".

13   See Timeline, "1957 Mohawk River Valley Re-establishment". With villages like Canajoharie (the Upper Castle) and Tionondogen (the Lower Castle), the Mohawk River Valley in New York State was considered the heart of Mohawk land (Kanièn:ke) before the Sullivan-Clinton Expedition drove them out during the American War of Independence; see Timeline, "1779 Sullivan-Clinton Expedition".

14   The Indian Act, originally passed in 1876, is the primary act that defines how the government of Canada interacts with Native peoples, setting out the rules for reservations and defining the procedures through which to determine who is or is not legally considered Native.

15   See Timeline, "1754–1763 French and Indian War".

16   See Timeline, "1968 Akwesasne International Bridge Blockade".

17   Michael Kanentakeran Mitchell, dir., *You Are on Indian Land* (Montréal: National Film Board of Canada, 1969), accessed March 10, 2022, https://www.nfb.ca/film/you_are_on_indian_land.

18   See Timeline, "1970 High School protest".

19   Rastewenserontah Peter Diome (1903–1971) was a prominent Roiá:ner and the editor of the journal *Longhouse News* in the late 1960s. He had been placed in a French-Canadian orphanage and only spoke French as a child but rapidly learned his language and traditions when he reintegrated the longhouse in Kahnawà:ke, devoting his life to sharing with other communities. Akwiraes Frank Natawe Curotte (1927–2000) was a major knowledge keeper and Bear Clan Roiá:ner in Kahnawà:ke. He played a prominent role in the reoccupation of Ganienkeh, where he acted as a teacher in the Aboriginal Way school.

20   Ronald Kirby (1937–2011) was the grand chief of the Mohawk Council of Kahnawà:ke between 1972 to 1976.

21   See Timeline, "1799 Handsome Lake".

22   See Timeline, "1928 Kahnawà:ke longhouse".

23   Carmelite priest David Scott Blanchard published a schoolbook for the Kahnawà:ke Survival School; David Scott Blanchard, *Seven Generations: A History of the Kanienkehaka* (Kahnawà:ke: Kahnawà:ke Survival School, 1980).

24   See Timeline, "1877 Chief Joseph".

25   A Mohawk immersion school, Karihwanoron, also opened in 1988 next to the Indian Way School.

26   See Timeline, "1972 Indian Affairs Occupations in Washington and Ottawa".

27   John Ciaccia has successively been the minister of energy and natural resources, (1985–1989), of Indian affairs (1989–1990) and of international affairs (1989–1994) for the Liberal Party of Québec. He would later be involved in the 1990 Oka Crisis as a negotiator for the Canadian government.

28   Before Canada became a country, money promised to Indigenous nations to compensate them for the loss of their lands was placed in the Indian Trust Fund, which were later transferred to Canada and placed in the Consolidated Revenue Fund. Although part of this money served to provide basic services to the reservations where Indigenous peoples were confined, it was also used by the government for its daily operations and invested in infrastructure projects that had nothing to do with Indigenous peoples—and which often even conflicted with their needs and wishes. No account was ever made of how much money was accumulated this way, a big part of which was simply spent by successive governments. Had it not been managed and spent by the Canadian government based on the racist pretext that Indigenous peoples were incapable of managing their own funds, those funds, along with the compounding interest accumulated, would today amount to trillions of dollars.

29   Mohawk Irvin Goodleaf was a special assistant to Jean Chrétien in the Canadian Department of Indian Affairs and Northern Development. He later became a businessman, reintegrated into the longhouse tradition and now lives in Kahnawà:ke.

30   This same bus, nicknamed the Freedom Bus, was later used by Mohawk warriors in the reoccupation of Moss Lake.

31   See Timeline, "1973 Kahnawà:ke evictions".

32   See Timeline, "1704 Deerfield Raid".

33   Through illegal land sales, rentals and occupations, it is estimated that Kahnawà:ke had lost two-thirds of its original territory by 1890.

34   See Timeline, "1853 French Dauphin Controversy."

35   Born in 1934, Jean Chrétien was the minister of Indian affairs from 1968 to 1974 before becoming the prime minister of Canada from 1993 to 2003.

36   See Timeline, "1985 Bill C-31".

37   See Timeline, "1974 Ganienkeh".

38   The John Birch Society (JBS) is a conservative anti-communist advocacy group that was established in 1958 in Indianapolis, in honor of John Birch, a US military intelligence officer and Baptist minister killed by Chinese communists just before the end of World War II. Minutemen refers to militiamen active during the American Revolution and a number of armed groups inspired by them that exist in modern times.

39   A five-minute drive from Moss Lake, the Big Moose Inn still exists today, close to Big Moose Lake.

40   See Timeline, "1613 Two Row Wampum".

41   See Timeline, "1977 United Nations conference".

42   *Ganienkeh Manifesto*, included in this book; see pages 130–38.

43   See Timeline, "1973 Wounded Knee".

44   During the massive 1971 riot at Attica Prison in New York State, Governor Nelson Rockefeller refused to comply with the prisoners' demand that he personally come to the prison to negotiate with them. Sending heavily armed police forces instead, Rockefeller's stubbornness cost the lives of at least forty-three people, thirty-three inmates and ten correctional officers and civilians.

45   After having been a bomber pilot in the World War II, Blackfoot tribe member Forrest Gerard (1925–2013) became the first Indigenous secretary of Indian affairs, from 1977 to 1980.

46   See Timeline, "1977 Ganienkeh moves to Miner Lake".

47   See Timeline, "1979 Fort Kanasaraken".

48   In Eeyou Istchee (Cree territory, northern Québec), the construction of the James Bay hydroelectric complex was highly contested by Crees, who successfully blocked the project in court in 1973. The project, one of the biggest in the world, was nonetheless completed at the end of the 1970s, flooding 11,000 square kilometres (approximately 6,800 square miles) of boreal forest.

49   Vernon Bellecourt (1931–2007) and Dennis Banks (1937–2017) were two prominent AIM leaders, both Ojibwa.

50   Shawnee leader Tecumseh (1768–1813) helped to form a large multinational Native American confederacy at the beginning of the nineteenth century, which was intended to form an independent Indigenous country, fighting American troops in the 1812–1815 War of 1812; see Timeline, "War of 1812". Odaawaa leader Pontiac (1720–1769) created a federation of many Indigenous nations living around the Great Lakes to fight the British after the latter had defeated the French in 1763; see Timeline, "1754–1763 French and Indian War".

51   The Three Fires Confederacy; see "Bodéwadmi" in the list of "Other Indigenous Peoples".

52   Louis Taypotat was elected chief of the Kahkewistahaw Nation of Saskatchewan on three occasions, conserving his position for twenty-seven years.

53   See Timeline, "1981 Raid on Listuguj".

54   See Timeline, "1999 Burnt Church".

55   See Timeline, "1969 Chicago Indian Village".

56   See Timeline, "2006 Kanonhstá:ton"; Glossary, "Kanonhstá:ton".

Kakwirakeron Interview

After traveling throughout North America as an ironworker and construction foreman building bridges and high-rise buildings, Kakwirakeron Art Montour was appointed by clan mothers to become a mediator, negotiator and spokesperson for the Mohawk Warrior Society during the reoccupation of Ganienkeh. A fluent speaker of his native language and well versed in Kanien'kehá:ka traditions, Kakwirakeron always strived for peaceful solutions amidst volatile situations. He was part of the Rotinonhsión:ni delegation to the United Nations in 1977 and was involved in the Raquette Point standoff in Akwesasne in 1979. In 1997, he helped organize Native resistance to New York State taxation of gas and cigarettes on Onondaga territory. Kakwirakeron passed away in 2017, leaving behind fifty-nine grandchildren and thirty-six great grandchildren.

Origins

My name is Kakwirakeron, also known as Art Montour. I'm a Mohawk, Kanien'kehá:ka, I'm originally from Kahnawà:ke, near Montréal. I was born and raised there. My grandparents on my mother's side were longhouse people, and my grandfather was a Roiá:ner for the Bear Clan. He was what they would call a war chief, at that time.

At the age of seventeen, I left to go to New York to be an ironworker. I remember stopping after work in the evening at this bar where all the Mohawks and Natives used to go. Some reporters came in and wanted to know what we thought about what was going on in Wounded Knee and whether we agreed with it or not. I was listening to everybody doing their interviews. I realized there was such a lack of knowledge about what was going on and what it all meant. This was before I became involved, so it really sparked my attention. I was very interested, but I felt like I had to learn more.

I had to come back to Kahnawà:ke for health reasons in 1973, and there were a lot of things happening there politically. There were two sides to it as always; there was the band council's side, which was the same as the colonial government, and there was the traditional side. I went back and forth between the two sides to see what each had to say and to see if I was going to support one side or the other. I was very impressed with the arguments of the traditional people. This is when people were starting to become aware of the Rotihsken'rakéhte', the Mohawk Warrior Society. They explained the Great Law, the Kaianerehkó:wa, to me. I was reinstated into the Kaianerehkó:wa during the Harvest Festival and became an activist. I have been with the traditional people ever since.

I had known Louis Hall since I was a child. He was a well-known figure in the community, always talking about the Kaianerehkó:wa. As for the Warrior Society, it really began with Tekarontakeh, who was really very young at the time, around sixteen or seventeen years old. Along with others, he had formed a singing group where they were trying to learn all the old songs and bring them back to the community. They had been attending all the longhouse meetings, hearing the elders talk about the Kaianerehkó:wa, about who we are and how sovereign we are. They realized that what they were hearing was not consistent with the way things were organized in Kahnawà:ke at that time. So they wanted to form a group, the Rotihsken'rakéhte'. It's an all-encompassing word in our language. It doesn't just mean warriors but can also mean husband, father, grandfather, uncle, nephew and so forth. It includes all men, the everyday person just as much as the Rotiianérshon. Louis Hall, who had done a lot of studying, suggested using the term *Warrior Society*, because of the fear it would cause the people opposing them. They still called themselves Rotihsken'rakéhte', but when they spoke in English, they would say the Warrior Society. They were just a small group of young men, boys almost. They decided that they wanted to reform the Rotihsken'rakéhte', so they came to a council meeting and asked the elders. One of the elders was Tekarontakeh's grandfather, Ahnionken Louis Diabo, who was a chief of the Bear Clan. They requested to be sanctioned by the council, and Tekarontakeh's grandfather replied that you don't need to ask for sanction, you're already part of the Kaianerehkó:wa, the Great Law, you have a very important place, and we will support you in your reformation of the Rotihsken'rakéhte'. So that's how, in modern times, it came back together. It came back less than a year before I became involved, so I became part of the original Rotihsken'rakéhte', but I was older at that time; I had just turned thirty-one. Many young men joined it, and Louis Hall had been studying and learning about the Kaianerehkó:wa and the warriors and what their duties and functions were. He helped the group to really know who they were, what they were, why they were, how they fit into everything; he had an excellent understanding of what the warriors were. He was very instrumental in the warriors being reconstituted according to the original ways and their original purpose. We have tried to maintain that same impulse ever since. There are a lot of misconceptions about the warriors, many of which are intentional.

Ganienkeh

The evictions in Kahnawà:ke brought the Rotihsken'rakéhte' to the forefront in 1973. People heard about it so quickly. Whenever there's an action in any of our communities, members of other communities come out and support. The next thing you know, there were Rotihsken'rakéhte' throughout Mohawk territory, then throughout the confederacy and beyond. You would hear about Warrior Societies all the way from the East Coast to the West Coast.

There were many conflicts between the band council people and the traditional people, but the majority of the community ended up siding with the traditional people. We felt that if we stayed in Kahnawà:ke and wanted to continue with our line of thinking we would probably just end up fighting among ourselves. It would have been Native against Native, and that wasn't feasible. We talked about going back to the Mohawk River Valley or somewhere within the Mohawk territory that was unceded. That's how we ended up at Moss Lake.

We went there to promote the Kaianerehkó:wa and our traditional way of life. We had decided before we went there that there would be no electricity. We were not against electricity, but if we had electricity in there, then the government could just conveniently shut it off and make us suffer. Being in the mountains, there was no running water. We had to get spring water and carry it into the house. We decided to have wood stoves for heating. We brought our children in right from day one and decided that they would get their education from Native people. People in their seventies and eighties came too. People came as families. None of us considered it as an occupation. It was a repossession of what had always been ours.

Once people grew aware of what we were doing, they wanted to know more about it. That's how the word of what we were doing spread beyond Mohawk communities. In fact, the initial group that went into Moss Lake included Kanien'kehá:kas, Oneidas, Onondagas, Cayugas, Senecas and Tuscaroras. All six nations had some presence there, and almost immediately we had the presence of young people from other Indigenous nations both from Canada and the United States. Moss Lake was a cross section of all of North America. People from Ganienkeh would go and participate in other people's movements all the time. It was taken for granted that people were going to show up from all the different communities. That probably influenced Louis Hall when he created the Unity flag, which displays the profile of a Native person, a profile that all Native people can relate to. Behind that profile is the sun and behind the sun the background is red, because we were popularly known as the Red man at that time. It became a huge symbol. I remember when Louis Hall presented it to the group inside Moss Lake, he said that the single eagle feather represented the unity of all Native peoples throughout North, Central and South America. He also noted that the feather was standing up because in some cultures the feather facing downward is a sign of defeat. The sun was also a symbol that all Native people look up to. It represents good energy, strength and power.

A lot of thought and discussion went into creating the philosophy of our group. Our main objective was to return to our land, to live as traditionally as we could and to follow and promote the Kaianerehkó:wa. Living a simple type of life could have easily happened, but New York State didn't want it to happen. There was nothing but talk about eliminating us, annihilating us. Living a natural and traditional lifestyle is what we all wanted, but it became very difficult, virtually impossible, for some people to let it happen. We did not plan to go there to get into a conflict. In fact, we made sure that the location where we would set up our camp would not be on private land but New York State land. We figured that it would help us avoid conflict. We knew what it was like to be displaced, and we didn't want to evict anybody and have them turn against us, but it still ended up going that way. The state's plan was that if we didn't voluntarily leave on our own, they would go in there and wipe us out. In fact, one of the state troopers who was commander at the time, Major Bob Charland, testified later in a federal court that he was given instructions to go in and use all violent force to remove the people. Then he looked right at the judge and said "including the use of flame-throwers". Can you believe that? They knew there were men, women, children and even newborn babies there. It was a real revelation when he said that in federal court.

Yet the people that lived in the rest of the state became very supportive of us over time. In addition to all the churches that supported us, there was a support group called RAIN—Rights for American Indians Now. People brought us supplies, food, clothing and whatever essentials we needed. It was a harsh winter climate there. People said that we wouldn't make it to winter, then that we wouldn't make it to fall, then to spring. They stopped saying that after about six months. Life inside the encampment was good; we really enjoyed it.

I was chosen as the spokesperson. I had to travel a lot. I ended up speaking at many colleges, universities and high schools, doing interviews. That was very helpful in getting and maintaining support for us. As one of the spokespeople, I listened to everybody's concerns and tried to take them all into account when I spoke in public. I remained a spokesperson through the whole thing. My grandfather was a good speaker, so I probably inherited it from him. I spoke well right off the bat. Within the first week or so, people approached me about talking to the news people. I was learning fast. In our way, we always give credit to the spirits of our ancestors, so I give credit to my grandfather who helped me understand many things I didn't know.

Tobacco and Gaming

My family and I moved to Akwesasne in 1984. The conflict on gaming in Akwesasne happened in 1989, so I was involved in it from the beginning. The media turned it into a conflict about gaming, but that was not really the issue. There was much propaganda to support the idea that we were just greedy businessmen, but I was part of it, and casinos are not what I was fighting for at the beginning. My involvement had to do with jurisdiction and the issue of our sovereignty. Those opposed to gaming were so small in number that they had very little influence in the community, so they went to the Canadian government, the Canadian band council, the American tribal council and New York State for support. Since the conflict was happening on the so-called American side, New York State tried to claim jurisdiction, but they knew that they would have to force their way into it, because New York State has no rights over Mohawk territories. Neither does the federal government. But they have might and violent force, if necessary. So the small anti-casino group turned to them to create their own "Warrior Society" with the state police, the sheriff's department, federal marshals, the National Guard, etc. They reached out to all the forces the enemy could muster. Being Mohawks, people involved in the band and tribal councils had grown up always believing those police forces were the enemy, but suddenly they were reaching out to them. Journalists made up the idea that it was a civil war, but you cannot call it a civil war when a group in a community stands up for its territory against soldiers from a foreign country. We call that an invasion.

For our part, we stayed internal; we didn't reach out to outside forces, only to our own people. Again, my part in it had to do with our sovereignty and jurisdiction over our own lands. If you're not supportive of gaming, then you don't have to participate in it. If you're supportive of gaming, then you can take part in it. If you're neutral, then you can stay neutral. Tobacco trade was also part of the controversy at that time. It was new, and New York State said that it was illegal for Native people to sell tobacco without charging New York sales taxes. It was the same thing with the gasoline; the state said that we could not sell gasoline unless we followed their rules. But because we never relinquished our sovereignty, they knew that they could never convince the entire community to follow their rules. From our point of view, our trade had nothing to do with smuggling; we merely transported tobacco from the southern to the northern portion of our territory.[1] We knew it wasn't wrong or illegal. We were just exercising our sovereignty. The cigarettes were purchased, not stolen. We purchased them and resold them with a profit. People that supported the band council were also opposed to the tobacco trade.

Within the longhouse, there were those who were fully supportive of the Kaianerehkó:wa, but there were also a few supporters of the Handsome Lake religion who strongly opposed gaming and gambling as a matter of faith.[2] That's how gaming became an issue within the longhouse; there was a real split. We had to decide whether we would remain within the Kaianerehkó:wa or give ourselves to Handsome Lake's religious cult. Yet the vast majority of people in Akwesasne did not side with the longhouse, Handsome Lake or the band council. We would even learn later that those who said they were opposed to gambling actually just wanted it for themselves. They must have felt that the people who had started the casinos had beaten them to the punch. They don't talk about anything anymore, as many of them ended up working at the big casino that the tribal council now controls.[3] It was mostly the religious people, the Handsome Lakers, as we call them, who were sincere in their opposition to gambling, because their religion told them it was forbidden.

However, I've spoken to many of them since then, and most of them agree that their opposition was a mistake, since tobacco brought so much economic benefit to this community. Once they realized that, many of them dropped their opposition and began working in casinos themselves. That's been the story here since 1989. Many who were opposed to the casino and gasoline industries embrace them today. Why buy gasoline from settlers when you can get it in your own community and pay less? I don't have any animosity against the anti-casino people today. I realize that a lot of them revised their outlook on things, and hopefully that can prevent some unnecessary future conflicts.

The Rotihsken'rakéhte' longhouse in Akwesasne represents the real spirit of the Kaianerehkó:wa, as it was established by Dekanawida, the Peacemaker. The Kaianerehkó:wa is based on consensus. It makes no exception. It has no dispute. It makes one big circle. Because we've always been free people and free thinkers, each of us has a mind that can think for itself. You can pass all the laws you want, but you cannot stop us. The fire where we have our councils is right inside each one of us, culturally. It's really a spark, not a fire. When the sparks from each individual human being are put together and kindled by collecting their thoughts together, then they make a fire, Kahwá:tsire'. We still put our sparks together here. According to our culture, the fire comes. You collect the thoughts together to make a fire. The people who have left our Rotihsken'rakéhte' longhouse and built another fire are free to do so. They have absolute freedom. That's why there's no civil war here. One side can say what they want if they want to, but on our side we have the Kaianerehkó:wa, and we have to follow it. If we stray from that, we are violating ourselves.

We continue living life as Kanien'kehá:ka people. We continue our festivals, marriages, wakes for people who have passed on, baby-naming ceremonies, social dances and gatherings. Life has always been that way for us, even going back five or ten thousand years. We merely continue the spirit of life here. That is where our spark, where our fire, comes from. It's indivisible. Even though they have always tried to divide and conquer us, they never succeeded. I was physically imprisoned, but they never imprisoned my mind. That's what I said on the day of my sentencing: "You can imprison me, you can take my body, but you can't imprison my mind. My mind will always be free".[4]

Notes

1   The US-Canadian Border does not apply to Indigenous peoples, as acknowledged by the Jay Treaty; see Timeline, "1794 Northwest Indian War and Jay Treaty".

2   The Handsome Lake Code explicitly forbids gambling, along with alcohol, witchcraft and adultery.

3   After spearheading opposition to the Warriors' casino in 1989, the tribal council opened its own casino and resort, the Akwesasne Mohawk Casino (AMC), in 1999.

4   Kakwirakeron was arrested on July 24, 1989, and charged with conspiracy, impeding the execution of search warrants and use of weapons in relation to the conflicts over gambling in Akwesasne. On April 10, 1990, an all-white jury at the Syracuse federal court sentenced him to ten months in prison.

Kanasaraken Interview

Kanasaraken Loran Thompson was born to a Roiá:ner father and an Iakoiá:ner mother. He spent his youth traveling between Akwesasne and various construction sites, where he worked as an ironworker on bridges and high-rise buildings for over forty years. After becoming a council member representing the Bear Clan in 1974, he found himself at the forefront of local resistance efforts directed against the erection of a fence around Akwesasne in 1979. As a result of a grand council decision, his house at Raquette Point was designated as a headquarters for that resistance, and his property became the site of an armed siege on the part of local anti-warrior vigilantes and New York state troopers that lasted for two years. In 1990, Kanasaraken was chosen to lead a delegation sent to Kanehsatà:ke Mohawk territory, as it was being surrounded by the Canadian army, to negotiate a peaceful resolution to the Oka Crisis, wherein he earned his nickname "Warrior General".

Our people have gone through centuries of oppression. All the trauma that people go through winds up in the DNA, so our DNA is full of problems and issues that will be carried into the next generation. That's what we're living through. It's been a struggle all the way. Way back, the pope told the explorers to go out and look for land, but there were people on the land. The pope said, "They're not people like us. They live like animals in the woods, so they have no souls, and they don't have any title to their land". That gave the explorers and the new people coming onto our lands the right to just do as they pleased. It gave them the right to shoot us like any other animal, which they did. They had no second thoughts about it. In growing, they just got rid of all the Native people that were in the way. There used to be millions of us when explorers first got here, the ocean's shorelines were covered with campfires. In our language, we understand what you are as a person, your soul, *Atónhnhets*, as being a spark, Ó:tsire'. This spark is what gives you life. When one sits down with a person to talk about issues, our language says that their sparks have come together and made a small fire. When the clan discusses its issues, it creates a clan fire. When the nation talks about its issues, it's a national fire. When the grand council has its meetings, it's called a big fire, Katsenhowá:nen. It's very different from what the English language suggests by saying grand council.

When the Peacemaker, Dekanawida, made the longhouse, he called it *Kanonhsionni'ón:we*, the *one real house*. He explained that the house extends from where the sun comes up to where it goes down. The length of its roof is the sky, and Mother Earth is its floor. To this day, the longhouse has remained within our circle. Our Circle Wampum, *Teiotiohkwahnhákton*, is encircled by two interwoven strings. One string represents the Kaianerehkó:wa and the other one represents the four ceremonies, while the people are understood to be contained inside both of these circles. If people leave the circle, they lose their voice and can no longer speak on either traditional or political issues. That's what we're living through right now, as many Native people changed their status and exited our circle by accepting European laws. The Iroquois Confederacy was the first one to deal with those settlers on a political level; we taught them how to govern themselves. They didn't know how to be free, because they came from monarchies, but our people taught them. In teaching them they put their government together; they taught them how to unite their thirteen colonies instead of keeping them separate. But they stayed monarchies in many ways, and they attacked our people instead of returning the favour.

It all goes back to square one. The first settlers wanted to get land from us, but the Iroquois never wanted to sell land. Since they could not deal with the Mohawks in this neck of the woods on land issues, they went to individuals in different communities that were Christian and made agreements with those converts who had abandoned our circle. That's how we lost nine million acres of our land. When they have us file land claims today, they're only trying to legalize and legitimize illegal land thefts that took place a long time ago, thinking we've forgotten about it. As the original people of this land, we permitted non-Indigenous people to live on our land, but we never allowed them to control it. We gave them permission to live here on the condition that they would govern themselves. We would govern our own people, and if conflicts happened between us, we would sit down together to see how we would deal with it, but we would be the ones judging our people, and they would judge their own people. That was the original agreement that we made with the first settlers through the Teiohá:te, the Two Row Wampum.[1] According to the Teiohá:te, the settlers had to keep all their language and culture on their own ship and leave us to lead our own way of life on our canoe, but the colonial governments never stopped trying to assimilate us into their society, and they never stopped trying to assert their authority over our territories.

Both my father and my mother were really active in holding on to and promoting our traditional values. I came into the world in that environment. We had a big family, and when I was really young, we had five huge gardens, we had cows and horses and chickens, so we were always busy working. As we grew up, whenever people came, we always opened the house, letting them stay a couple of nights. They all sat downstairs in the living room talking about our rights, our historical agreements, our issues with the courts and the other problems of the day. They would talk all night, and I would go to sleep in the stairway trying to listen. My father was a little hard of hearing, so he talked loud, which made the rest of them talk loud as well, so I had a pretty good understanding of what was going on. Whenever we went to the longhouse for ceremonies, for meetings and gatherings, my parents always made sure that we sat and listened. That's how I grew up, watching the longhouse issues take place. I was absorbed in them. My father didn't want his children to have anything whatsoever to do with any kind of religion. He didn't want us to learn anything about European religious values. What we had to learn was our own culture.

When I got older, I started working in construction, traveling to different cities and observing what was going on there. I got married a year after I graduated, and I concentrated on working full-time. I went to work in Virginia, and I got hurt down there, so I moved back home on disability leave. That's when one day people showed up down the river at my father's driveway. Three people came knocking on the door. They called me out of my house and encouraged me to get involved in what was happening at the longhouse. They were starting a "Warrior Society", as they called it, and they needed to get the longhouse up and actively moving again. I wasn't doing anything special at the time, so I started to hang out with them, and I gradually understood what was going on. There was always a pocket of traditional-minded people around. At one time, they had to go underground, because they were so oppressed, but once the community started to sympathize with the positions they took on different issues, they slowly became strong again. I was too shy to stand up and say or do anything publicly back then, so I just sat and listened. The North American Indian Travelling College on Cornwall Island offered me a job where I would travel to different universities and colleges and talk to students. I learned quite a few things from longhouse people who were part of the same traveling troupe, especially from Jake Thomas,[2] who was from Six Nations, and who was in charge of reciting the Kaianerehkó:wa at the longhouse. One day, a Bear Clan meeting was called. They had a vacant position in the clan, and they wanted my brother to fill it, but my brother said that he was not interested in becoming a chief. So they looked at me, and I told them, "I don't know anything, but if you want to take a chance with me, I'll try to help you with what I know". They were fine with that, so they put me in the position.

Land claims were becoming a really important issue in Akwesasne at that time. The Iroquois Confederacy was discussing the matter, and I was listening to their debates. We were discussing the treaty signed in 1796 between the United States and the Seven Nations of Canada to delimit the lands belonging to the Mohawks in Akwesasne, which they called Saint-Regis back then. The Seven Nations of Canada were Christianized, and the treaty was not agreed upon by the real Iroquois Confederacy, so it was an illegal treaty.[3] But the 1796 agreement was larger than the reservation land, it included nearby towns like Massena, New York, which is just next to my family's property. Afterwards New York State had purchased more of our land inside the tract, and that was contested. It was in the middle of these discussions that the Saint-Regis tribal council suddenly decided to put a fence around the reservation using a grant from the federal government. I saw that if they put a fence around Akwesasne, it would limit our land claim to the small territory of the reservation, and I did not agree with the idea of reservations or with limiting our territories and our land claims to their narrow borders, so I told the tribal council that when they got to my home in Raquette Point, they could not go any further, as they had no right to be on that land, which belonged to my family, which did not recognize their jurisdiction and their boundaries.

Around that time, my friend Joe Swamp and I were working on a building outside one day, when we suddenly heard chainsaws. I said, "Boy that sounds really close, let's go check it out!" So we took the tractor and a trailer and went down there. We stumbled on really young kids, all eighteen or nineteen years old, who were cutting down trees on a sixteen-foot path to put up a fence there. I asked them, "What are you doing? You've come too far. We told you that you cannot come onto our family's land. Where's your boss?" One of them answered, "Oh, he's not here right now". I said, "But you're doing damage. I'm going to have to confiscate all your equipment". It was perfect for them, since they didn't want to work, so they all started running around picking up their chainsaws and equipment to help us put them in the trailer. I put it all inside a garage at home and went back to my business.

There was a small police force on the reservation at that time; "Indian police" as they were called. The chief of police was my next-door neighbour; he lived in a trailer right next to my house. I guess they found him drinking at a bar, and they put him in his uniform. Anyway, he showed up with another guy asking about all of the equipment, and I told him what had happened. I told him I did not steal their equipment, I just seized it, because they were doing damage on my family's land. He asked to see the equipment, so I said, "Sure, it's all in the garage". They looked at it and left. Later that evening, I was babysitting my two kids and that cop came back, this time with a state trooper and a guy from the Bureau of Criminal Investigation, and they said they had a warrant for my arrest. I said, "What for? You have no authority here". They said they were arresting me for theft, and they tried to take me in. A fight started, the state trooper got aggressive and tried to grab me, and we started wrestling in the kitchen, while the kids were standing in the archway. The trooper got me in the corner. I had long hair, so then he grabbed me by my hair. I told them, "I'm not going to walk out, so if you're going to take me out, you're going to kidnap me!" I just went limp, and they had to carry me out of my house. They took me to Malone, a city nearby, and I had to spend the night there. The next morning, my wife brought me back home, and a longhouse meeting was called. It was jam-packed, even outside it was full of people all wondering what was going on. Longhouse people were really angry about what had happened.

We convinced the Iroquois Confederacy to have a meeting in Akwesasne, so everybody here could understand what was going on. In that grand council meeting, it was decided that we would have to get rid of the police, because they were getting too strong as a colonial government agency in our territory. People got up and walked straight to the tribal council building, while others shut the roads down to make sure the police could not get in. When we got there, the tribal council came to the door, and the Akwesasne police chief Harris Cole stood there. We told them that we were there to disarm their police force. A big fight broke out with the tribal councillors, the police and their supporters. After that incident forty sealed indictments were issued. Even those on the council didn't know if they were on the list, so the decision was made that we would need to stick together in one place and be protected from the outside. So they came to my place at Raquette Point. They said it was a good place to stay, as it was next to the river, which would help in case the police blocked the roads to stop our food supplies from coming in. The roads were barricaded with trenches right into the ground for over a year, and all traffic coming was closed right off. When it became public that they were going to stop all food from coming in, everybody in the area started bringing us food by boat, so we never ran out of food here.

One day in August, they suddenly told us, "We're going to give you ten minutes, and we're coming in". They were all lined up on the road up the hill. I had binoculars, and I saw them with their helicopters flying around. They said, "Give up your weapons and come out; you have two minutes", then, "You have one minute", but then they did nothing; they postponed it. We had bunkers all over the place, all the way around the treeline, and there were tents all over. They called it Camp Kanasaraken; that's my Indian name. We had security patrolling different areas, and at one point they caught state troopers crawling on the ground, trying to sneak in. Our guys said, "You're surrounded, stand up, put your hands up!" and they obeyed; they were shaking. We said "Take your gun belt off, turn around and walk back". That became a big thing, because we had their guns now. So negotiations took place to get their guns back. We didn't want trouble, so we gave them back a month later. While it was happening, we had no idea how long it would go on. We got rough lumber, and we built a place to house most of the people that were there. The basement of my house was just filled with people. We had three-tier bunks, everybody was packed there. We stayed right here, we never moved, and we ended up winning the battle without even setting foot in court. They had no jurisdiction over us.

It was the same when the taxes went really high for cigarettes, later in the 1980s, and tobacco became an industry that allowed our people to put food on the table. They thought I was involved in what they referred to as "smuggling cigarettes" back then, but I answered, "What do you mean? How can I smuggle cigarettes, if I stayed in my Indigenous territory all along?" But the tribal and band councils always opposed it, because they wanted to collect taxes on the businesses. This is what has always been going on here. When they built the seaway here in Akwesasne,[4] the tribal and band councils wanted it to happen, because they would get money out of it. It wasn't a lot of money. Today, we'd laugh at it, but the traditional people had trouble fighting against it, because they didn't have any money, and they didn't have any media power, so they were always presented as the bad guys, because the government put out propaganda against the traditional people. The governments only follow the interests of the corporations, which have the money to sway the politicians. They call it lobbying, but it's just the almighty dollar. They always have to keep making more and more.

You see this river they call the Saint Lawrence? It's beautiful. But back in the 1980s it was a lot better. General Motors, my neighbour right here, they're responsible for so much pollution. They dumped lots of polychlorinated biphenyl (PCB) underneath a hill and put grass on top of it, but it's so deep that they keep finding PCBs sixty feet below. There was a lot of stuff blowing from their dump onto our family property. They started churning this black oil up out of the ground, and it smelled kind of good: it was PCBs. A lot of kids didn't know how poisonous it was. They would dump it out, let it dry up, and a lot of local kids would go in and walk through the dump. We had no idea what it was back then. My brother and sister-in-law took them to court; they are very active in making sure General Motors is held responsible for what they did. My sister-in-law found out that the pollution coming from their PCBs is directly related to high blood pressure and diabetes, and this place is overrun with those things; it's just an epidemic here in Akwesasne. They lied to us left and right. You cannot drink the water here; people get cancer from it all the time. They wanted to put an incinerator up here too. It seems like they want to bring pollution from all over the world and burn it right here, but we won't let that happen. Mother Earth is getting raped day in and day out, and it's just going to get worse before it gets better, because they will always want to take more natural resources than what Mother Earth can handle. All nationalities are going to suffer because of that, not just the Indigenous people.

Non-Natives should understand that when we are fighting for our rights, we are also fighting for their rights. Most non-Natives in North

America don't know what freedom is. They have to get up in the morning and go to work. They have a leash. But the only true freedom is when you can let nature support you. The European understanding is that the sovereign is the individual holding the crown, and not the people. In our understanding, each and every one of us holds the sovereignty of our people. To be sovereign requires peace, *Skén:nen* in our language, whose root is *slow*. Peace requires to think slow, to keep cool, not to go off and create a war situation. That is our responsibility.

Notes

1   See Timeline, "1613 Two Row Wampum".
2   Hadajigre:ta', aka Jacob Ezra Thomas (1922–1998), was a Cayuga knowledge keeper from Six Nations of the Grand River. Aside from holding the title of *Teyohowe'tho*, representing the Cayuga Sandpiper Clan at the confederacy's grand council, he was also among the first Indigenous persons to become a tenured professor in a Canadian university, teaching at Trent University for thirteen years. Jake Thomas was one of the few persons capable of reciting the entire Kaianerehkó:wa, and his knowledge was widely recognized both by his fellow community members and academic anthropologists and linguists.
3   See Timeline, "1796 Seven Nations of Canada".
4   See Timeline, "1959 Saint Lawrence Seaway".

Ateronhiatakon Interview

Ateronhiatakon Francis Boots is a Kanien'kehá:ka knowledge keeper and speaker for the Snipe Clan. He has acted as Akwesasne's *Aión:wes, keeper of the house*, since 1974. Ateronhiatakon's deep knowledge of Kanien'kehá:ka traditions brings him to travel to various Native communities across Turtle Island to teach the native language and culture, as well as to officiate Thanksgiving Festivals, marriages and condolences. Ateronhiatakon played a central role in creating the Akwesasne-based journal of Indigenous struggles, *Akwesasne Notes*, before getting involved in the White Roots of Peace initiative, sharing Indigenous traditions across the Americas and beyond.

The first action I participated in was on December 8, 1968, literally in my backyard in Akwesasne. I was working in the shipping department of this big lacrosse stick factory on Cornwall Island, shipping sticks to England, Australia and Japan, and I was told that there was a roadblock just a half a mile away. They had started collecting tariffs at the border, and traditional people from the longhouse were opposing it. We're not supposed to pay taxes or tariffs. Not long after that I joined the roadblock, and I remember big fat policemen walking in unison towards us, and before you knew it they threw us in cars and drove us away. In jail, we asked what they had arrested us for. Is just blocking the road against the law? That was my first political activity, and it changed my life. I quit my job after that, and I became involved in *Akwesasne Notes*, which was born at that time. Shortly after we formed a communications group and started traveling to Vermont and neighbouring high schools and universities. At the same time, I got involved in the traditional chiefs' council. People need to know that in this community we have an elected system of government that is imposed on us, and then we have a traditional government that is struggling to maintain cultural, treaty, environmental and land rights. That's what traditional people are all about. I participated in what the traditional chiefs were doing. It was a newfound identity. When I joined the roadblock, the Indianness just hit me in the face; I walked right into it, and I've been involved ever since.

In its prime, *Akwesasne Notes* was the major Indigenous news journal, not just in the Americas but all over the world. It became a real hub of information. How it all started is that right after the protest of 1968, the local newspapers had a few articles about what happened, so we reproduced them and made copies that we just distributed in the community. The next week we did the same thing. All the reservations were getting more active, and we were getting all this information. And then this man came to us, he was a federal government employee, and he was there to help people who were starting businesses. He quickly saw the potential there. He's the one who organized the information. He knew just how to write the articles, always on the typewriters. So Indian Affairs ordered him out of the reservation. But the women said, "No, he's going to stay here. We invited him to stay here, and we want him to stay here". Eventually the Bear Clan adopted him into our community, and he was given the name Rarihokwats.

The way we did it is that we sent the newspapers to the subscribers, but they had to send us a letter within a few weeks to confirm that they were reading it or send us a few bucks or send us some new information if they wanted to stay on the mailing list. We never charged a subscription fee, and we didn't have any advertisements. That's how it just kept getting bigger. Pretty soon, the post office in Rooseveltown was completely overwhelmed, they couldn't handle all the mail they received for us. People would send all kinds of things, a few dollars, information, recipes; it was a big job to open all that mail! Then all of a sudden, the universities, libraries, institutions, they all started buying the newspaper, so we received piles and piles of checks. I'll never forget how we had to make all the packages by hand in my mother's kitchen, thousands of them, sending all the bundles for the different zip codes. It was very hard labour, but we were really happy doing it. My mother had to move her kitchen to the other room! There were people coming from all over Indian country to see how our newspaper worked; they were sleeping in tents all around my father's house. It was the hub for the community; people were sitting around reading these letters from all over the world. Nobody ever got a salary, not even Rarihokwats. We gave out all the money we received to people who needed it, for funerals and other things. That's the way it was.

When I was twenty-eight years old, some forty years ago, I was designated as the Aión:wes. This is the title of the head of the Kanien'kehá:ka men's fire under the Kaianerehkó:wa—what they call the war chief in English. But the true role of the Aión:wes is to be the *keeper of the house*, meaning to protect your community, as much in the case of everyday family issues as for emergencies, like when the territory has to be defended against an attack. According to the original instructions of the Kaianerehkó:wa, the role of the Aión:wes is based on three principles: the power of a good mind, peace and strength. Since our confederacy was established, there has always been a men's fire, the Rotihsken'rakéhte', whose responsibility is to organize the defense of the territory. There's a long history to it; it has been part of our way of life since time immemorial. In the past, whenever other Rotinonhsión:ni territories needed assistance our chiefs would counsel and send the Rotihsken'rakéhte' there if necessary. We would put up defenses and bear arms to defend ourselves. Throughout my time as head of the men's fire, I was called to give assistance to other Indigenous peoples all over the continent.

We were in Alcatraz when it was occupied by Indigenous protesters. It had been chosen as a site of occupation, because as a barren prison it was a symbol of the oppression we were experiencing in reservations.[1] One of the leaders in Alcatraz, Richard Oakes, was from Akwesasne.[2] It wasn't easy to coordinate, because all the people who went there were from different backgrounds, and there was a lot of pressure from the media. I was there for about four months. I remember often being cold and hungry.

We were there when the Trail of Broken Treaties crossed the United States to occupy the offices of the Bureau of Indian Affairs, which was disenfranchising Indigenous people across the country.[3] There were hundreds of us from all over when we arrived at the Bureau of Indian Affairs in Washington. When all the employees left the building, people broke into the office on the second floor. People were riffling through files, looking for documents related to their community, land easements, things like that. People were rightfully looking through all this paperwork; it was all over the place. The most militant were the Tuscaroras from the Carolinas. I don't know who let them in the building. Boy, they were mad, they were angry, they were hurt. They started taking all the equipment from the offices and putting it at the top of the stairs in case anybody were to come. There were medallions and certificates of all kinds all over the floor. The Tuscaroras started making weapons out of the table legs. To me that crossed the line, so I told my folks, "This is not going to have a happy ending. I think we better do something". We talked to the old Lakota people asking them what ceremony we could do to calm the people down. This was supposed to be their building. Do they act like this at home? So there was a pipe ceremony, and everybody settled right down. The people came down from the roofs, and the cops were all outside. The ceremony was so intense, the Lakotas were able to quiet people down.

When we went to Wounded Knee in 1973, we would not influence the Lakota though, because they already had it right in our opinion. We supported them the best way we could, but they had everything. They had their pipe, they had their sacred hoop, they had all these beautiful things. And they had a clear negotiating position. It was the other side that wasn't interested in resolving anything, and the United States government, they were only interested in sending the army in. So we really didn't have a lot of influence. The only thing we could do was add maybe four or five people to the front, and we weren't prepared to do that, so we left. We tried our best to help them monetarily and in other ways, but I have to say that Wounded Knee is one of the saddest moments in American history. The first Wounded Knee and the second Wounded Knee: there were massacres at both.[4] We always had good relationships with the American Indian Movement (AIM). It didn't have to do with our politics; it had to do with our spirituality. Most AIM people were not from reservations. They were from the cities, so Indianness was new to them. Wearing beadwork and Indian designs was all new to them. They didn't speak the language. They didn't know any of the songs. They were in the poorest part of cities. That in itself was quite a contribution, because it awoke a lot of people. The message of AIM was: "You better get out of this city and go back to your grandfather and maybe learn from him. Go home. There's no future in these cities for you". But as a national organization, there wasn't just AIM, there were the women, the Women of All Red Nations (WARN).[5] They were just as political as AIM. They were organizing day care centers, birthing places, schools, food pantries. That made more sense to me than marching up and down the street with a sign. The leaders of AIM meant well, but they had such a gigantic opposition. They were going to be assassinated, and everybody knew it, so they had to operate in the shadows.

In 1977, we attended a United Nations conference on the rights of Indigenous people in Geneva.[6] We took a very strong position there, saying that we owe no allegiance to anybody else except ourselves. It was accepted. Representatives from almost every Indigenous nation of North and South America were there. We made a statement called *Basic Call to Consciousness*.[7] I was selected as a delegate to travel to many parts of the world, including what was then called People's Republic of Jamahiriya, also known as Libya.[8] We were invited there to partake in solidarity and an understanding about our right to live according to our own ways. We were well received and were invited to feast, the same way that we do here; when you're finished with words, you sanction it with a feast. The Libyans honored our traditional ways, and in return we honored them by offering sacred tobacco. I've been to many other countries, and original peoples understand each other immediately. No words are needed; there's an immediate sense of brotherhood, of unity.

The early 1970s were really amazing times. We had communication between many Native communities throughout the Americas through *Akwesasne Notes*. There was a lot of networking going on, and our people really came together. We had something called "Unity Conventions", with Native people from many different areas traveling around and visiting each other, reviving our spirit of "Indianness". We went to many places— Oklahoma, Florida, New Mexico—developing our relationships as nations, not as tribes or reservations, as well as our spiritual connectedness. We did it by talking of our continent as one and of all Native peoples as sharing a responsibility to the universe and the environment. That's when we started using the term *Turtle Island*, which has become very common now. The same with caretaking the land for the "seven generations" that are coming towards us: we realized that we have to think in those terms. That was an amazing transformation, when you consider that we were confined on reservations, where there were so many things we couldn't do. We broke out of that. We liberated our thinking. We liberated our hope. We sensed that hope in our unity. It was an amazing time. Our chiefs, the Rotiianérshon, had very clear minds and were acting in ways that immediately inspired the other nations that met them, and the women, the Ka'nisténhsera', understood their role and made sure that they would be listened to. We were able to get back what we believe to be our way of life, not according to what somebody else believes to be our way of life, you see. Before that we used to behave like Hollywood portrayed us; we bought into that. So it was a big transformation at that time, to use what really belongs to us. And our leaders were up for it. It was amazing.

We had the sense that somebody was listening to us; that's what made the difference. Before that nobody wanted to hear from those Indians on the reservation, but now we had an audience. Lakota people were speaking up, talking about the Sundance again. The Ojibwa were coming back to their Seven Fires ceremonies. The fire became a symbol of requickening and lovingfulness, what we call *Kanoronhkwáhtshera*.[9] It became trans-Indian; it was everywhere! The fire is what brings people together. When you think of it, a fire is warmth, light, sparkle, but when you don't think of it, it's just a fire. Once somebody puts tobacco in the fire, it becomes a sacred fire; it's very different. That's what we were experiencing. We were seeing everything that was happening, and we wondered what our role was in that context. Should we start traveling to meet all those people, or should we weave the fabric of our life stronger first as Kaianerehkó:wa people? That was a critical decision. You have to understand who you are before someone asks you to explain it. We couldn't go there empty-minded; we had to have the fullness of our own ways. We've had conflicts since the Europeans have come here to take our land, our resources and our spirit away. We always had to defend ourselves against these attacks, basing our defense on the Kaianerehkó:wa. We have to maintain the vision of our original instructions in order to defend our people. Our language is key for remembering these instructions; it was given to us to access our own identity. When we do our ceremonies, our festivals and our thanksgivings in our language, with our children listening, it's the words of our ancestors from time immemorial that we are reviving through our ceremonies.

Akwesasne appears to be the focus of every destructive force associated with American government policies. I remember that when I was a young boy I lived in a pristine area. The rivers were natural and beautiful. Today, it has all changed; it has all become man-made. We live in a complicated geographic location, straddled between Québec, Ontario and the United States, on the Saint Lawrence River. But since I can remember we've always declared ourselves an independent people. We are not American or Canadian citizens; we are Kanien'kehá:ka people. The defense of our sovereignty is something that we have always advocated for very strongly. The elected systems of government which they call tribal councils in the US and band councils in Canada have been imposed on us. Akwesasne is a prime example of the governments' oppression of

Native peoples. All of the examples are very clear here. When you cross the Canada-US border that passes through our community, you have to present a foreign government's identification card. They won't even accept our own documents. The foreign border brings us to experience economic and psychological oppression every day in Akwesasne. We raise our children to be very aware of this, and not to buy into their Canadianization and their Americanization. We are sovereign Kanien'kehá:ka people, and we should proudly stand up and declare so at every opportunity.

More recently, in 2009, we had problems with the Canadian Immigration Customs building on Cornwall Island, which is right in the middle of our territory. The Canadian border agents wanted to have a sidearm, a gun. They didn't have guns on the Canadian side up until that point. We had a long history of conflict with border agents, and we thought that if those people were armed they were going to shoot somebody. Our people said that we couldn't allow them to have guns on our territory. We set up a camp near their offices, and the border control officers' response was to run away and leave the building. The bridge that passes through our territory was simply shut down altogether, so we had no way to circulate through our own community anymore. Today, their building there is still vacant. They set up a different office on the south side, in what they call Cornwall, which they use now, and they ended up keeping their guns, so we only half won. At least they're not in our territory, but they're still harassing us on a daily basis. Our people used to go shopping for groceries on the American side, and some of them were so poor that they bought their groceries on credit for the week. Then the border agents wanted them to pay taxes on their groceries when they crossed the border. How the hell are you going to pay a tax on groceries if you barely have the money to buy the groceries? We also shut down the bridge, and the government finally acknowledged that those tariffs don't concern us Indigenous peoples on our traditional territory. We're always in conflict with oppressive laws here. It's because we understand our freedom, and we're ready to defend it.

We have so many different so-called "law enforcement agencies" trying to control us in Akwesasne, because it is divided between New York State, Ontario and Québec, with all their different federal, provincial, state and county police departments. One time, it was Franklin County that tried to impose its county police here in Akwesasne. Those cops started harassing our people all the time, ticketing us for having bad signal lights and stuff like that. So we went to them and said, "Look, from what we understand, the police department is supposed to be there to help people, but here you are harassing them for things that we don't think are necessary". They would not listen. They had a badge on their chest and a gun on their hip and thought that it gave them some authority. We occupied their building, and we threw them right out, as a symbol that we mean business.

In 1990, before anything happened in Kanehsatà:ke, there was already a conflict relating to casinos in Akwesasne, and the army was already there with the state police. They had all the roads blocked and controlled the waters both on the Canadian and the American side. There had been two men killed there, and there was an investigation. I got a phone call from a friend, David Gabriel, asking me to go to Kanehsatà:ke to perform songs for the graduation of the seniors' adult education program, which happened to be happening at the time. So four or five of us grabbed drums and rattles; we jumped in my van and went there. We went straight to the Pines of Kanehsatà:ke, where ceremonies usually take place. There was a dirt pile at the entrance, but everything seemed normal. We sang, and, meanwhile, people told us what was happening, that the city of Oka wanted to cut trees in the cemetery in the Pines of Kanehsatà:ke to expand their golf course. We said, "What? Why don't they build it on their side?" So we decided to stay, and on the morning of July 11, 1990, at 5:30, we woke up to burn tobacco and say a thanksgiving address. We were waiting for the city people to come for the Pines, and suddenly there was this massive percussion grenade that went off, and you could see this whole sea of tactical police coming at us with tear gas. That's how it started, you know; we were just burning tobacco. There was a seventeen-second exchange of gunfire, and that's when Corporal Marcel Lemay got shot. There was a long investigation about that, and they never discovered who shot him. We think they did; they think we did. That's a long story, but it was over the principle of how much land you can give up for a golf course. Should you give up your ceremony for a private golf course? Should you give up these pristine pines where people have been coming for hundreds of years to celebrate all the small things that they're happy about in their community?

In all these difficult times, the guiding flame has always been my understanding of the Kaianerehkó:wa. We were given these instructions; we were given a way to have a good mind, a way of peace and a way of strength—plus our four original ceremonies. That has been the guiding light, and the pleasure and the resolution for any internal hardship, the solution when one is scared or anything like that. That's how I've been able to continue. And my family, they have been the strength for everything I have done. In the last fifteen years, the people started coming back to the Kaianerehkó:wa. At one time, in the 1950s, there were almost only Christians in Akwesasne. The longhouse people were underground; they would practice their way of life in the privacy of their homes with the windows curtained off so nobody could see. Today, it's wide open; our young people are coming home in droves, and they know their songs and their ceremonies. I believe that we're going to survive. There was a time in my life when I had some doubts about that, but today I'm confident that we're going to survive. In the future, I believe that we will not allow our way of life to be tampered with by the colonial powers. The settler peoples also have got to come back and understand that they too have those instructions to be kind to Mother Earth, to be kind to the rivers, to be kind to the trees and all life. They seem to have forgotten that, and that's where the conflict is. They too have to come home now.

Notes

1   See Timeline, "1971 AIM occupation of Alcatraz".

2   Born in Akwesasne in 1942, Richard Oakes worked as a high steelworker before becoming a prominent leader in the 1970 occupation of Alcatraz Island. In 1972, at the age of thirty, he was brutally shot to death by a YMCA camp manager in Sonoma California.

3   See Timeline, "1972 Indian Affairs Occupations in Washington and Ottawa".

4   See Timeline, "1973 Wounded Knee".

5   The Women of All Red Nations was established in 1974, in Rapid City, South Dakota. It included more than three hundred women from thirty nations, many of whom had previously been AIM activists and had been present in Wounded Knee. WARN fought on many crucial fronts related to the experience of Indigenous women, including education, pollution, representation, health, and land issues. It notably revealed the widespread abuse in regard to sterilization procedures being practiced on unwitting Native women, bringing the United States Department of Health and Human Services to issue regulations on sterilization in 1979.

6   See Timeline, "1977 United Nations conference".

7   Akwesasne Notes, ed., *Basic Call to Consciousness* (Summertown, TN: Book Publishing Company, 1991).

8   See Timeline, "1991 Visit to Libya".

9   *Requickening* is a term used for when new Rotiianérshon are installed, following the condolence ceremony of a deceased Roiá:ner.

PART III
Rekindling Resistance

——

This section delves into the cultural roots of Mohawk resistance, explaining the protocols, symbols and traditions that support its sovereigntist stance. The first text, by Kahentinetha, lays down the basic principles of the Kaianerehkó:wa, introducing its complex system of consensual decision-making to the larger public. She tells the story of the formation of the confederacy, the meaning of the Kaianerehkó:wa's 117 articles and their corresponding wampums, as well as the spatial organization of councils. The second text, by Ateronhiatakon, explores the deeper meaning and function of wampums in the Iroquois tradition, revealing how they are materially built to keep the words and enclose the memory of past agreements, making them available for future generations to interpret. The third text, by Karhiio, explains how being a warrior is an everyday responsibility that pertains to every free and sovereign Indigenous person.

Basic Principles of the Kaianerehkó:wa

Kahentinetha Rotiskarewake

Kahentinetha Rotiskarewake is a Kanien'kehá:ka from the Bear Clan in Kahnawà:ke. Initially working in the fashion industry, Kahentinetha went on to play a key role as speaker and writer in the Indigenous resistance, a role which she has fulfilled consistently for the last six decades. During this time, she witnessed and took part in numerous struggles, including the blockade of the Akwesasne border crossing in 1968. She has published several books, including *Mohawk Warrior Three: The Trial of Lasagna, Noriega & 20–20*,[1] and has been in charge of running the Mohawk Nation News service since the Oka Crisis in 1990. She now cares for her twenty children, grandchildren and great-grandchildren. *Kahentinetha* means *she who is always at the forefront*.

To understand the principles of the Kaianerehkó:wa, four aspects must be considered: (1) the *structure* of the longhouse, i.e., the people within our clans and our rights and duties; (2) how an *issue is passed* from one party to another so that there are checks and balances; (3) the basic criteria when deliberating, those of *peace, righteousness and power*; and (4) the *symbols*, such as the small condolence ceremony when we cleanse our eyes so we may see clearly, our ears so we may listen well and drink clear pure water so we may speak directly and truthfully. In the process, the will of each individual is preserved. These are different parts of the Kaianerehkó:wa that must all work together so we can function communally in our best interests. Today, some groups have formed which use one aspect to the exclusion of the others, such as using only the structure without the philosophy or using the symbols and turning it into a religion or using the structure and putting another ideology onto it, such as the Handsome Lake Code.

To acquire peace, Dekanawida did not base his ideas on faith and hope. He described a giant white pine that reached into the sky, symbolizing the sisterhood and brotherhood of all human beings. At its roots were the five nations of the original Rotinonhsión:ni Confederacy. A structure was designed to make the individual the center of power so that no dictator could seize control. The people met to discuss issues and came to an understanding. The governmental structure included the separation of powers of the judicial, executive and legislative branches. The Rotinonhsión:ni nations were made up of democratic social units to form a democratic and peaceful confederacy of all Indigenous people. After the upheaval of Indigenous culture by the European invasion, the Iroquois and many other Indigenous nations, such as the Aztec, Blackfeet, Sioux and Hopis, had the same ideas about the return of Indigenous thought.

Dekanawida saw that if war continued, greed and suffering would continue, and eventually our extinction would be inevitable. We would distrust each other and the principles of peace of the confederacy. We would become involved with the "serpents" (the Europeans) of materialism, who would become so powerful that they would almost destroy the Indigenous people. Dekanawida told our people that when the worst time came to gather our minds as set out in the Kaianerehkó:wa. He, meaning his message, would return as a light coming from the east. After the fight among the serpents, at which time the Indigenous people would remain neutral, we would reassemble and renew our knowledge of the principles of the Kaianerehkó:wa. Dekanawida said that the fight between the serpents would become so violent that there would be an environmental catastrophe, "the mountains would crack, and the rivers would boil, and the fish would turn up on their bellies". He also predicted that all the elm trees would die. Once Dekanawida's message returned, the Indigenous people would be greater nations than ever before. The abuse by the Europeans was seen as a time for us to renew our minds and help lead mankind to respect the natural world.

The Rotinonhsión:ni established separate nations along the Great Lakes, the Saint Lawrence River, in Upper New York State and farther south. We, along with the Tuscaroras, Hurons, Eries, Wenros, Cherokee and Minquas, spoke an Iroquoian language. Each nation had national territories and trade relations with our Iroquois and non-Iroquois neighbours. All Iroquoian peoples were organized into clans and shared the same basic structure and ceremonies of thanksgiving to creation. In particular, the *Ohén:ton tsi karihwatéhkwen*, the *words that come before*, as provided in Wampum 7, was common to all Indigenous peoples. It indicates that the Kaianerehkó:wa is an interdependent system of relationships of all elements of nature, which are all equal. For many generations there had been blood feuds within and between Iroquois nations, usually over seeking justice for the death of someone from their clan. These blood feuds threatened our systems of law, order and social unity.

The Five Nations Confederacy was at first a confederation of five Rotinonhsión:ni/Iroquois nations—the Mohawk, Cayuga, Onondaga, Oneida and Seneca. The Tuscarora, who came north from the Carolinas, joined the confederacy in 1722, making it the sixth nation. According to Rotinonhsión:ni mythology, the Kaianerehkó:wa was meant not only for us but for everyone, a United Nations of people who united for peace. To illustrate how effective the philosophy was, their weapons of war were buried so as not to fight among themselves again, vowing to uncover them only for defense against invaders.

The Kaianerehkó:wa reflected the "blood" ties which strengthened the unity of the five nations. Dekanawida knew that the blood ties were a positive force which brought together Rotinonhsión:ni politics, culture and social order. These were the ties the newcomers had to alter in order to possess the land and establish themselves in North America. The colonists have not succeeded.

Rotinonhsión:ni women are the "progenitors of the soil" (Wampum 44) and hold the land for the future generations. The land cannot be alienated. Thus, the Europeans had to displace the Indigenous women so they could manipulate the men in order to take the land and resources. They had no fondness for or understanding of the women's traditional position of power.

The Kaianerehkó:wa has 117 articles called *Kaión:ni* or *wampums*. Each law is associated with a wampum belt or string of wampum beads and is structured as follows:

Wampums 1 to 16: the organization of the confederacy: Dekanawida and the Chiefs plant the Tree of Peace; Thadodáho and the Onondaga chiefs become the caretakers of the council fire; the nations are divided into three parties; Mohawks are appointed as the leaders of the confederacy; how issues are passed and how new laws are made.

Wampums 17 to 27: the rights, duties and qualifications of statesmen: the roles of the clan mothers; how chiefs are deposed or resign; the qualifications and roles of chiefs.

Wampums 28 to 35: condolence of chiefs: how condolences are conducted; how titles are passed on.

Wampum 35: Pine Tree Chiefs: temporary chiefs.

Wampums 36 to 41: war chiefs: their titles, names, functions, installation and duties.

Wampums 56 to 65: the meanings of symbols, such as the wampum strings; the bound five arrows meaning *unity in one body and one mind*; who are traitors and how they are punished; the confederacy belt, reading the Kaianerehkó:wa; rites of installation and burying of the weapons.

Wampums 79 to 92: war: the Warrior Society; establishing peace with an outside nation; conducting warfare; relations after war; the peace chiefs and related protocol.

Wampums 93 to 104: rights of the people: referendum; men's council; women's council; all council fires; the rights of ordinary men and women; the festivals of thanksgiving.

Wampums 108 to 117: funerals: the rites of passage.

Not every wampum will be discussed, only those that illustrate the basic philosophy and structure of the Kaianerehkó:wa.

Great White Roots: Wampum 2 provides the possibility for those other than the Iroquois to trace the roots and take shelter under the Tree of Peace, as long as they obey the laws of the Kaianerehkó:wa and live according to the philosophy of the Rotinonhsión:ni.

Confederacy Structure: Wampums 5 to 11 set out the structure of the Rotinonhsión:ni Confederacy, the Five Nations Hereditary Council. *Rotinonhsión:ni* means *those who make the longhouse*. Each nation keeps control over its own affairs, its dealings with other nations of the confederacy and with non-member nations that the grand council becomes involved with. Within each nation, local settlements and clans are autonomous and independent. Clans and settlements have their own meetings. Nations meet in a national council. All of the nations meet in the grand council as the issues warrant. The Rotinonhsión:ni confederate council consists of fifty civil chiefs

Individual Family

Clans (Turtle, Wolf, Bear)

Territories Kahnawà:ke-Kanehsatà:ke-
Akwesasne-Tyendinaga-Ganiengeh-Wahta-Six Nations

Mohawk Nation (National Council)

Confederacy (Grand Council)

Figure 3.1 The organization within the confederacy

> referred to as the "Circle of Chiefs": Onondaga fourteen, Mohawk
> nine, Seneca eight, Oneida nine, Cayuga ten.

The Rotinonhsión:ni Confederacy structure is not hierarchical. It is a series
of circles within circles with a process to form relations between each
segment of society. They operate on a cyclical basis, just like the natural
world. The most important is the unborn individual, surrounded by a
circle of the family, then by the circle of the clan, then by the circle of the
chiefs, then by the circle of the Kanien'kehá:ka/Mohawk national council
and finally by the Confederacy grand council. Every individual belongs
to a clan, which is organized within each community. Each community
is the responsibility of the particular nation, and each of these nations is
part of the confederacy.

Sovereignty and self-determination begin with the individual: all
people are recognized to be free and equal, from the very youngest to
the eldest. It is provided in the Kaianerehkó:wa that liberty and equality
demand great moral fortitude, and it is the nature of free men to defend
freedom.

The warriors are the Rotihsken'rakéhte'. In his medicine pouch a warrior carries tobacco, soil and his umbilical cord. *Skén:nen* is a state of complete peace, tranquility and enlightenment. The people of the clans select the chiefs, clan mothers and war chiefs. Based on the people's decision, the clans can depose the chiefs, who are the spokesmen for the people, not the decision makers. The Warrior Society is actually the power of the people in action. The war chiefs are not a distinct class and can only give orders on military expeditions. They sit in on council meetings and make sure the Kaianerehkó:wa is followed. The clans can depose the war chief when necessary and can even call a war party back from the field. It is said that when war is declared, it is based on factual evidence with no doubt, allowing the men to wage it with all their might. It is said that all Rotinonhsión:ni are born warriors, and that it is the duty of every person to become a protector of the people and the land.

The *Rotinonhsión:ni*, the *makers of the longhouse* or *confederation*, do not rule by force but by the power of the mind, O'nikòn:ra'. They are powerful, because they are able to make complex alliances based on persuasive debates on the reality of issues which people share.

The Five Nations refer to themselves in Mohawk as *Onkwehón:we*, which means *people forever*. It is the basis for universal action. In case of war, "Skanawitith's Law of Peace and War" provides that after a war with a foreign nation, the foreign nation is to be persuaded three times by reason and urged to join the Great Peace. If this fails, the chief of the offending nation is clubbed to death, and warfare continues until won by the Five Nations. If a nation willingly joins, their internal government system may continue so long as it is consistent with the Kaianerehkó:wa. They have to treat people as equals with human rights.

In Wampum 6, the Kanien'kehá:ka/Mohawks are recognized as the heads and leaders of the Rotinonhsión:ni Five Nations Confederacy. The Kanien'kehá:ka were the first to accept the Kaianerehkó:wa and helped one of the founders, Dekanawida, to gather the other nations together. It is, therefore, a violation of the Kaianerehkó:wa to introduce measures in the confederate council if the Kanien'kehá:ka have protested against them. The decision-making process gave the member nations an actual power of veto, which equalized all the nations. This position may make the Kanien'kehá:ka feel they have to take on the duty to maintain the Kaianerehkó:wa and its philosophy and to not make any compromises with the Handsome Lake Code. On the other hand, the requirement of complete understanding on all decisions of the confederacy council gives all nations a de facto veto power and, thus, does not set the Kanien'kehá:ka apart from our brethren. Those Mohawks who refuse to compromise with the Handsome Lake Code find it is contrary to how they see the natural world. We are constant in our adherence to the original constitution.

All members of the confederacy have a duty to understand and explain the philosophy of peace and power throughout the Six Nations, to other Indigenous nations and throughout the world when asked to do so. There are, however, Rotinonhsión:ni people who do not realize this and have embraced the Handsome Lake Code, not realizing that it is not intrinsically "traditional" to Indigenous thinking but is colonial.

Consensual Decision-Making Process

In Wampums 5 to 11, Dekanawida outlined the decision-making process. The Mohawk Council is divided into three parts, with each having three chiefs for a total of nine. The three clans are: the Bear Clan, the first part and the *firekeepers*; the Turtle Clan, the second part; and the Wolf Clan, the third part.

The well keeper announces the subject for discussion and passes the issue over the council fire to the Turtle Clan and Wolf Clan. The Bear Clan listens to the discussions of the Turtle Clan and Wolf Clan. If an error is made or the proceedings are irregular, the Bear Clan calls attention to it. When a case is decided by the Turtle Clan and Wolf Clan, the Bear Clan confirms their decision.

If the Turtle Clan disagrees with the Wolf Clan, then the Bear Clan, as the firekeeper, asks the two sides to deliberate again and to provide new information. Usually, the two sides are now likely to agree. The decision is then accepted by the Bear Clan.

Should the Turtle and Wolf Clans again disagree on their second deliberation, the Bear Clan, as the firekeeper, then pass the decision that it sees fit. Should the Bear Clan disagree with the decision of the Wolf and Turtle Clans, whose decisions are the same, both the Turtle Clan and the Wolf Clan must deliberate again. If their decision is the same as before, the Bear Clan has no choice but to sanction their joint decision.

In the decision-making process:

- all opinions have to be considered;
- all must be completely reasonable;

- all should come with an open mind;
- all must fully understand the other's viewpoint;
- no participant can repeat a position once it has been fully explained and understood;
- if a person does not agree with the views that have been stated, then they must fully explain their dissenting view;
- no one can impose their will or make decisions for another;
- all must understand the viewpoint and agree of their own free will. The goal is not total agreement, but total understanding;
- if there is no agreement, then the consensus is to retain the status quo. If there is understanding by all, then they go ahead with the decision.

Although no one can ensure that all will fully understand the other's viewpoint, one must try to explain as fully as possible, and the respondent must try to understand.

The chiefs and the war chief who preside over the meeting make sure that the Kaianerehkó:wa and collective rational thought and behavior are followed. Persons are asked throughout the process if they fully understand. If not, the process stops until all explanations have been provided. One cannot be stubborn and refuse to understand, as they will be questioned and must follow the criteria of peace, righteousness and power at all times. All human beings are capable of rational thought, which leads to solving even the most difficult problem. The underlying philosophy is that human beings are loving, caring and wish to interact in a positive way. It is known that people cannot think clearly when they are in psychological pain, have feelings of rage or lose hope. The consensual decision-making process must bring people from despair to hope. Every person has a responsibility to develop their mind. To think is to create a sane world for the present and future generations, a world safe from the emotional, irrational behavior of people controlled by fear, hatred, greed, jealousy, suspicion and conflict. The main obstacle to our survival is fear.

Three criteria

The clans consider the pros and cons of the issue. Three criteria must be met:

1. *Skén:nen, peace*: Does it preserve the peace that is already established?

2. *Karihwí:io, righteousness*: Is it morally correct, just as the natural world is correct?
3. *Ka'shatsténhsera', power.* Does it preserve the integrity of the nation? What does it do for the present and how does it affect the future seven generations? The *seven generations* concept means that decisions made today must benefit the people seven generations into the future.

Dekanawida raised the idea of reasoned thinking to a principle. Every human being has the potential to use their mind to create a better life through peace, power and righteousness.

In entering the consensual decision-making process, whatever ideas are put into the process, the needs and attitudes of each is considered and complements the decision. Also, the individual has a duty to be directly involved and to bring their ideas into the discussion within their clan. The final decision will be fully satisfactory to some, satisfactory to others and relatively satisfactory to the remainder and will reflect elements from every group. This is a slow careful process requiring the reaching of a full understanding by each individual, and not a decision made by a "leader". The person who explains the decision is a spokesperson.

Iroquois Justice System

If the issue concerns a person's behavior, the accused may defend themselves. Depending on the severity of the infraction, the accused have the right to be heard before the council fires of the men and the women of their clan and the chief statesmen of their nation, as well as the chief statesmen of the confederacy. Basically, this is a trial by jury. Decisions have to be justified, rational and follow the process. The defendant's voice is lost only after a final decision.

In Iroquois society, those performing the "court" function are persons who represent the people according to their own selection process. In the Iroquois constitution, the people select the clan mothers, chiefs and war chiefs, who can be recalled by the people at any time. Adjudication is carried out with the advice, guidance and wisdom of the people as a whole, who keep in mind the continuity of the genealogical information, history, traditions and values of the nation. Carrying out responsibilities is a burden, a duty and a privilege. The crucial feature is that the people make the decision. Should a clan feel unable to deal with an issue, they may pass the issue to other clans to be dealt with. Depending on the issue, the Six Nations Iroquois Confederacy serves as a court of appeal for individual community issues, as well as a court of first instance in disputes that cannot be resolved at the community level. Great councils meet where the wisdom of the communities is pooled and applied. The four principles of Indigenous law are:

1. natural law;
2. truth, as the highest point of being, and justice, as the application of truth;
3. applying respect in dealing with all matters;
4. liberty, based on the first three principles.

Ohén:ton tsi karihwatéhkwen—The Words That Come Before All Matters

Wampum 7 provides that the opening thanksgiving is recited at every gathering of the people. Thanks is given to all that helps human life. It does not mean that the people worship these useful gifts, but they thank the power that produces them.

The Kaianerehkó:wa thanksgiving opening address puts people within an interdependent system of relationships among all elements of nature, which are equal. The Handsome Lake Code outlines a hierarchical order of the "spirit" forces, as well as a hierarchy of offices in the longhouse and a hierarchy of medicines arranged according to power.

An elder provided the following insights into the basis of the Kaianerehkó:wa as set out in the Ohén:ton tsi karihwatéhkwen, "the words that come before every matter".

The opening begins by paying respect to the people who still follow the Kaianerehkó:wa, reminding them of the necessity of good relations among themselves in order to be more productive and happy.

Then respect is extended to the Earth, which is our mother, and how female functions parallel the role of the Earth. The immunities and medicines they inherit come from living on her. Their mother is one of the family, not more important than any other member of the family. She has a specific role and way of doing things.

The waters are the cousins with whom each person associates every day and are a necessary part of their lives. From there, respect is extended to the contents of the waters, the fish, plant life and other beings. Food and medicines needed to live healthily come from the waters.

Plant life, such as corn, beans and squash, strawberries and other foods, is referred to as the "sisters". They are given the same respect as their mother and cousins. Then respect is given to their brothers and sisters, the animals, insects and birds, who too are beneficial to the people. The people grow up with their relations, who constantly help one another and are all part of the continuation of life.

Then respect is extended to the grandfathers, the four winds and thunders, who too are part of the family. They help to renew elements of nature for the people and continually show their natural and beneficial functions. The grandmother is the moon, which has a lot of knowledge. From the moon, the people learn the best time to put seeds in the ground and to pick medicines. She controls women's cycles and when new phases are coming onto the Earth.

The sun is the eldest brother, who is the example for the men to follow. The sun gives support to the Earth by warming it so things can grow. He helps give support and reinforcement to the people. He beautifies everything that has been put on the Earth. The men also protect and support the people, particularly the women. They help raise the children and ensure their well-being and the continuation of life.

Then respect is given to the distant cousins, the stars. They were used by our ancestors for direction as we traveled. We do not always see them, but when we do they are at their brightest. They have a lot of knowledge and strength, should we ever need their assistance.

All elements of creation are an important and necessary part of everything else in the world, not above or beneath anything. Every individual in the family has a different function. In raising the names in the longhouse, every child is a child of the people, who together must support that child and recognize and develop their natural abilities. Thus, the natural world is the family, and respect is given to all the relatives equally. There is no hierarchy.

Now, let us turn our attention to the Ka'shatsténhserakó:wa, the *Sha'oié:ra*, the *great natural power*. We shall never know the face of this power or the name of this power or where this power dwells. All we will know is the creation of this power, and that it is logical. It is neither male nor female.

Kaianerehkó:wa comes from the word *Kaienere*, which means the *great, good path*. *Roiá:ner*, the word for *chiefs*, means *he has a path*. *Iakoiá:ner*, the *clan mother*, means *she has a path*. In other words, a natural direction has already been set for everyone to follow which is good and beneficial to all members of society.

There is an eagle that sits at the top of the tree, which will scream a warning if we go off that path. The eagle is symbolic of the people. They are told to be watchful, as well as to emulate their "great vision" to distinguish the situation at hand from past experiences. They are to look in all directions with an open mind.

The forty-nine chiefs are equal in power. None is higher than another. Some nations have more clans, greater territory and larger populations, but all are equal. The people are not rulers but have a specific path that was set out for them. The path they must follow is the *great path*, which is the *Kaianerehkó:wa*.

The term *chief* is inaccurate and misleading. The Roiá:ner does not lead the people according to his own will but only according to the Kaianerehkó:wa.

The elder notes, "All family members come from the same creation—mother, father, grandmother, grandfather, sisters, brothers, cousins, nephews and nieces. How can there be peace and harmony when one is above the rest?" The Kaianerehkó:wa is real democracy based on natural righteousness which acknowledges all that is real. According to the Kaianerehkó:wa, everything is reality. *Karihwí:io* means *it is real* or *it is perfect*. This concept has been erroneously used to describe the Handsome Lake Code, which is an ideology based on Christianity.

The elder said, "There are some things that are not understood and are unexplainable, such as creation". People have mixed the European-Christian school of thinking with the Kaianerehkó:wa. For the Iroquois, confusion is created through unsubstantiated explanations for unexplainable powers; creation has been made perfectly with all forces and facilities necessary to help the people. Praying to unexplained "spirits" will not resolve their problems. Facing reality will. These fears are exploited to make people dependent rather than independent and self-sufficient. Indigenous people have been convinced that they must live in peace. In nature, any creature that succumbs to such exploitation or does not defend itself becomes extinct. The Indigenous people are threatened with extinction if they rely on this principle.

Dekanawida warned that the chiefs must never seriously disagree among themselves. If they do, it will cause them to disregard each other. Quarreling with each other could lead to bloodshed. The law stipulates

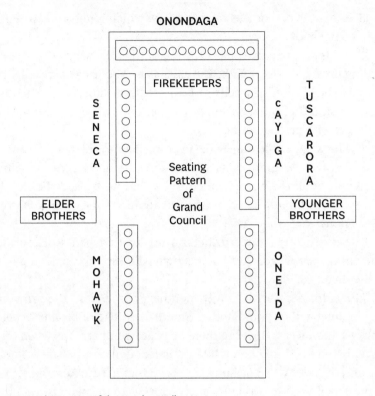

Figure 3.2 Seating pattern of the grand council

that no "sharp utensils" will be used in order to avoid the spilling of blood in any way. If blood is spilled, they lose their rights and privileges. Then their grandchildren would suffer and be reduced to poverty and disgrace.

Dekanawida warned that their grandchildren would suffer hardship from such an eventuality. Should it occur that the heads of the people of the confederacy shall roll and wander away westward, our enemies would say to them, "You belong to the confederacy; you were a proud and haughty people once". They would kick the heads [of the confederacy] with scorn and go on their way. But before they got far, they would vomit up blood, because the confederacy would still have enough power to take its revenge.

The grand council process is established along the same three-party system. The Kanien'kehá:ka and the Seneca are the first part, the Cayuga and Oneida are the second part and the Onondaga are the firekeepers, the third part. The Tuscarora speak through the Cayuga and Oneida.

In Wampums 9 and 10, the law outlines the decision-making process at the grand council level and involves seven separate steps:

1. All decisions start with the Kanien'kehá:ka/Mohawk. The Kanien'kehá:ka statesmen are divided into three clans, which must all consider the measure separately and arrive at a joint decision.

2. When the Kanien'kehá:ka have agreed on the outcome of the decision, it goes to the Seneca for consideration in the same manner.

3. When the Seneca have the question and agree with the Kanien'kehá:ka, they then give their opinion to the Oneida and Cayuga statesmen for their decision, again arrived at in the same manner.

4. After the Oneida and Cayuga have agreed, they return their decision to the Kanien'kehá:ka and the Seneca for their confirmation again.

5. At this time, the Kanien'kehá:ka and Seneca give the question to the two separate bodies of the Onondaga statesmen for their decision. This step operates like the veto power.

6. When the two bodies agree, then Thadodáho gives the decision to Honowirethon to confirm their decision, if it is unanimous.

7. Honowirethon then gives the decision of the Onondaga to the Kanien'kehá:ka and the Seneca, so that the decision may be announced to the council as the will of the council and the policy of the Five Nations Confederacy.

These are the checks and balances in the Kaianerehkó:wa. The council fire system is the confederacy's dispute resolution system.

In selecting a new chief, the clan mother, the men and the women of the family and clan of the deceased chief must all agree. The name is selected by the people and then submitted to the chiefs. If they confirm the nomination, then the candidate is submitted to the other two clans. If confirmed, he is raised by the condolence ceremony before all of the people.

In Iroquois, the chief is the Roiá:ner, from the word *path*, which means *one who follows the footprints of the previous Roiá:ner*. When he goes off that path, he cannot lead the people.

The custom is that no one shall put themselves up as a leader, but that they shall be invited to be a leader. There are, in fact, no leaders, as such.

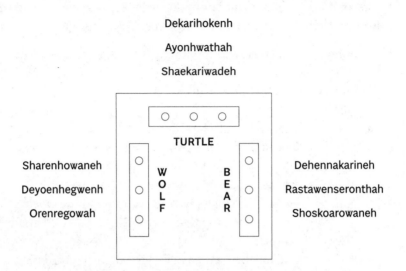

Figure 3.3 Council of the Mohawks—Wampum 11

They are "spokespersons" or "representatives" who carry the will of the people. They are asked three times to be a representative. The candidate refuses each time, asking if others are more suitable. If none is found, then the candidate is asked a fourth time, when he must accept. By this time, he has received the majority backing of the house and has been confirmed at a people's meeting, where he "stood up" as a representative. After this process, it is difficult to remove a person as a spokesperson or from any position.

Power of the People

Wampum 16 provides one of the most powerful rights that citizens have in making government policy, particularly when the leaders do not heed their wishes: "If the conditions call for an addition to or change of this law, the case shall be carefully considered, and if a new beam seems necessary or beneficial, it shall be called, 'Added to the Rafters'". The clans tell the war chiefs, who must tell the council to heed the will of the people. The chiefs do not go against the will of the people because of the people's power of impeaching those who commit treason.

Wampum 25 provides that if a chief of the league should establish any authority other than that of the Kaianerehkó:wa, he shall be warned three times and then dismissed by the war chief on behalf of the people.

Wampum 35 provides for the election of Pine Tree Chiefs. Should any men, inside or outside the nation, help with special ability or show great interest in the affairs of the nation, the chiefs may elect him to sit with them. He shall be proclaimed a Pine Tree sprung up for the nation, but he has no power except as an advisor. Joseph Brant was sprung up as a Pine Tree Chief to be a translator for the Rotinonhsión:ni. A Pine Tree Chief has only one duty and can only do what they are stood up for. Brant became a Freemason, which is part of colonial society. He broke the Two Row Wampum agreement and Wampum 58 of the Kaianerehkó:wa by submitting to the laws of a foreign people. He was deposed by the fifty confederacy chiefs in 1805. This was a precedent, because a Pine Tree Chief traditionally cannot be cut down, only ignored for all time. He signed treaties and agreements as a "chief" when he was a British subject as a colonel in the British army.

War Chief and His Men

Wampum 36 provides definite functions for the war chief and his men (Warrior Society). The war chief is the mediator between the people and the chiefs during both times of war and times of peace. He is charged with the protection, defense and welfare of the people. These duties may take many forms, such as peacekeeping, teaching, speaking to the people, repossessing lost lands, maintaining human rights, diplomatic relations with other nations and any other work that promotes the welfare of the people. If there is no council or the national council and Thadodáho are not functioning properly, the people then assume the functions of government, and the war chief and his men carry out the wishes of the people's council.

Clans

Wampum 37 provides that the women head the clans, are the sole title holders of the nation's soil and in them are vested the birthrights. The Europeans, not being members of any of these clans, have no right to own any land in this part of the world. Karoniaktajeh stated, "In the true matriarchal society, the women are the chiefs and fight in the wars. In the Iroquois matrilineal society, the women have political equality plus other rights, because they are the source of life and are considered closer to nature than are the men". The line of descent, rights of inheritance and chieftainships are derived through the female line.

Wampums 42 to 54 provide the structure of the clans, which are political families. The clan mother is called *Iakoiá:ner*, meaning *she follows the footprints* of the previous Iakoiá:ner. They carry out the decisions of their clan, put their clan on the right course of action and make sure their clan upholds the Kaianerehkó:wa. The clan mothers possess the chieftainship title wampum strings. The people can depose her if she does a serious wrong. Through the war chief, based on the will of the people, she can depose and replace an errant chief. Children automatically belong to their mother's clan.

Condolence Ceremonies

Wampums 32 and 54 provide that a condolence ceremony is performed when a chief dies and a new one is installed. The Mohawk, Seneca and Onondaga chiefs are installed by the Oneida and Cayuga chiefs and vice versa. The chieftainship titles are the names of the original forty-nine chiefs at the formation of the confederacy, which must never be buried.

Line of Descent

Wampum 44 provides that the line of descent shall follow the female line, women being the progenitors of the nation and titleholders of the land and soil. The clans oversee the adoption of strangers, ceremonies, burial places and meetings of the clans. The women are in charge of maintaining the blood lines of the people. This explains why the European colonists had to destroy the women's powers in order to occupy and take political and economic control of North America.

Land Title Held by Women

The Kaianerehkó:wa does not provide for the sale or alienation of land. The territory belongs to the unborn. No living being has the right to sell any part of it, just like no one has a right to sell their mother or any part of her. Both Wampums 44 and 72 provide that the titleholders of the land and soil are the women on behalf of the Rotinonhsión:ni. The Rotinonhsión:ni legal opinion is that the Indigenous peoples of A'nowarà:ke—Turtle Island—are the first humans here, and that foreigners have no right to take over the land. The so-called "conquest of America" is simply theft of Indigenous land. Women never relinquished ownership, because they have no right to do so.

No treaty between the Onondaga and the newcomers involves the women. Further, it is not proper to pursue constitutional jurisdictional issues in the colonial court. Jurisdiction over the land still lies with the Indigenous people, and its reappropriation is the responsibility of all the people. Therefore, all land transactions since contact are fraudulent and illegal.

The Kanien'kehá:ka say that when the women of the nation are weak, the nation is weak. The strength of the Kanien'kehá:ka is derived from the women, whereas the males and their children gain their identity, power and relationship from the universe. The women are the connection to the Earth, and their men depend on this connection to give them the energy and courage to protect their people and their territory.

Naming Ceremony

Wampum 46 provides for the clan mothers to bestow names on the children. In the past, we were born and lived in longhouses. A child is born a Kanien'kehá:ka, Oneida, etc., but when they are ceremoniously named according to the Kaianerehkó:wa, they become a *Rotinonhsión:ni:onwe* (*Rotinonhsión:ni person*). They are Kanien'kehá:ka by blood and Rotinonhsión:ni:onwe by law. The parents are instructed to teach them the native language and to live according to the Kaianerehkó:wa.

These clan ties perpetuate the position of the Kanien'kehá:ka women within the confederacy. They take part in the daily lives of their family members. If a mother is having problems with her children, she sends them off to meet with the clan mothers. The clan mothers then explain to the children their roles within the Kanien'kehá:ka organization and the behavior expected of them, leaving the final decision up to the individual. This system keeps the group working together as a whole and removes any disruption that could cause dissension within the nation.

Fifty Chiefs' Names

Wampum 46 provides that the women shall be the holders of the authorized names of the fifty chiefs of the confederacy for all time to come.

Deposing Chiefs

Wampums 52 and 54 provide that the women select and depose the chiefs. They are also responsible for reciprocal obligations of help, defense and redress of injuries to outsiders. They maintain strategic marital ties.

Symbolism

In Wampums 56 and 65, Dekanawida used symbolism to explain his ideas. He told them to bind their nations together as a bundle of arrows to be left beside the great Tree of Peace and the Confederate Council Fire of Thadodáho. This symbolizes that all these bundled arrows are stronger than one arrow. He said the confederacy shall in the future have one body and one head.

He warned that if any evil should befall the nations, they should stand or fall united as one person. This is how the Kanien'kehá:ka and other Rotinonhsión:ni nations are today. Although divided on certain issues, we are united in our pursuit of sovereignty and justice.

Dekanawida instructed the chiefs to cultivate the good feelings of friendship, love and honor among themselves. He had, thus, fulfilled his duty in assisting them to establish and organize this great confederacy, which, if carefully guarded, would continue from generation to generation, as long as the sun shines. His instruction was that no one else should ever be given his name, and he then left. It is possible that this was because he was the Peacemaker from another Iroquoian nation (Wendat). He brought the message. His job was done.

Chief Submitting to Foreign Laws

In Wampum 58, "Anytime a confederate chief chooses to submit to the law of a foreign people, he is no longer in but out of the confederacy. [They] shall be called *They have alienated themselves*. Such people ... shall forfeit all birthrights and claims on the Five Nations Confederacy and territory". This provision is used as the reason for the majority of Rotinonhsión:ni:onwe not voting in the colonial band council, federal or provincial elections. In most Mohawk communities, there are two main systems of authority operating, the traditional longhouse chiefs and the Indian Act band council set up by the colonial government of Canada or the federal Indian law tribal council set up by the US. Some vote in the band or tribal council elections because they are beneficiaries of jobs, social assistance and other government programs. Less than 10 percent of the "eligible voters" take part in the Indian Act elections. Even so, the colonial governments transfer all monies, programs and benefits to their band or tribal councils for distribution to the members. Given the lack of jobs, the social, economic and political divisions and the constant campaign to weaken our traditional ties, this system has gained some influence on the territories.

Accepting the band council system and the Handsome Lake Code are considered a violation of Wampum 58 of the Great Law. Karoniaktajeh stated that the charge against these chiefs is treason. There are persons who have taken part in the band council system who are considered to have "lost their voice". These persons may remain in the longhouse by sitting in meetings and listening but not speaking. They may be asked for an opinion or assistance. They are not discarded, because the longhouse way means getting along with each other and bringing people back into the fold. The policy is one of inclusion, not exclusion. These persons can eventually regain their voice. We attempt to understand, learn and bring harmony to the people.

In Wampum 59, if a chief does not heed the warnings of the people, then the council of the women or of the men have the duty to return him to the right course of action. If he seriously endangers the people, the war chief drops the Black Wampum, and the men spring to their feet and club the erring chief to death. The right to decide on execution is held by both the general council of the men of the Five Nations and the general council of the women of the Five Nations. If the erring chief grabs the black beads before they hit the floor, then he is given a chance to make amends.

Tree of Great Long Leaves

Wampum 60 provides that those who are farseeing have a duty to bring any insights to the people's attention. Should a great calamity threaten the generations rising and living, then he who is able to climb to the top of the Tree of the Great Long Leaves may do so. Should he see that evil things indeed are approaching, then he shall call to the people of the Five Nations Confederacy assembled beneath the Tree of the Great Long Leaves and say: "A calamity threatens your happiness". This is the ancient way of warning the people to be ever on the alert to danger and to discuss and do something about it.

Reciting the Kaianerehkó:wa

Wampum 62 provides for reciting the Kaianerehkó:wa every five years. Now that it is written down, Dekanawida would probably have recommended that the people read it often. There are chiefs who don't realize when they are violating the law, because they refuse to read it. Once a year, every community would recite the Kaianerehkó:wa for its members to hear. Every five years, the entire confederacy would gather to have a

Kaianerehkó:wa recital to eliminate the excuse of being ignorant of the law. "I did not know" is not an acceptable excuse for breaking it.

Temporary Adoptions

Wampum 67 allow for temporary adoptions of persons of another clan or of a foreign Indigenous nation by bestowing "a name hung about the neck".

Holding Confederacy Land

Wampums 72 and 73 provide that the confederacy territory is the soil of the Earth from one end of the land to the other and is the property of the people who inhabit it, and that none other may hold it. The nations agreed on boundaries for hunting grounds and territories. The confederacy's role is to protect these boundary lines and any changes have to be made in the grand council with all nations concurring.

Blood Claims

Wampum 76 provides that the rights can only be claimed through family lineage. Otherwise, not knowing all the traditions of the confederacy, someone might go against its Great Peace without realizing it. In the national or grand councils, only the Roiá:ner has a voice, unless an individual is asked to speak.

Weapons of War

Wampum 91 provides for the right of the warriors to take up the weapons of war to defend their land, people and sovereignty. All living things in the natural world possesses the "instinct" to protect themselves, their territory and their own kind, especially their young.

People's Right to Meet

Wampum 93 provides for the inherent and constitutional right of the people to assemble anytime and at any place within their territory without having to seek permission from any national council. The Kaianerehkó:wa sets the path to follow; no new path can be made, and no one may stray from that path: "Whenever there is an especially important matter, the chiefs of the league must submit the matter to the decision of their people, and the decision of the people shall affect the decision of the league council [which] shall be a confirmation of the voice of the people". When the people hold a general council, their decisions are as valid as a grand council decision, provided that they do not violate the constitution. The grand council has to accept the people's decisions, as the confederacy is the people's government.

What the Constitution Represents in Terms of Philosophy

The constitution gives the Rotinonhsión:ni:onwe a strong identity, a philosophy upon which to base our lives, unity with our brethren and a sense of who we are as a people. This has created a momentum to recover control over our destiny. Today, the constitution provides a platform for negotiating political disputes with Canadian and American colonists, as we did in the stand-off in Kanehsatà:ke (Oka), and as we did in the past with the French, English, Dutch and Americans. Using the constitution, we are also able to deal with disputes within our nation and make decisions using its basic principles. It outlines everyone's role and purpose in the confederacy, as well as a philosophy and structure within which to deal with our environment.

Women are an integral part of Kanien'kehá:ka survival and are the backbone of Mohawk society. Both men and women have our roles to fulfill in keeping the nation strong. Duties are divided and complementary.

Women, as heads of our families and clans, are said to better understand controversies among people. In war, we would not unnecessarily risk the lives of our people over petty squabbles. The Kanien'kehá:ka men depend on this feminine wisdom to decide whether going to war would provide the greatest good for the ultimate effort.

The Rotinonhsión:ni, being a matrilineal society, hand down property through the females. A Mohawk bridegroom is expected to live in his wife's community and in her home, which was a longhouse with the extended family. Marriages are considered seriously. Children are highly regarded. During marriage ceremonies young couples are instructed that "if creation wants to, it will send you children". Children are gifts from creation and are to be treated as such.

This philosophy unites the Rotinonhsión:ni, which is now a force that Canadian and American authorities have come to respect. Challenged for hundreds of years, the Rotinonhsión:ni have emerged as a cohesive group. We are reaffirming our sovereign nationhood, reclaiming our lands, powers and possessions and making our presence felt nationally and internationally. Outside threats from the colonial states that are squatting on our land have forced the Rotinonhsión:ni to consider our political position.

We are falling back on our traditional longhouse philosophy, the treaties, our history and, of course, our constitution, the Kaianerehkó:wa. Young Kanien'kehá:ka people are studying the Kaianerehkó:wa and relearning the Kanien'kehá:ka language. No doubt, the tried and true philosophy of the past, which has withstood attack and near annihilation, provides direction to the young people.

Kanien'kehá:ka activism has shown other Indigenous people that it pays to exercise their rights. The mainstream public is seeing a new Indigenous image emerge. Even on the international stage, Kanien'kehá:ka and other Rotinonhsión:ni are asserting themselves, for example, at the United Nations, where we are eloquently presenting our cases. No doubt the philosophy embedded in the ancient Kaianerehkó:wa constitution is a major factor as to why the Rotinonhsión:ni still struggle, resist and exist.

Unity of the Rotinonhsión:ni nations is based on the philosophy of the Kaianerehkó:wa. The more unified the clans and communities of the Kanien'kehá:ka nation become, the stronger we become. It is this philosophy that affirms the sovereignty of the Kanien'kehá:ka nation and the Rotinonhsión:ni Confederacy. The Rotinonhsión:ni being geographically located in both the colonies of the United States and Canada must constantly exercise diplomatic acuity in dealing with these states on various matters, such as land claims, programs and services. It is the Kaienere'ko:wa that provides the will and spirit to exercise this identity.

Note

1   Kahn-Tineta Horn, *Mohawk Warrior Three: The Trial of Lasagna, Noriega & 20–20* (Kahnawà:ke: Owera Books, 1994).

—

The Iroquoian Use of Wampum

Ateronhiatakon

My name is Ateronhiatakon. I am Kanien'kehá:ka (Mohawk) from
Akwesasne and a student with many interests, most importantly to learn
about knowing. I grew up in a large family, raised with strong cultural
and community values and identity. From a very early age, I learned about
identity, language, customs and ways. These ways are hard and sometimes
painful. I cherish them all today. It is a gift. What I understand about
the intent of this gift is that it is to be shared. My interest in stories and
teachings goes back beyond memory. It all comes with duty and responsibility, for when one learns of these teachings, what is to be done with
that knowledge?

I owe a lot to my teachers, for their strength to continue their instructions nurturing us with wisdom, and to my friends, who help me discover
these gifts in a meaningful way. This is reflected in the oral and written
transmissions of "The Iroquoian Use of Wampum". The goal is to continue
to learn. In my learning, perhaps I can also teach the values I find in
the teachings and traditions. I believe that within these ways is strength
medicine for all who care to seek its guidance.

The Iroquoian Use of Wampum

On well worn tourist trails, main and back road museums join
"made by Indians" traders in describing wampum as "Indian money".
However, the use of wampum by the Iroquois as a trade item was of
secondary importance at most. Sir William Johnson wrote in 1753, "It
is obvious to all who are the least acquainted with Indian affairs, that
they regard no message or invitation, be it of what consequences it

will, unless attended or confirmed by strings or belts of wampum,
which they look upon as we our letters, or rather bonds".
—Letter of Sr. William Johnson, 1753. Doc. Hist. N.Y., vol. ii. p. 624.

Onkwehón:we, the original people, have been instructed that when, for
whatever purpose, the people come together, before all else comes the
Ohén:ton tsi karihwatéhkwen, the thoughts which bring our minds
together to collectively express our gratitude. We address each other as
brothers and sisters of the same creation, as friends and human beings,
which is the way we are instructed to greet one another. We greet each
other in peace and goodwill. We say "good health" to one another, so be
it in our minds. And the people reply "to" or "nio". We give thanks to the
Earth, the giver of life, to the waters, to the plant life, to all of the animals,
the insects and the fish, to the life and forces that are in the sky world,
eldest brother sun, grandmother moon and our distant cousins the stars.

I want to share the words of the people who are no longer with us,
who when teaching me intended that I should pass on these words to a
younger generation. There are many variations of these teachings, but
I am going to share a version that I heard while I was growing up and
sitting in the longhouse listening. What I saw that impressed me was the
respect and honor that my grandparents would show when they handled
Onekò:rha, wampum.

To the Rotinonhsión:ni, the Iroquois people, wampum held, and holds,
the special significance of a message given through a spiritual means. We
are told that wampum was given to us a long time ago by Ayonwentha
(Hiawatha), one of the very special men among our Iroquois people, who
helped Dekanawida, the Peacemaker, establish the Kaianerehkó:wa, the
Great Peace, known as the Five Nations Confederacy or the Iroquois
Confederacy. At the time Ayonwentha received these wampums, he had
lost his daughters. He was in great sadness, and he did not know what to
do next. A message came to him as he was walking beside a lake, and in
one version of the story a flock of geese came to this lake and picked up
the water. On the remaining lake bed lay strings of wampum. Ayonwentha
said, "If I ever meet a man who has this same grief, who has this same loss
that I am feeling, here is what I would begin to say to him in condolences".
He would say to him that life has to continue. Although we acknowledge a
great loss in our life, we have to look at the life cycle that will continue. The
sun will shine tomorrow, just as it did today. The moon will continue her

direction. Mother Earth will continue her cycles. So it was that he found the words that are still used for the condolence messages today when our leaders, both men and women, pass away. Ayonwentha, a great statesman, in his grief, found in his heart what he would say to his fellow man who would be in the same condition as him. The wampum is the evidence of the sincerity of the condolences.

Onekò:rha is made from the quahog shell. The quahog shell has two colors, an area where it is purely white, almost ivory, and areas that are more purplish. Wampum is made from both the ivory and the purplish areas. There are notations as to how the combinations of purple, white, and purple and white beads are to be strung. It is the significance of how they are strung that the interpreter or orator must remember and recite. This requires considerable insight and training. We say that a man who can do this has a gift given to him by a spiritual power, and that gift belongs to the people. It just flows through the orator: the gift does not belong to him; it is a gift that the people have been given through the orator.

The Mohawk, Onondaga, Seneca, Cayuga and Oneida comprise the confederacy. Each has a string of wampum beads. We refer to that string of beads as the nation's council fire, and it is a symbol present during councils. A fire is burning, and whatever words we use while this wampum is displayed have to be kind and gentle words. The nation's Council Fire Wampum is brought out for important national, international and multi-national meetings. It is known and acknowledged by the people that the bearer of this wampum belt represents the nation's one-minded consensus. When he speaks, he speaks with the collective in mind. That means the men elders, the women elders, the chiefs, the clan mothers, the faith keepers, the children and even the future generations. So you can perhaps imagine the commitment, the thorough peace, that wampum bearers must find in their own minds when they take wampum in their hands.

There are many, many different types of wampum. The Messenger's Wampum, for example, would be used for an announcement of a grand council (meeting of all nations of the confederacy) or for a nation's meeting. This wampum string is a short one fastened to a wood stick, and the man who carries it is recognized by the nation. He is given this wampum and a message announcing a meeting. Often there are marks on the stick which indicate in how many days the meeting will be held. He will travel directly to the nation, where he will deliver this message, and only this message. Then he will return immediately to the source which sent the wampum out. The main purpose of the Messenger's Wampum is to give a specific message about a meeting or an issue which needs to be discussed and relates to the people as a whole.

Wampum is the symbol of the authority that the women hold, and when there is a specific and important message that is to be delivered, this wampum is brought out. The people will then know that this person is speaking from a particular family with an urgent message, and that all should hear and adhere to the message that is being delivered.

Historically, wampums were used to record agreements between the Rotinonhsión:ni and other nations or governments. For example, when the Rotinonhsión:ni met with the Dutch, they acknowledged each other's existence and developed a relationship. The Rotinonhsión:ni understanding of that relationship is recorded in a belt called the *Kaswénhta*.[1] The Kaswénhta is also known as the Two Row Wampum belt, and there is a very special meaning for us in that belt, even today. The Two Row Wampum belt is about two and a half feet long and has two purple parallel lines which run the length of the belt on a white background. This particular belt denotes the type of relationship the nations of the Rotinonhsión:ni were expected to have with the Dutch and other arriving nations for all time to come.

The Kaswénhta represents the continuous flow of life. One purple row signifies the Onkwehón:we. In that row would be the canoe, and in the canoe would be the Onkwehón:we people, their language, their culture, their customs and their ways. Whatever is important to their understanding of their own identity is there, complete for future generations. However, the Rotinonhsión:ni acknowledged another row, and in that row would be the vessels of other nations, the Dutch in this case. The Dutch had their own language, culture, customs and ways; their past and future are in their vessel.

In their agreement with the Dutch, the Onkwehón:we said, "We are not your sons, we do not have a relationship in which your king will be our father, but rather we are equals, and we are brothers; we are created as brothers, and we can flow down the river of life, each in our respective vessels and canoes. We can have a relationship, a communication, an understanding about one another, but we are not to steer the other's vessel or canoe". This meant that neither the Dutch nor the Rotinonhsión:ni were to legislate laws or influence in a detrimental way which would redirect each other's full heritage, language and culture. The example given is that if anyone crosses from the canoe to the vessel or the vessel to the canoe, there is a concern that there may be rough waters. A wind might come, and if there are people who are straddling these two vessels, there is fear that they might not survive that storm; the people might fall. That message, ancient as it is, has a very important significance today.

There are many, many ways in which the people symbolized words and happenings or future direction through wampum. One of the more common ones, and there are different versions of this, is the Teiotiohkwahnhákton, commonly referred to as the Circle of Unity Wampum. This wampum commemorates the establishment of the Kaianerehkó:wa. The people wanted to remember how important unity is, so they strung two rows of wampum beads and made a circle which has two interwoven strands. From this circle hang the strings which denote the positions, the authority of Rotiianérshon and Iakoiá:ner, the chiefs and clan mothers, which is to say the families. In this circle of wampum are the spaced denotations of nationhood. Where the strand is much longer it represents Thadodáho, who is the keeper of the central fire of the Rotinonhsión:ni, in Onondaga. The special message in this wampum, we are told, is that there is no issue more important than the peace and unity of the people. We should not allow anything to creep into the minds of the men and women who sit on this council which would be a deterrent or cause destruction to the total unity of the confederacy. The message specifies that each nation has to maintain unity and peace, and their responsibility is expressed in words. Words are what we were given, and words are very important. Oratory is an important part of our teachings.

At Six Nations' meetings the wampum belts are very regularly taken out and stretched, to make sure the wampum beads are, in fact, intact. At the same time, it is ascertained that someone has the same strength as the leather thongs that hold the beads together. This represents the orator's strength, the strength of living life that emanates from the wampum, to be able to speak and present the oratory surrounding the wampum belts, beads and strings. An old piece of leather, as in nature, deteriorates over a number of years. Parts need to be replaced, fresh thongs are necessary, the belt must continuously be made strong. More importantly, the message that belongs to the belt must be fixed in memory to make sure that someone has that message to hand down.

The interpretation is part and parcel of the wampum's message, and life experiences are crucial in the interpretation of this message, so the wampum is alive from one generation to the next. Today, our wampums are in glass cases in museums throughout the world, and many of our own young people, our own Iroquois people, pass by these glass cases and look at our wampum belts in awe, wondering what they could have been used for, because the museums do not include the tradition and the words of the belts in the displays. The wampum belts, beads and strings are used as reminders for the speaker, but it is the speaker who knows the words. The wampum belts themselves do not speak; one has to know the culture, the language, the words, the feelings, the life around what happened with these wampums to understand the real significance, and when wampum belts are in display cases they do not generate that kind of spirituality. Sometimes I think that historians, although they don't mean to, perhaps want to put us in a historical timeline, and they don't allow us to say, "But it is alive today". This oratory is here today, and we can still hear these things. We know the words today. Historians perhaps want us to say, "Well it used to be like that". Yes, it used to be like that, but it still is, and it will be in the future.

Note

1   See "Teiohá:te", in the "Skakwatakwen—Concept Glossary".

I Am a Warrior

Karhiio John Kane

Karhiio John Kane is a Kanien'kehá:ka from Kahnawà:ke, who currently lives on the Cattaraugus Territory of the Seneca Nation. John has been involved for most of his adult life in in contemporary issues affecting Native people and has battled local, state and federal government and raised awareness on issues ranging from taxation to Native mascots, missing and murdered Indigenous Women, land use, land claims and environmentally destructive infrastructure projects like the KXL Pipeline, the Dakota Access Pipeline and Line 3. He hosts a popular radio show "Resistance Radio" on WBAI 99.5 FM, in New York City, and WPFW 89.3 FM, in Washington, DC, and the podcast *Let's Talk Native with John Kane.*

I am a warrior. I'm not the Hollywood version or the kind slapped on the side of a football helmet. I am not something man devolves into but, rather, something we aspire to. I am not a soldier in an army of mindless pawns. I don't fight to defeat an enemy; in fact, I hardly "fight" at all. I have never killed a man, although I have carried weapons for that purpose.

I am a warrior not by anyone else's definition other than our own. My purpose is not war; it's protection. But I protect both by nurturing and defending, and that applies to my loved ones, the people closest to me, and the ones we describe as those faces still in the ground—the future generations. I am a warrior, not a holy man or "warrior in spirit", nor do I possess a warrior spirit. I don't live my life to fulfill some mythological "warrior culture". I don't pray for peace; I work to maintain balance and harmony, whether it is in my family, community or with complete strangers.

I say all this because the word *warrior* is so abused. I know it's not ours. It's like so many other words that have been applied to us. Around fifty years ago, Louis Hall told a group of young men who began to pick up our traditional songs that they didn't need permission to do so, nor did they need permission to start playing a bigger role in defending their community and advancing our sovereignty. He told them that they had more than the right to do so; they had an obligation. Not many used the word *Rotihsken'rakéhte'* back then. It was generally used to describe the men, and Louis taught many about the importance of *Rotihsken'rakéhte'* and its deeper meaning. Its usage grew and some wondered how it came to mean the *men*. I heard it said that it was the *men*, without titles. It wasn't specifically fighting men, although some claimed it literally meant *he who carries the burden of peace*. Some say it means *he carries a gun*, and still others said it means *he carries a bundle*. What was told to me by the ones I trust most in the etymology of our words was that it means *he carries his medicine bag*. Not a doctor's bag but our own pouch with our own medicine: our umbilical cord that connects us to our mother, the soil from our birthplace that connects us to the mother of all, some tobacco and other objects and medicines that may only relate or have meaning to the owner. That bag is a reminder of the responsibility of men to protect our women and children and to know at all times that we are to honor motherhood and what sustains us. It reminds us of who we are and where we come from. At some point, as our men began to push the envelope of our sovereignty, *Rotihsken'rakéhte'* gained only one meaning, a meaning taken from the English language: *warrior*! I know it is certainly nowhere near the best definition, but it has its usefulness, and it is a word I will never run away from.

Louis Hall believed in symbols. He was an artist and a teacher when I came to know him. His artwork told stories, and he certainly didn't mind incorporating some text in his artwork, so there could be no misinterpretation. He thought we needed a flag. A flag that all Onkwehón:we (Indigenous people) could hold and fly as a symbol of unity. The Unity flag he created would become the most iconic image of Native unity and resistance in the world. I have purchased over a hundred of these flags over the years, sending them all over Turtle Island, whenever and wherever Native people were standing up for themselves and the land. Some were sent beyond our homelands to lands where people were in the same fight we were in. I sent a dozen of them to the Kanaka Maoli in Hawaii in solidarity with their fight for their sacred mountain Mauna Kea and against the American military presence there.

Louis's *Warrior Handbook* was required reading for the folks I hung around with. We aspired to do great things: defend and promote sovereignty, regain lost lands and re-establish life under the Kaianerehkó:wa, the path re-established when the people of our five regions stopped fighting among ourselves and reunited. Many of those battles were against our own people, those who were far more content with the personal comfort they found within the systems that had killed and oppressed our people for centuries than with what they found in our traditional ways. Too many took the attitude "if you can't beat them, join them", having never even attempted to fight them. Others got educated and thought they could work the system, more often for personal gain than for the advancement of our people. This was the prevailing philosophy of tribal councils whose strength and authority were established by Canada and the United States, not by those they claimed to lead and represent.

Who were these "warriors" living by the principles laid out in the "handbook" and having the audacity to stand up in the face of genocide? Were they desperate individuals with few options in life and little hope for the future? No! While I may not have been typical, I certainly wasn't atypical. I was among many who were articulate, thoughtful and hard-working. I graduated at the top of my high school class and went off to college. As the son of a high steel worker, well-liked and well-read, I was expected to be a professional… something. But what is a warrior? The men I associated with were ironworkers, veterans, lacrosse players, artists, teachers and craftsmen. They were tough, smart and passionate. None were desperate or without hope. Many came from Christian families but had cast that off along with many other colonial influences on our culture. They were family men with wives and children who struggled to balance the responsibilities of being a Rotihsken'rakéhte', in an age where the paychecks that supported your family carried the imprints of the countries you fought on their currency. In order to make a living, some, like myself, were ripped from their families, not unlike those children ripped from their parents and shipped off to residential schools. This time it was fathers ripped from their wives and children, who depended on them.

We fought law enforcement, local and federal. We stood up to armies, the FBI and the Bureau of Indian Affairs. In the case of the latter, we also fought their puppets who lived among us. I am Kanien'kehá:ka, what most people know as Mohawk, but my wife and three children are Onyota'a:ká, or Oneida. As with many Native communities, corrupt men seeking money and power knew that path led through the BIA and the false claims of authority it allows for. As a warrior, I was proud to take a stand for my family and the Onyota'a:ká people, even though standing up to the power of the US federal government has a cost. Mine was a sham federal trial and a two-year prison sentence.

There's a legacy that was born out of the redevelopment of the Warrior Society, and we're seeing it every day. There's real solidarity. We're seeing a lot more people who are willing to resist the policies of assimilation and land control. People try to associate that with AIM, but I don't think AIM was nearly as effective as a real sovereignty movement—that came with the Warrior Societies. They were parallel movements in many ways, but for us the idea of the Warrior Society wasn't about creating a movement, it was about revitalizing our culture. It was about asserting the importance of our land, not just our people, and really pushing back against a dominant culture at our doorstep.

When you are young and looking at what your previous generations did or didn't do, you can build a certain amount of resentment, because you can feel like the folks before you didn't do enough. You're grateful that the language and some elements of the culture continue, but our young people who are now involved in resistance, they have something to look back on. They got to see what my generation and the folks older than me were involved in, and it's inspirational. Even though they may have been too young to experience our taking back land at Ganienkeh or Oka, they know what took place there. What we're seeing now is a generation that doesn't feel like they are pioneers of resistance. They're taking it to the next level and, hopefully, taking it beyond where we took it.

I knew Louis Hall, and I know the amount of work that went into the *Warrior's Handbook* and the newsletters he was banging out on a regular basis. Louis Hall made us think critically in ways that nobody ever had before. Louis Hall was unique for the generation he represents, even for those considered iconic individuals and Native voices; there was nobody doing what Louis did. Some of the names like Oren Lyons or Vine Deloria,[1] their bigger message still had too much capitulation for my liking, and unfortunately their actions never met their words. Louis Hall wasn't just a mouthpiece, he was physically engaged. Louis Hall led me to a place and prepared me to experience the things I needed to become knowledgeable. I was privileged to know him and those who knew him even better than I. I continue to learn from people he has influenced, mostly from those who were closest to him. This is the warrior I am.

Note

1   Born in 1930, Oren Lyons is a Seneca faithkeeper. Lyons taught Native American
     Studies at the University of Buffalo. Vine Deloria Jr. (1933–2005) was a Standing
     Rock Sioux author and activist who taught at a number of universities, including
     the University of Arizona, where he established the first American Indian Studies
     graduate program.

PART IV
On Karoniaktajeh

This section pays homage to Louis Karoniaktajeh Hall's legacy in uplifting the Mohawk people's fighting spirit through his artwork, writings, activism and everyday behavior. A famous and polemical figure in Mohawk communities, Karoniaktajeh has not received the attention he deserves outside of the confederacy, despite the fact that his Unity flag is today the single most popular symbol of Indigenous resistance in North America. Kahentinetha's text tells the story of Karoniaktajeh as an ordinary yet exceptional human, deeply committed to Indigenous sovereignty in his everyday life. Kahentinetha's memories are elaborated by a second text, which gathers the words of many of his friends throughout the Iroquois Confederacy and beyond.

Who Was Karoniaktajeh?

Kahentinetha Rotiskarewake

The Artist

Everybody has seen the famous Unity flag. From Zapatistas in Mexico to Aborigines in Australia, from Idle No More through the Elsipogtog anti-fracking struggle to Standing Rock, this flag has been used as a universal symbol of Native resistance to colonialism. Few know that it was designed by a man they called Louis Hall, who called himself Karoniaktajeh, "he travels on the edge of the sky". They called him a Mohawk from Kahnawà:ke, and he called himself a Kanien'kehá:ka.

I have known Karoniaktajeh most of my life. My father, an ironworker like many Mohawks, died by falling off a bridge in Vermont. I was left without a father at thirteen years old. As a devout longhouse person, my father was insistent that I retain my knowledge and language, and, as a family friend, Karoniaktajeh was instrumental in helping me fulfill that promise. He encouraged all of us to stand up for our identity. Everything I learned about our culture came from visiting him and the clan mothers.

Above everything, Karoniaktajeh was known and renowned as a brilliant artist throughout our Indigenous communities. He painted several hundred paintings, often marked by a strong sense of humour. He was a self-taught artist and built his own unique Onkwehón:we style that no one could duplicate. For the most part, he tried to paint us as attractive and strong. His works were very detailed and colorful. Without a shop to work in, he used to do his painting in his kitchen, often using materials at hand like wall paint and plywood boards. I became interested in art watching him paint or make a drawing that he would give away to someone. Known for his artwork, Karoniaktajeh was contacted in 1973 by the American Indian Movement to make a poster to illustrate their spirit. In this way, he helped connect the American Indian Movement with Mohawk communities and the Warrior Society.

Apart from his visual art, Karoniaktajeh was also an accomplished writer. His books, including the *Warrior's Handbook* and *Rebuilding the Iroquois Confederacy*, are still standard reading for many of our people today. These textbooks are representative of the revival of Indigenous resistance in the 1970s. His teachings were often found in the internationally acclaimed publication *Akwesasne Notes*, as well as in local newspapers like *Longhouse News*.[1] He would also send many letters to mainstream newspapers criticizing Christian influence and doctrines, advocating that Native Americans must take hold of their own traditions. Much like his paintings, Karoniaktajeh always wrote humorously. He saw things through our own lens, and those who were the object of his critiques were dealt with using ridicule, sarcasm and a great deal of wit. These stories would constantly poke fun at the band council, the settler politicians and the Church. This treatment I'm sure came from the nuances and sayings of our old language. He had a small desk that he built himself to put his typewriter on, which I still have in my house. His art and writing weren't only art and literature; they were political expression.

Political Vision

Karoniaktajeh used to receive constant visits from the American Indian Movement and other Red Power activists to learn about Mohawk resistance culture and the Kaianerehkó:wa. They would come visit and stay for a few days or even weeks, camping out in the yard. He would sit with them all and discuss the Kaianerehkó:wa, its history and culture, and they would learn our songs and dances. He would always praise visitors for speaking about their culture and criticize the Church for swaying them away from it. Eventually these families would return home, and at some point some of us would go visit them. In one case, we went to visit a family in Tobique, New Brunswick, to discover that they had become completely enamored with tradition. It was Karoniaktajeh who helped change that community.

His participation in the refoundation of the Rotihsken'rakéhte', the men's council fire, was a direct extension of this will to empower community life based on our traditions. When Rotihsken'rakéhte' decided to repossess land in Ganienkeh, he was immensely supportive and provided guidance. He was always exchanging letters with prisoners, notably from AIM, many of whom he kept a correspondence with for years.

He saw a greater direction, further than just Kahnawà:ke, and always supported movements of the people, respecting their right to choose their own direction. After the Oka Crisis in 1990, people used to come to Kahnawà:ke to seek him out. Some Native people came and camped out at the longhouse. They were searching for their way and wanted to do rituals and ceremonies. But we are a people of action. We had our festivals and other ceremonies, but we didn't stop at just praying. We always saw that when disaster strikes, you gotta get up off the chair and do something.

Though Karoniaktajeh could not sit on the council because he was not married and had no children, the people appointed him as a spokesperson to carry out their wishes for specific issues. All his life, he was always ready to receive people and discuss matters with them. Anyone could go to his house for a cup of tea and long discussions about our history and the Kaianerehkó:wa. During the repossession of Ganienkeh, despite him not having a family, he was appointed as the secretary of the Ganienkeh council fire because of his wisdom. He envisioned a return to the original Rotinonhsión:ni through our original constitution, not only in Ganienkeh but throughout Turtle Island, A'nowarà:ke. Even when he was old and sick, Karoniaktajeh never ceased to paint, to write and to inform the people of their own sovereignty.

Sovereignty and the Great Law

Karoniaktajeh took freedom and independence seriously. He took treaties at their word, all the while recognizing them as illegal agreements made under threat. He understood that the philosophy of the Kaianerehkó:wa served as the basis for the US Constitution, which had perverted it into a hierarchical system. In Karoniaktajeh's view, we all have an absolute right to the land, because our Mother created us alongside every natural entity. At the same time, a constitution is the will of a free people. This means that the Kaianerehkó:wa favours nature; it represents creation's design for all living things to live in harmony with the natural world. Our title is based on us holding the land for the future generations, *Tahatikonhsontóntie*. It is *them* who own all the assets and have all the power.

Karoniaktajeh said that Canada runs a business using the resources of the future children of the original people. Canada is concerned with banking, railroads, oil, insurance companies, pipelines, real estate and so on, with no end to the damage that could be done. Karoniaktajeh said, "There is no statute of limitation on mass murder!" He foresaw that future business ventures must be based on the Kaianerehkó:wa, where everyone serves nature. In fact, today corporations have to get our prior and informed consent to use the land and resources of our children. Knowing that, how can we sit at the table with these artificially created illegal entities who rape our land? Regarding war and peace, Karoniaktajeh would have said that the government knows that "this country is yours, and they can't take it away from you without your consent if you are at peace, but if you are at war they can take it by conquest".

His thinking was far more advanced than that of many of our "appointed" leaders and the self-serving corporate medicine men. There are many who say they met Karoniaktajeh, and that they learned from him, but we find that some did not get his message. Being the opposite of the "corporate" Indian leaders paid by the colonial state, Karoniaktajeh always took the idea of Native sovereignty seriously. That's why he promoted the idea of a complete separation from Canada and the United States to form an independent republic based on the Kaianerehkó:wa. But it had to come from the people. Karoniaktajeh didn't consider himself separate from the whole of the community. When he worked at Lafleur's supermarket as a butcher, people would visit him and ask him questions while he waved around his knives. He was comfortable with the people. He never hid his views from anyone. Because he was so dedicated to his work, he lived the life of a pauper. He could live without a lot of things, like running water, electricity and bathroom facilities, and although he appreciated them when he had them the lack of these things did not bother him at all.

Instead of complaining, Karoniaktajeh always insisted that our time should be spent on how we are going to accomplish what we are doing. There is no word for saying *I'm sorry* in our language. When we excuse ourselves, we say we will *make things better, Enskerihwakwatá:ko'*. As we traveled and spoke, we acknowledged but did not cry over what the white man did to us. We told them to correct their wrongs, respect our rights as human beings according to creation—to exist as we were designed to by creation, not to deny us our natural way of being. The colonizers have brainwashed themselves by believing that they are godly, that they should have dominion over all creation. In this way, we say, they are not people of the natural direction, Onkwehón:we.

That's why Karoniaktajeh always pointed out that even though our people had the ability to develop into the culture of possession, we chose to develop within a culture of humanity and balance with nature instead. All this came from the Kaianerehkó:wa, the Great Law. The Kaianerehkó:wa is the will of a free and independent people. Our way favours nature. Creation has designed everything to live together in harmony with the natural world. We look at nature to see how we shall conduct ourselves. As my aunt Ganyetahawi advised, "If you need answers, sit in the woods, and they will come to your mind".

A man of such intelligence, Karoniaktajeh was never awarded any titles. His words, etchings and actions speak for themselves. He was never afraid to be in the midst of the people. His tactic was to recognize and help us see what is real and what is artificial. There are many who call themselves "longhouse elders", but what are they passing to our young people to enhance our natural existence as the people that we are? Are they giving them actual formulas to survive? Like our ancestors, he encouraged us to look into ourselves and take responsibility for our survival. Other teachers say, "Pray to the Creator", but tobacco abuse in ceremonies can lead our people to use prayer instead of getting up and actually doing something.

In Karoniaktajeh's view, prayer sidetracks you from taking responsibilities. He advised us to go to communities throughout the continent and get involved. He believed in offering kids the opportunity to travel throughout the confederacy, to learn what no institution could teach you by experiencing life. By encouraging the people to take back what is theirs by whatever means, Karoniaktajeh merely followed what his language told him to do. He and his politics were one with his language. This philosophy and these principles made the Onkwehón:we a great people who lived without settlers for tens of thousands of years. In the end, the Kaianerehkó:wa aims to maintain peace between all living things. It was maintained this way until Jacques Cartier came into the picture. Even there, we always tried hard to maintain peace and a welcoming spirit by keeping the Kaianerehkó:wa open to all nations. All of Karoniaktajeh's life was dedicated to this task.

On Faith

Before he began writing, Karoniaktajeh was a devoted Christian and was even being groomed for the priesthood. Like many of our people, he was deceived by religion, but soon he saw the contradictions in Catholicism. He searched for something real and found the Kaianerehkó:wa, and he committed himself to reintroducing it to all Onkwehón:we and to all people. Karoniaktajeh escaped the Christian prison and its imaginary to find his way back to the real world. He totally immersed himself in the Kaianerehkó:wa and started a huge movement of revitalization and resistance.

He read a lot about history, both ancient history and what we may call the *Jesuit Relations*, or "how the church attempted to destroy us". He knew as much about Western culture as he did about Onkwehón:we. The priests hated and feared him. They could never win an argument with him, because he was more learned than them and thought more deeply, using his own mind rather than dogma. He saw that Christianity was set up to degrade and annihilate our people. It attacked everything about what we were as a people, wanting total control of us. Karoniaktajeh discovered that religion was barely even an illusion—there was nothing real about it. On the other hand, we had the perfect reality, the natural world and a part of all living things on our side. He knew that this was because all life had the same original instructions—to use our instincts in order to survive.

Karoniaktajeh openly defied the Church, British and French institutions, Indian band and tribal councils, as well as federal Indian law. He encouraged our people to understand that through creation they had natural rights to breed, eat, access medicines and all the bounties of nature. Our mother gave us the right to choose, exercise our own mind, preserve ourselves, along with all life, plants, insects, fish and all that fight to survive. Nature always prescribed that one had to work at something to benefit from the good things in life. Creation has provided us with everything that we need to survive, but it is up to us to use it. Evil is not based on anything in nature. It is unnatural, destructive to humans, animals, birds, insects, trees, flowers, plants, land, fish and the waters. Those following the unnatural way are in a reality of their own minds. People are misled into believing there is a greater afterlife, while great suffering goes on among those living right now. We are supposed to let this happen, because God and Jesus are going to reward us in the afterlife, but it is right now, on Earth, that we are concerned about our children and our environment. Teaching evil neglects the responsibilities that creation designed for us.

Europeans didn't just steal our land, they brought Karihwiiohstónhtshera', a man-made reality that you cannot prove, but which all are forced to believe. It is a made-up reality of the mind based on faith, not knowledge. Karoniaktajeh could see the difference within the language. Indoctrination numbs their minds. Europeans brought religion. Religion didn't exist for us as a thing separate from other aspects of life. Our way is Sha'oié:ra, the movement in the same direction as reality, which is, in fact, the opposite of faith. These Europeans who supposedly represented God said we were heathens: children of the devil. Those who questioned them were seeds of the devil. Karoniaktajeh saw the white man's education system as a means to override the natural minds of the people, to confuse us and make us incapable of reaching into our minds for our inborn understanding of life. Emptied minds more readily carry out carnage and devastation without a second thought.

Language

Karoniaktajeh recognized what our ancestors passed on to us through language. He found all our answers in our language, which contains all our ways and history, past, present and future. Our language is the expression of our culture and natural way of being. *It contains, in itself, all of our politics.*

Karoniaktajeh always insisted that we bring him to the socials at the longhouse, so he could listen to the songs and watch the young people dance. This, he said, was therapeutic. Our language is not just about words; it is the *tone* naturally buried deep in our minds. We are born with the tones which form the bond with our Mother Earth, the natural world and our people. This tone raises pictures that are buried deep in our minds. When the past, present and future pass before us, we can feel the tones and see the pictures, and then the words come to us. When a mother hums and sings these tones to her baby, the baby learns to describe the pictures in his mind using the tones. A picture cannot be changed to something else. It is the truth, and we cannot say it is something else. We make imprints and memories of our land and people. When we walk on it, we know that it is ours, and that is the basis of our life.

Through language, Karoniaktajeh asserted his identity. Our identity is equivalent to our way of being, which we call *Karihwí:io, how we carry ourselves naturally on this Earth.* We are part of every living thing—trees, sun, water, land, animals, everything—this is the reality of our existence. By encouraging people to learn the truth about themselves, by knowing their *Onkwehón:we:néha* language, Karoniaktajeh brought forth upon the world what would be his main legacy. His struggle was always directed against those who tried to cut us from these roots.

Karoniaktajeh's last will was to spread his knowledge about the Kaianerehkó:wa, to make it available as the knowledge of all of our people. We wrote down everything we knew about the Kaianerehkó:wa. It took us a long time to write it, Ganyetahawi and Karoniaktajeh were always arguing about the spelling of Indigenous words—which had never been a written language, but finally we got the transcription complete. Then we started to film the lecture, which we did in bits and pieces over a year, and which is now available on my website, Mohawk Nation News.[2] Today, we have something nobody else ever did, the Kaianerehkó:wa in our language and in English, in film and book form.

After we completed that video, Karoniaktajeh moved into an apartment which was built for him on top of my house. He continued to work. He was a stubborn man. I knew he was sick, but he refused to let me take him to the doctor. He led by example. Even in his final days, he never abandoned the struggle. His artwork, his writings, we will never forget what he did for the people. His spirit still inspires us, like other figures from the past. That's why we too will never abandon the struggle, because, in the end, the message is more important than the man.

Notes

1   See Timeline, "1968 Akwesasne Notes"; *Longhouse News* was the official organ of the Kanonhsionni'ón:we Kahnawà:ke Branch of the Six Nations Iroquois Confederacy, edited by Rastewensertontah Peter Diome.

2   Mohawk Nation News, accessed March 15, 2022, https://mohawknationnews.com.

Karoniaktajeh Remembered

Billy Tayac, South Maryland Piscataway chief

Karoniaktajeh was an ordinary man who was inspired. His mind gave him greatness. He was the most feared Indian in the United States, Canada and even South America because of his great mind. His greatest accomplishment was *unity*. I asked him, "Why did you create the flag?" He said, "All people throughout the world have a flag that unites them. Now we have one, the Unity flag. Today, wherever anyone resists against corporations, states, provinces, countries, that flag pops up. It means they're going to resist, and not give up". His flag continues to inspire today. We had the LISN [League of Indigenous Sovereign Nations] plan that was intended to unite our people.[1] We took it to Leon Shenandoah, the "official" Thadodáho "grand chief" in Onondaga, to help implement it. Ninety days later, he had not read it. So we went to see Karoniaktajeh, who said, "I always thought unity would come from the Rotinonhsión:ni. I never thought it would come from a Piscataway!" Unity was his lifetime dream.

Dana Lee Thompson, Akwesasne scholar

Karoniaktajeh was an educator. We used to go listen to him in the cookhouse. He was a historian who made history. He taught us to be proud and fight back. He was ahead of his time. He brought people back to the Kaianerehkó:wa. In the 1920s, the Catholic Church got a big stone fence built in Kahnawà:ke to keep us from going to the river to get water. A young Mohawk, Ronakarakete, refused to accept it. He went home and got some dynamite, returned and blew that fence to smithereens. The Church kicked out the family. Even though he had been forced to be a Christian when he was young, Karoniaktajeh always fought the Church.

Danny Delaronde, Kahnawà:ke Rotihsken'rakéhte'

Karoniaktajeh had lots of stories for us young guys, encouragement which flowed naturally from him. He was creative with his writing, words, art and speaking, especially when he talked about the Kaianerehkó:wa. He would always give us examples. When he started to make the Warrior flag, we would help him with other youth. He made a draft, asked us for suggestions, left and then came back, asking us again what we thought. We all said "That's it!" We were part of making this Warrior flag. And now it's all over the world! It was for everybody. We were all moving in the same direction with the same power and determination.

Irvin Goodleaf, Kahnawà:ke former special assistant to Jean Chrétien, Canadian minister of Indian affairs

Karoniaktajeh thought deeply about the people and how the Rotihsken'rakéhte' were a great part of it. He always exposed the "store bought" Indians (band councils). Karoniaktajeh had his own spirit. He did not fear anybody, which gave spirit to the men. We should remember him. His flag is the symbol of the whole struggle. Other movements had started in cities. He was here to witness the resistance against the seaway. He was always there where it happened. He trained us to be fit in mind and body and helped us create a rallying point, giving us inspiration. He pictured our way of life as based on nature. During the 1990 crisis, he went to the lacrosse rink in Kahnawà:ke to talk to the people about our sovereignty and the role of the Rotihsken'rakéhte'. He put his thoughts in pictures. The philosophy was made simple; every day is the last day. I am fortunate that I was with him. I remember seeing a pamphlet he wrote in the Mohawk Nation Office explaining our sovereignty and the Kaianerehkó:wa, instructing us to never follow anybody else's law. He encouraged us to bring these principles to every negotiation with anybody. We need people like him to continue.

Kaniehtiio Horn, Kahnawà:ke actress

I used to feel so special when Karoniaktajeh would close one eye and point his fingers like a gun at me and my cousin when we would be running around playing or sitting quietly listening to him speaking. I was eight years old when Louis passed away at my house. I remember being told when I got home from school and feeling like I lost my grandfather. I cried and cried. He was the wise old man figure in my young life. I knew he was an amazing artist. I knew he made the Unity flag and knew of all of those great things he created and wrote. It wasn't until I was older that I understood how powerful his knowledge, passion and love for his people was, and that anyone that knew him and spent time with him was fortunate and carried with them a piece of him. When I was in my early twenties, I moved into the apartment he passed away in, and I lived there for ten years. I still talk out loud to him sometimes, because in a way I feel like his spirit has permeated the walls of my mother's house. I think of him often. There are reminders of him everywhere I turn: his art, the flag, his teachings. I have always felt that it was my duty to make him proud, to be part of the future he was moving towards and envisioning for our people.

Karakwine June Simon, Kanehsatà:ke elder

Many years ago, when I was about twenty-two years old, Glenna Shilling-Matoush took me to see Louis Hall. He told us many stories about the Mohawks. For instance, how the warriors climbed the cliffs at Québec City during the Wolfe and Montcalm battle and won it for the British. I was totally engrossed with all his stories. He told me about the Jesuits too. None of this stuff was in history books. Looking back, I realized one of his missions in life was to educate the young, especially young Mohawks. I am forever grateful to Louis for telling me and others the real history that the education system refuses, up until this day. I shall never forget Louis Hall.

Karakwiniontha Waneek Horn-Miller, Kahnawà:ke water polo Olympic champion

Karoniaktajeh was thinking and writing an offensive strategy for our survival. Where are we going as a people? We want our children to think for themselves. There was a place for everyone who was willing to work for the people. The longhouse, the 1990 crisis, Ganienkeh, our sovereignty made us look at Karoniaktajeh and his knowledge based on the Kaianerehkó:wa. He said we are in the final stages of colonization. Our young people want to belong to the greatness of the Great Peace. We can contribute throughout the world. We don't want ways designed by outsiders. He trained thinkers. As an athlete, I have always had to use thinking to develop an offensive strategy and a good defense. He lit that fire, looking at what is possible beyond the Indian Act and colonization. To be forward-looking with an eye on the past. Now we have defined the narrative. We had no fear. We go out and do stuff, knowing what is possible. In this game we cannot just wait and try to keep up. His writing, art and fearlessness made us understand sovereignty and nationhood our way. He helped us build strategies based on what was organically good for our people. We feel it. We know it. We fight for the freedom to face fears and wrongs—and the right to survive. Karoniaktajeh wanted us to live offensively!

Katsi'tsakwas Ellen Gabriel, Kanehsatà:ke activist

Karoniaktajeh was a visionary. I have realized that his manifesto was carried out by the true warriors and peoples during the 1990 siege of Kanehsatà:ke and Kahnawà:ke. He was referenced on many occasions during 1990 and afterwards. His words conveyed the frustration and indignation of multiple generations who suffered under oppressive Canadian colonial laws that threatened their land, identity and survival. Reclaiming land is the most precious part of his vision for our survival. He knew that an offensive position was the only way. His words ring true even today, as we witness so many other Onkwehón:we peoples continue the centuries-old resistance to assimilation. It is time to dust ourselves off and listen once again to the words of Louis Hall and to demand with louder and stronger voices: land back and restoration of our beautiful democracy, so that we will live in peace and always remain vigilant in the protection of our lands, living with respect on Mother Earth.

Kawenaa Liz Montour, Kahnawà:ke archivist

We were Karoniaktajeh's neighbours. I knew him in the 1960s. He was a good farmer of the land, a great artist and spoke the old language. We traded farm lots with him. He spoke to the people and was always ready to back up what we said. I went with my mother to visit him often. When they were talking, I would go into the back room and stare at his great oil paintings. In high school, he helped me with a story on our history about the "Patriots". He said the Americans were heading towards us from Châteauguay to attack us. Our people were in the old church. A woman was out tending the cattle and saw the army hiding in the bushes. She ran into the village and into the church and screamed for them to get out, because they were going to be attacked. She saved them. My teacher was appalled and did not accept my paper, because it was based on oral history, which did not count.

Mark Maracle, Tyendinaga Rotihsken'rakéhte' and iron worker

I am honored to have known Karoniaktajeh. He was and remains one of my great teachers who taught me of our proud traditional history. His spirit is always with us through his writings and the great works of art he left us. He is honored and greatly respected throughout Turtle Island and around the world. In July 1989, he came to Akwesasne when hundreds of New York state troopers invaded our land, and he was also present in 1990 when Kanehsatà:ke, Kahnawà:ke and Akwesasne were invaded. He was always there to give us insight and to help us understand the Kaianerehkó:wa's way of dealing with hardships.

Mike Thomas, Kahnawà:ke Rotihsken'rakéhte'

I am a warrior of the Great Peace, the Kaianerehkó:wa. Karoniaktajeh taught me responsibility towards our people. Standing up no matter what, even if you stand alone. Before I went back to the longhouse, I spent a lot of time with him and John Beauvais. I began to follow the roots that lead to the Tree of Peace. I was passionate about being Onkwehón:we and being a Rotihsken'rakéhte'. To this day I try to live and work on that path that was shown to me. Listening to him was powerful. I even became a war chief. The Warrior Society would meet in the cookhouse next to the longhouse: Nias Hemlock, Mitch Deer, Cookie McComber, Steven Stacey and the others. We talked about responsibility and picking the fight. Our agenda was the people. Karoniaktajeh laughed, "It's not going to be easy! Dealing with the foreign government is a very important duty". We all stepped forward and walked down that road. We risked our lives. It was a rewarding journey. The legacy was carrying the peace, developing the warrior's endurance, seeing it through and finding out what it meant to be Rotihsken'rakéhte'. Karoniaktajeh's message was that we would fall and get back up. He warned, "Watch out! You will always be under the watchful eye of the foreign government". He said that our duties were greater than ourselves. He made us warriors for a lifetime.

Ojistoh Horn, Akwesasne and Kahnawà:ke physician

Karoniaktajeh was always in and out of my family's life, and his colorful and unique art was all over our home. I was in university taking extra courses in history and Native issues and was fortunate to be able to visit him regularly and listen to his stories and incredible recitations of our history. My mother, my grandmother Frances and Karohiaktajeh were an incredible trio, and I find that even today phrases and memories of them flash through my mind. I remember the anticipatory grief I felt when I saw him dance for the last time in the longhouse. I think of him often and am pleased to see him live on in our collective mind.

Rick Pouliot, Wabanaki warrior

Karoniaktajeh's writings brought his deep thinking to many people. I had the honor of sitting with him and hearing his words in person. He provided a roadmap for people of all ages to be role models for the youth. Karoniaktajeh said the most important part of being a warrior is to help close to home, especially when women and girls face continuing violence. Karoniaktajeh's paintings, including the Unity flag, brought visualization and symbolism to a global level. It is a symbol of the Native people's resistance and their endeavour to assert their aboriginal rights and sovereignty. These flags are displayed by Native people throughout Turtle Island. They demonstrate our collective commitment to stand together.

Takawirenteh Allen Delaronde, Kahnawà:ke Rotihsken'rakéhte'

Early on Karoniaktajeh worked with elder Pete Diome to deeply understand the Kaianerehkó:wa. He tried to teach it to the young people. He was a great writer, explaining our true history and the Great Peace, which made a great difference all over. Today, many people are fighting for their rights because of him. Many don't give him credit for what he did. He understood because of what he saw, heard and touched in natural things. He did not look up to the sky and ask someone to do his work for him. He proved that the Church was bad by making fun of it. He liked telling stories and made them amazing and humorous. His writings and paintings showed that. His ideas were successful. He helped reclaim our land at Ganienkeh. He provided lots of information on our rights during the 1990 Oka Crisis. He knew this was a national political issue, not domestic. He knew our way is based on the Kaianerehkó:wa. He said, "Don't learn from the top down. Learn about life, food, everything natural from the bottom up. Without insects we would not survive. They are the first step in the chain of life".

Teiowí:sonte Thomas Deer, Kahnawà:ke graphic artist and historical and cultural liaison for the Kanien'kehá:ka Onkwawén:na Raotitióhkwa Language and Cultural Center

The single biggest contribution that Karoniaktajeh gave to his people was a vision of what we can become. Through his writings and artwork, Karoniaktajeh idealized what Kanonhsionni'ón:we society could be if we all embraced our traditional teachings, pushed fear aside and put in the work to make that dream come true. Karoniaktajeh was a true visionary and made people search for knowledge—myself included. The "Oka Crisis" led me to the longhouse, but it's Karoniaktajeh's teachings that kept me there. I consider myself a student of Karoniaktajeh, and many of my life choices were heavily influenced by his own life. His writings inspired me to be a writer like him, and his artwork encouraged me to use my art as a teaching tool. In a lot of ways, I feel compelled to continue where he left off and help make his vision come true.

Tekahonwasa Lance Delisle, Kahnawà:ke artist and musician

It was Karoniaktajeh's *Warrior Manifesto* and the way that it honors our people that affected me the most. I realized what our responsibilities were going to be. He was always concerned about those who are coming by dedicating himself to the resurgence of our identity. His ideas were an eye-opener which caused me to stop drinking. He encouraged me to continue my art and music. He explained the principles around the design of the flag. He said where the sunrays touch the Earth is where we have to be to protect our people. One night, he came into the Warrior's Office where I was working as a dispatcher. He sat down, and we talked about how people are motivated through art. He asked me what the story was behind my drawing and what I was writing. He advised, "Always think about your message". His art is really striking, vibrant, showing us as healthy and strong people. Many people around Kahnawà:ke have prints of his art hanging in their houses. He inspired me as a writer and musician, and, above all, he was a genuinely funny guy.

Watio Wat'kwanohwera Splicer, Ganienkeh artist and Rotihsken'rakéhte'

I remember when I was a kid seeing Louis Hall in the longhouse and knowing that that old-timer created all those paintings with his own distinct style. He definitely influenced me as an artist. Also, knowing that he had a Christian background but worked so hard at going back to our own ways was really inspiring. He influenced a lot of our people, encouraging us to think for ourselves. What he helped to create is our own state in Ganienkeh, and that is where I am now, trying my best to carry on what he had started.

Wendahawi Elijah, Kahnawà:ke language teacher

I was always amazed at how Karoniaktajeh always kept painting in the middle of whatever he was doing. After he passed, his family gave me one of his paint brushes. I thought, "Holy smokes! How did they know I was into art?" Maybe it was meant to be. His main influence is that he put pride and a sense of empowerment back into us after the residential schools and other ills and pains we suffered. You can see that strongly in his art and the strength he portrayed in the women and men. I wish his art could be shown to everybody. As a youngster, I did not understand the politics, but I knew he was very important in our community. I pursued art to get at our history and culture and to feel proud. I will never forget how his art helped me realize my strength. I always remember Louis's gym with the bench and the weights. He said, "You're never too old to exercise". I went into sports and kept fit. At his apartment next to the longhouse, people came from all over to visit him and hear him talk about the Kaianerehkó:wa.

Note

1   The League of Indigenous Sovereign Nations, established in 1991, brings together representatives from fifteen Indigenous nations.

PART V
Karoniaktajeh's Writings

This section gathers a selection of Louis Karoniaktajeh Hall's most influential writings. Even though these texts have circulated widely throughout Rotinonhsión:ni territory through self-published books, inspiring generations of Indigenous warriors to take pride in their traditions and to defend their sovereignty, this is the first time they are officially published for a wider audience. The texts here include the *Ganienkeh Manifesto* which was written in 1974 after Mohawk warriors reoccupied an abandoned summer camp near Moss Lake, in New York State, declaring it sovereign Indigenous territory. The manifesto shares the vision of the people who built the camp to make it a cornerstone for reviving traditional land-based and cooperative Indigenous lifestyles beyond the boundaries of the reservations. Written in 1979, while Karoniaktajeh was surviving a harsh winter in Ganienkeh without electricity, the *Warrior's Handbook* is considered to be his most famous text, staunchly celebrating uncompromising resistance as necessary for the survival of Indigenous peoples and cultures in North America. The booklet originally included pieces which Karoniaktajeh had already published in other outlets, such as *Longhouse News*, the most important ones being included in this book. Finally, *Rebuilding the Iroquois Confederacy*, published around 1985, shares Karoniaktajeh's understanding of the "Peacemaker" Dekanawida's original intention of "extending the rafters" of the confederacy's Great Peace to all nations. It explains how this universal vision was gradually forgotten by way of Christian and colonial influences and envisions the re-creation of an independent Indigenous nation on Turtle Island as a promise for the future generations to enjoy.

Ganienkeh Manifesto

Ganienkeh—"Land of the Flint"—ancient homeland of the Mohawk Nation, whose descendants, with traditional Natives from other Indian nations, are moving back to repossess their natural heritage. Other Native nations throughout the world have regained their lands and governments. The North American traditionals are sure that the government of the United States and its general public shall see the justice and the rights of the American Indian people making such a move.

Ganienkeh shall be the home of the traditional Red man. Here, based on the rights accorded everyone else in the world, the Red man shall exercise his proven government and society, in keeping with his culture, customs and traditions. Based on the rights of the human, he has the right to operate his state with no interference from any foreign nation or government. Here, the people shall live according to the rules of nature. Here, the Great Law of the Six Nations Iroquois Confederacy shall prevail. The people shall live off the land. The co-op system of economy shall prevail. Instead of the people competing with each other, they shall help and cooperate with each other. Here, they shall relearn the superior morality of the ancients.

It is not a backward step. The way to a proper, moral government, a practical and worthy economic system and a proper, moral human relationship is true progress. What is regarded as progress in this day and age is a road to destruction. Advanced technology abuses nature. The result has been the pollution of air, land, water and the human mind. A brief reflection reveals how abused nature repays in kind: the competitive society. The main objective of human intelligence should be the peace and happiness of mankind on Earth, not the profit saturation of a few tycoons and the worship of advanced technology. This kind of progress has brought the world to the brink of destruction.

Let there be a ray of light somewhere. Instead of abuse of nature, let there be an appreciation of nature. Ganienkeh calls all Native American Indians who wish to live according to their culture, customs and tradition. Traditional Indians who answer the call and participate in the project shall be asked to prepare to meet unusual situations. Indians lived a million years without money and technology. They lived off the land. (Today's existing cooperative communities refuse family allowance, welfare relief, old age pension and still live very comfortably.) Utilizing the co-op community system, the Indian State of Ganienkeh shall be a moneyless state. The requirement is enough land to grow food for all, enough grazing land for beef cattle or buffalo and enough timber land for building materials—and people who are ready to work towards its success.

The Mohawk Land was lost in an earlier century by fraud, and its possession by New York State and the State of Vermont constitute illegal usurpation. No deed signed by Joseph Brant and the New York State agent can extinguish the rights of the Mohawks to their own country.[1] Native North Americans not only have the rights but are duty bound to *correct the wrong committed by Joseph Brant and the New York State agents against the Mohawk Nation.* No individual Indian or any individual nation of the Six Nations Confederacy has the right to sell or give away land without the consent of the grand council of the Six Nations Confederacy. This was one of the findings of the New York Senate investigating commission, which ended in 1922.

Joseph Brant, who was not even a member of the Six Nations Confederacy, having previously disqualified himself, did on March 29, 1797, with an alleged "power of attorney", make a deal with the New York State, in which he gave away all the Mohawk land to the said New York State. Several months earlier, in November of 1796, the same Joseph Brant, with the same "power of attorney", gave away large tracts of land in Ontario to his British friends. It was called 999-year leases *at no cost,* that is, no revenue was to accrue. Brant loved white people so much or was mesmerized by them that he pauperized outright his own people to please his white friends.

In a letter to the representatives of the United Nations at San Francisco, California, April 13, 1945, the Six Nations Confederacy stated strongly that Joseph Brant was never given the right to give away their lands. Even if they had given Brant the alleged "power of attorney", it would still be invalid, as the deal would have to be consummated in the grand council of the Six Nations Confederacy. The fee simple is still vested in the Six Nations, and the Mohawks have the aboriginal title to ancient Kanièn:ke. No self-respecting nation on Earth would accept the dirty deal handed out by Joseph Brant and the New York State agents.

The Mohawk Nation, supported by traditional North American aboriginal Natives from other Native nations, such as Ojibwa Crees, Algonquins and others, shall move into the Mohawk homeland of Ganienkeh. The combined nations shall establish the Independent North American Indian State of Ganienkeh. The Great Law—the Kaianerehkó:wa—which has lately spread all over Native North America, shall be the constitution of the Independent North American Indian State of Ganienkeh. The Mohawk Nation is not breaking away from the Iroquois Confederacy. It is repossessing its homeland with the help of other Red Indian traditionals and, at the same time, exercising the human rights accorded to everyone else in the world. Other Native nations of Asia and Africa have regained lost lands and human rights. The United States restored Okinawa to Japan. We expect that the United States should see their way to render the same justice to American Indians.

To any premise that the Mohawk project is an internal matter of a white people's government, certain steps are hereby taken, along with pointing out that the Indian nations have long had their own organized governments and society, greatly preceding the people who have taken by usurpation authority of this area of the world, and these steps include declaring to the world news of this move on the part of the traditional Indians of North America. There shall be communication to every nation on Earth and to their embassies at the United Nations with a request of foreign relations with the countries contacted, even if only on paper. That the Indian State of Ganienkeh has this right is guaranteed by the United Nations, as the same right has been provided to other new nations, which are actually old ones that have likewise formerly been defrauded of their land and governments.

The US is a member of the United Nations and sworn to uphold its principles. The UN proclaimed its Universal Declaration of Human Rights in December 1948, and it provides in Art. 15: (1) Everyone has the right to a nationality; (2) No one may be arbitrarily deprived of his nationality nor denied the right to change his nationality.

We too are human and should have the rights accorded to everyone else in the world: the right to our nationality and the right of our nation to exist and the right to an area of land for our own territory and state where we can exercise our own proven government and society.

Notices shall also be sent to the president of the United States and to the governors of the States of New York and Vermont. A request for foreign relations will be submitted to the US government. The procedure being followed to regain the ancient Mohawk homeland is consistent with human rights. Nature did not give certificates of possession to people she consigned to certain areas. Ours is the strongest natural legal right known to man, aboriginal rights.

> Message to Congress, July 8, 1970:
> The first Americans—the Indians—are the most deprived group in our nation. On virtually every scale of measurement—employment, income, education, health—the condition of the Indian people ranks at the bottom. This condition is the heritage of centuries of injustices.... The American Indians have been oppressed and brutalized, deprived of their ancestral lands and denied the opportunity to control their own destiny.
> —President Richard M. Nixon

Today's white men say that the injustice was done two centuries ago, and it has nothing to do with them. The present Mohawk action is in 1974. Will the white man continue to keep justice from the Indians? The Mohawk project is the way to real self-determination—"control of their own destiny". It is the way for the Red Indian race to regain lost pride, lost belief in humanity and to offset escapes from reality like alcohol, drugs and suicides that are destroying the Indian people.

From the preamble to the Kaianerehkó:wa

> circa 1450, Onondaga:
> I am Dekanawida and with the Five Nations Confederate Rotiianérshon, I place the Tree of the Great Peace.... Roots have spread out from the Tree of Great Peace... and the name of these roots is the Great White Roots of Peace. If any man or any nation outside of the Five Nations shall show a desire to obey the laws of the Great Peace... they may trace the root to their source... and they shall be welcomed to take shelter beneath the Tree.

1945, San Francisco:

We the peoples of the United Nations determined to save succeed-
ing generations from the scourges of war... and to reaffirm faith
in fundamental human rights... and to establish conditions under
which justice and respect for law can be maintained... do hereby
establish an international organization to be known as the United
Nations.

The noblest work of man is to find the formula for peace and
happiness for everyone on Earth. To that end, the most urgent needs of
the nation of mankind are proper, moral governments and a practical
economic system that eliminates poverty and advances human relationships. Down through the ages, the world's wisest men have ever tried to
find a formula of peace and happiness for suffering and deprived humanity. We've read of the efforts of Socrates, Plato, Aristotle and many others.
Wise as they were, they all failed in this, mankind's greatest work.

Searchers for the formula have consulted the Holy Scriptures for
instructions on devising a proper, moral government, but the teachers
in the Good Book only spoke of kingdoms, which are total dictatorships,
and had no idea of the government of, for and by the people. As no one
has the right to be king or queen, it showed no idea of truly proper human
relationships. Not knowing how to eliminate poverty, the holy teachers
advocated poverty. Ask starving Indians in Northern Ontario reserves of
destitute areas if they are happy and at peace. People in the last stages of
poverty are repressed and live in absolute misery and wretchedness. The
Holy Scriptures laid no claim to have a formula for peace and happiness
on Earth, only in the "afterlife"—after you're dead. That's no good for
people suffering the tortures of the damned in this life.

The East had its own famous wise men, among whom was Confucius.
Wise as they were, they too could not find the key to peace and happiness,
a proper moral government, a practical economic system and human
relationship. It took the North American Onkwehón:we Dekanawida to
find the formula. He took from natural righteousness (Karihwí:io) and
made a code, which he called the Kaianerehkó:wa—known as the Law of
the Great Peace. The wise man of the ages, armed only with his Great Law,
conquered the five most fierce nations imaginable in history, the Mohawks,
the Oneidas, the Cayugas, the Senecas and the Onondagas, united them in
a confederacy (Kanonhsionni'ón:we, in Mohawk), put them symbolically

in one longhouse and created peace and happiness that lasted until the white man came with his Dark Age.

The Kaianerehkó:wa was the world's first national constitution and the first international law, the first code of human rights. The Iroquois Confederacy was the world's first people's republic, with sovereignty for everyone. All other countries were kingdoms, and in a kingdom only the monarch had sovereignty. Everything and everyone belong to the king. The entire world may thank the Peacemaker Dekanawida for whatever rights and freedoms its people enjoy, *but* not all the rights and freedoms in the Great Law were adopted. The copiers kept full justice from their people. They left loopholes through which they may continue subtly to oppress humanity.

There has been a continuous psychological warfare waged against the American Indian. It's every bit as deadly as the one with guns. The casualties are the drunks, drug addicts, suicides, renegades and traitors, all destroyed people. Indians are made to feel cheap and inferior, which results in identity conflict. Most Indians cannot find work in the white man's mainstream and have to go on welfare relief and are called "welfare bums" to help them slide down in their self-valuation.

The establishment of the Independent North American Indian State of Ganienkeh offers a positive solution to the problems of Indians. They get away from the deleterious effects of welfare relief life. They can get away from city slums. They will live in fresh unpolluted air. They shall help build an Indian state. They shall regain privileges. They shall do it themselves. No longer shall the white man's government say Indians are a burden on their country's economy via welfare relief. A well-run cooperative community needs no financial help whatsoever. The white man will no longer be hurt where it hurts the most, in the pocketbook. Wouldn't that alone be an inductive persuasion to the white man to let go of the captive Indians? There may be some broken-down, brainwashed Indians, who because of fear and inferiority complex shall be afraid to go to Ganienkeh—at first.

The vanguard of strong, resolute men, women and children who shall establish the Indian state are traditionals. They know their rights and are exercising them. The establishment of the Indian state gives the North American Indians an international personality and the right to establish foreign relations with other nations—all the rights mentioned above are guaranteed by the United Nations. Because of the nature of the movement, it is an international affair, not an internal matter.

The prospective members of the new Indian state shall be ready for herbal preventative medicine, to keep sickness to a minimum (see Chief Smallboy's healthy camp).[2] By following the above, the Independent North American State of Ganienkeh shall be free of the white man. For the protection of the rights, culture, customs and traditions of the Indian people who participate and join in the project, the following is proposed.

Articles of Agreement by the Nations within the Independent North American Indian State of Ganienkeh

Assembled this day on repossessed Mohawk land, representatives of various North American Indian nations have come to agreements with the host Mohawk Nation in matters attending the establishment of the Independent North American Indian State of Ganienkeh. Nations agreed on the following:

1. That the host Mohawk Nation was dispossessed of its land by unjust actions on the part of a foreign people, and its repossession was a result of a joint effort of the abovementioned Indian nations whose signatures appear below; therefore, the said North American Indian nations concerned shall share in equality the benefits, protection, privileges, resources, production and the government of the said Independent North American Indian State of Ganienkeh.

2. That the assembled North American Indian nations do make, ordain and publish an *alliance* and take the Pledge on the Wampum that they shall forever defend and protect each nation in the alliance and the Great Law of the Six Nations Iroquois Confederacy, mankind's first and greatest national constitution.

3. That the assembled Indian nations shall implement the cooperative economic system to run the Independent North American Indian State of Ganienkeh, and that each member nation shall take a certain area to lock its cooperative communities, and that every subject of the said Independent North American Indian State of Ganienkeh is a member of the co-op, with the right to an equal share of the production and, to this end, every subject of the said Independent North American Indian State of Ganienkeh

shall pledge to do his share of the work to so earn his share of the production.

4. That the assembled Indian nations shall live off the land, grow food on every available acre, keep livestock and preserve the environment.

5. That each member nation continues to exercise its own customs and traditional Indian spiritual ceremonies, and each member nation shall permit the other members to adopt any spiritual ceremony, if they so desire.

Pledge of Alliance

To make sure that the project succeeds in all its phases, it has been proposed that all traditional Indians joining and participating in the project take the pledge of allegiance to the Independent North American Indian State of Ganienkeh, while holding the string of sacred Pledge Wampum in hand. The following words to be used in taking the Pledge are hereby suggested:

> I_____, do pledge on the Sacred Wampum that I shall support, defend and protect the Independent North American Indian State of Ganienkeh. I accept the Great Law of the Six Nations Iroquois Confederacy as the constitution of the Independent North American Indian State of Ganienkeh and do pledge to obey its laws and to defend it to the best of my ability. I do pledge to work in the interest of all the people of the Independent North American Indian State of Ganienkeh, who are engaged in developing the Indian state into an example of proper moral government and society. I accept the cooperative economic system as the most practical and worthy of the human state and do pledge to do my full share of the work to help in its success. I pledge to cooperate fully with others who are taking this Pledge of Allegiance to the end so that the people of the Independent North American Indian State of Ganienkeh may realize fully their human rights and know peace and happiness.

Mohawk Camp

This area is part of the land under the legal and aboriginal title of the Mohawk Nation. We Mohawks have returned to our homeland. With the help of other traditional Indians, we shall make a home for any and all

Indians who wish to live according to their own customs, culture and traditions.

Native nations all over the world have regained their lands. The US restored Okinawa to Japan. We assume that this rendering of justice shall be extended to American Indians, and that this land shall be restored to the Mohawks.

This *camp* is out to prove that the traditional Indians can live off the land without electricity, money, welfare relief or aid of any kind. White people are asked to help by not interfering. All we need is to be left alone to live in our own way.

Any help from other nations, in the form of letters to the US government appealing to its justice and to render the same to American Indians or through pressure by way of the United Nations shall be greatly appreciated.

The facts in the above *Ganienkeh Manifesto* were compiled by
Louis Hall
Secretary—Caughnawaga Branch[3]
Six Nations Confederacy

Notes

1   Joseph Brant (1743–1807) was a Mohawk military and political leader, whose sister Molly Brant was married to a powerful British official, the superintendent of Indian Affairs for the northern colonies, Sir William Johnson, 1st Baronet. After having fought on the side of the British during the American Revolutionary War, the Rotinonhsión:ni were granted land in present-day southern Ontario, called the Haldimand Tract, to compensate for the lands lost to the Americans. Brant disposed of two-thirds of the Haldimand Tract, which originally covered two million acres, of which only the reservation of Six Nations of the Grand River is left today. Today, the legality of Brant's unilateral land sales is often questioned, as the Haldimand Tract still belongs to the confederacy; see Timeline, "1784 Haldimand Proclamation".
2   Once a trapper, hunter and farmer, Alberta Peigan chief Johnny Bob Smallboy (1898–1984) and 125 companions established a camp in Alberta's Kootenay Plains in 1968 to lead a healthy and natural lifestyle away from drugs and alcohol.
3   Karoniaktajeh used the spelling Caughnawaga, which was replaced by Kahnawà:ke in the 1980s.

Warrior's Handbook

Introduction
Who Made You? Or How Scientists Created the Red Race
The white man says Indians came from Asia by way of the Bering Strait. If they were Indians maybe, an Indian being a native of India. The particular Indian we're talking about is the Onkwehón:we, you know, the Native American. They say the Red man crossed over from Asia on a land bridge, or stepping islands (like stepping stones). Our mighty ancestors took mighty strides. The master storytellers say the time of this migration was twelve thousand years ago. Since it's a scientific estimation, therefore, it's impressive. They came to this conclusion by "reading the rocks". Now, you guys, you wanna watch out and avoid rocks. They can betray your passage, even if you passed twelve thousand years ago. The scientists can even detect, if slightly, your ancient fragrance, which you left behind as you passed the rocks.

Another set of scientists, after much reading and smelling of the rocks, said that many moons ago there was an Ice Age that lasted about one million years, and it covered the North American continent with a sheet of ice four miles high half way down to Mexico from the Canadian border. They estimated that the ice receded ten thousand years ago. If that's so, then simple arithmetic tells us that the Ice Age had two thousand years to go when the scientists say our ancestors crossed the Arctic waste and ice-bound Canada over ice four miles thick. Let us envision the ancestors coming over in the rarefied air, a four-mile-high and refrigerated atmosphere at least a hundred below zero, in thermal suits and space helmets, with bottles of oxygen strapped to their backs. It was a tremendous trip of thousands of miles.

Scientists are resourceful fellows. The first bunch decided to stick to their guns regarding the twelve thousand year estimate. They took a leaf from the Holy Scriptures, where Moses with his magic wand struck the Red Sea, which, thereupon, parted and allowed the Israelites to walk through, after which the sea returned and swallowed the Egyptian army pursuing the Israelite refugees. The Egyptians protest the story, saying there's nothing in their history about such an event. The scientists disregard that and have the leader of the future Indians in possession of an equally magical wand, which parted the ice and allowed the wanderers through. The scientists don't say it in quite that way, but they revised the ice picture and have an ice-free alley through which they have our ancestors walking out the Bering Strait theory. We too protest. There's nothing in our history about such an event.[1]

As far as we're concerned, our ancestors made their debut in this valley of happiness right here on this land of Onkwehón:wekeh (America), just as the white man originated in southern Europe, the Blacks in Africa and the Asiatics in Asia. The Bering Strait theory is tongue-in-cheek propaganda to make the Onkwehón:we think that they also are aliens in their own land, and that the Europeans have just as much right to be in America. The scientists are trying to justify in the white people's minds their presence on Red man's land.

Warrior's Handbook

The birth of man is an act of nature. Nature has produced several races of mankind. They all have the right to live. No one has the right to take another person's life, except in self-defense. Nature even provided an instinct of self-preservation, so that the person having been born shall defend and protect the life that was given to him.

Let's, therefore, introduce the first law of nature: *self-preservation*. If anyone is trying to destroy you, *stop him*! It's your duty.

Man also has another life. His national life. His nation also has the right to exist. The members of the nation are duty-bound to protect and defend their nation. The world has nations of people. Everyone has the right to a nationality. Man is a social person and has the right to belong to his own society. (The Onkwehón:we are denied this right. The man from Europe wants him to join the white man's society. He calls it assimilation.) It is hard to imagine anyone not belonging to a nation. A man's national life is as important as his physical life.

Besides having the right to exist, the nation also has the right to an area of land for its territory, where it may exercise its government, law, customs and society. No nation shall be so deprived that it has to exist on a reservation. At this moment, July 24, 1979, only Ganienkeh, which is part of the traditional Mohawk Nation, practices its right to live in a territory. All other Indian nations exist on reservations.

It is a deplorable state of affairs. There is a remedy for it. The situation was caused by people from Europe who somehow prevailed over the native Onkwehón:we, who lived on reservations while the Europeans developed the country. It was a great mistake for our ancestors to fall for the promises of the Europeans that reservation life would be free from worry, fear, trouble and poverty and would pass like a pleasant dream.

The Natives of America never should have permitted the Europeans to get a foothold in Onkwehón:wekeh, but they did and paid for it with their lives and liberty. It is now up to the present generations to make the best of it and to fight to regain areas of their land where they may live in freedom from the great white father. It can be done. There are ways and means. Many Onkwehón:we are too afraid to fight for their rights. They have been browbeaten into a state of hopelessness. They shall have to be inspired to stand on their hind legs and fight for their future and for the future of seven generations ahead. Again, there are ways and means to turn the meek and humble into courageous and resolute people. Then, there are those who can fight and are ready to put their nation in its rightful place among the nations of mankind. They are the leaders of the present and the future.

To combat oppression, let's take the famous Jewish people as an example of success. For many ages, they were a destitute people. They were hounded from pillar to post. Their leader came up with the Ten Commandments, which he said was given to him by the Creator God. It was recommended as the way to go to paleface heaven. The results shall be achieved after one is dead. It's for the afterlife. Our problem is different. We have to achieve a better life here on Earth, while we're still living. To gain their Israel, the Jewish people had to use a different strategy than the Ten Commandments. After more than thirty centuries of praying to Jehovah, they finally got tired of waiting for him to do their thing. They changed their style. They grabbed the bull by the horns and asserted themselves. They got up and grabbed a land base for themselves. They copied the European grab of the Red man's land. Behold the meek and humble Jew suddenly turned tiger, who even killed a lot of Arabs to set up Israel. It's not the way prescribed by the Ten Commandments. But the Ten Commandments is a good idea. It stood the Jews in good stead down through the centuries. The following is a warrior's Ten Commandments, which the writer did not go up a mountain to get from the Lord, as the white man says his ancestor Moses did, but they were conceived in the mountains of Ganienkeh Territory in the howling wilderness at fifty below zero temperature.

The writer lays no claim to be a prophet and divinely inspired or that these Ganienkeh commandments shall lead to any paradise in the afterlife, but they were designed to meet the problems on Earth and uncover the secrets of peace and happiness in this Earthly life. Certain Mohawks, oriented to think like their masters, shall not accept this, my:

Mohawk Ten Commandments

1. *Be brave and fearless*, as there can be no peace on Earth for those who are in fear.
2. *Be strong.* In this hard and cruel world, only the strong may know peace and happiness. To be weak is to invite aggression, oppression, tyranny, misery and woe.
3. *Fight for your rights*, for only those who fight for it can achieve human rights and respect. There is a right and wrong way to *fight*. Always propose to fight in a clever way, for he who fights in a clever way is equal to a thousand men.
4. *Maintain a strong national independence and sovereignty under the Great Law of Peace—the Kaianerehkó:wa*, and let your slogan be *Peace, Righteousness and Power*, for not one of these is possible without the other two. Let no power abolish your nation.
5. *Maintain your own national initiative*, and let no other nation control your destiny. Respect nature's first law of *self-preservation and stop any traitor seeking to destroy you and your people*, for any nation which ignores this law stands condemned to extinction.
6. *Develop the spirit of cooperation*, so that your nation can rely completely on its own efforts. To become a competitive state is to create tensions, strife, panic, frenzy, fear, hate, bigotry, weakness and divisions.

7. *Think right so that you shall do right and be right,* for only the truly justice-minded can achieve peace and happiness for all.

8. *Respect the rights of others* that your own rights may be respected, and these rights include the right to live and be free, the right to a nationality, territory, government, possessions, freedom of speech, to think and believe as one sees fit, to human rights and the pursuit of peace and happiness.

9. *Acquire wisdom and knowledge of the world,* for only through understanding among all people will misunderstanding and wars be eliminated. Let there be a special course of study on the subject of devising a proper moral government and that proper people be trained to operate this very important device to ensure the peace and happiness of mankind and that a study be included to produce a most worthy economic system to eliminate poverty, misery and wretchedness. Let only those who pass a most rigid test on the subjects of government and economic knowledge be allowed to run governments and nations.

10. *Acquire advanced human relationships.* Human birth is an act of nature, and all humanity is equally subject to nature's law of death. No one has the right of lordship over others. The more able only have the right to help those less able; the appointed leaders of governments only have the right to be the voice and will of the people that all may share the bounties of nature and know peace and happiness.

The Warrior Society

The term *Warrior Society* was supplied by the white man. The Great Law says "the war chief and his men". As the term *Warrior Society* seems to apply very well, and as we are using the English language in this confabulation, we shall use the term.

The Great Law provides definite functions for the war chief and his men. They are charged with the protection and defense of the people. Their duties take many forms: keeping the peace, teaching, public speaking, repossessing lost lands and human rights and work of all useful kinds to promote the welfare of the people. Upholding the Great Law results in "Peace, Righteousness, Power": a noble work entrusted to the care of the Warrior Society.

In recent years, girls and women of the Six Nations Confederacy have shown an inclination to participate in action programs, such as demonstrations and confrontations. They even made a declaration at the Loon Island takeover in 1970 that at the next war with the white men they would take part and have learned to handle firearms.[2] They took part in the repossession of Stanley Island two weeks before. At the confrontation with Québec Provincial Police in Kahnawà:ke, girls were there with high-powered rifles. At Moss Lake, they stood firm beside their men. In other demonstrations and confrontations throughout the continent, girls and older women were much in evidence. This being the case, the Warrior Society is hereby strengthened by the addition of Warrior Girls.

Long live the Warrior Society!
The government of the world's wisest man

The most important attributes of man are intelligence, wisdom and knowledge. The noblest work of man is to find the formula of peace and happiness for everyone on Earth. Wise men through the ages have tried to find such a formula. An impressive array of great men were they! There was Socrates, the most famous of them. Wise as he was, he failed to find the formula. His pupil Plato also achieved a great renown. His attempts are recorded in his writings, as he tried to form a perfect government and state. His own pupil Aristotle, whose theories on law still influence the lawmakers of today, also failed in this, mankind's greatest quest, the key to peace and happiness.

The wise men who wrote the Bible also failed to teach suffering and deprived humanity of how to devise proper moral governments. They spoke only of kingdoms, which are total dictatorships. They had no idea of the government of, for and by the people. Nor did the holy teachers advocate an economic system that would eliminate poverty. Not knowing how to eliminate poverty, they advocated poverty. Ask starving Indians in Northern Ontario reservations or the people in destitute areas in India if they are happy and at peace. They represent people in the last stages of poverty and live in absolute misery and wretchedness. The Bible's wisest man, King Solomon, had five hundred wives. That alone disqualifies him as a wise man. As he was a king, and no one had the right to be a king or queen, he showed no idea of truly proper human relationship. He also had poor people in his kingdom; he did not know of an economic system that would eliminate poverty. The Holy Scriptures lay no claim to have a formula for peace and happiness on Earth, only in the "afterlife"—after you're dead. That's no good for people suffering the tortures of the damned in this life.

The East had its own famous wise men, among whom was the noted Confucius. Wise as they were, they too could not find the key to peace and happiness on Earth, a proper moral government, a practical economic system and human relationship. It took the North American Onkwehón:we Dekanawida to find the formula. He took from natural righteousness (Karihwí:io) and made a code which he called the Kaianerehkó:wa, known as the Law of the Great Peace and the Great Law. The wise man of the ages, armed only with his Great Law, conquered the five most fierce nations imaginable in history, the Mohawks, Oneidas, Cayugas, Senecas and Onondagas, united them in a confederacy (Kanonhsionni'ón:we in the Mohawk language which was spoken by all the Iroquois nations at one time), put them symbolically in one longhouse and created peace and happiness that lasted until the white man came fresh from the Dark Ages. The Iroquois Confederacy became a powerful state and established a protectorate of twenty-eight Indian nations.

The Kaianerehkó:wa was the world's first national constitution, the first international law, the first code of human rights. The Iroquois Confederacy was the world's first people's republic, with sovereignty for everyone. All other countries were kingdoms, and in a kingdom only the monarch had sovereignty. Everything and everyone belong to the king. The entire world may thank the Peacemaker Dekanawida for whatever rights and freedoms its people enjoy, but not all the rights and freedoms in the Great Law were adopted. The United States of America was the first to borrow from the Kaianerehkó:wa to devise its constitution, and the rights and freedoms adopted became loopholes through which humanity could continue to be oppressed. International Law has provisions which are definitely Iroquoian.

The League of Nations of the 1920s was inspired by the old Iroquois League of Six Nations. The present-day United Nations, organized to bring peace to all nations and abolish the scourges of war, was patterned along the same lines. This world in 1950 made a special study of the longhouse with the objective of incorporating Iroquois principles into its deliberations.

Long live the Kaianerehkó:wa!
Long live the memory of the peacemaker Dekanawida, wisest mortal of the ages!

Psychological Warfare

The Europeans waged military wars against Indians and made the Indians fight against each other, including inducing the Iroquois protectorate nations to attack their protectors, the Iroquois Confederacy. The European holy men are proud to admit they started that one. It took a quarter of a century of urging and cajoling, but the men of God are persistent fellows. The missionaries kept at the protectorate nations, appealing to their fighting spirit, especially to the youth, who were most apt to do the fighting, with promises of military assistance from the French, Hurons and Algonquins. The purpose of starting such a war was to destroy the great Iroquois Confederacy, so as to make possible the conquest of the entire continent by the French. The Kanonhsionni'ón:we was in the way. It had to go.

Naturally, the holy men had no idea that the war they started would last about 150 bloody years, at the end of which time all the protectorate Indian nations would be extinct and the French would have lost their land possessions in America. The Six Nations were still on their feet, reduced in number but still fighting. They just had to be the toughest people on Earth. In fact, a thousand Six Nations warriors, with a little help from the British (as usual) beat nine thousand French at Québec City in 1759.[3] Want to hear about that, boys and girls?

It was this way. Twistory (twisted history) tries to say that there were no Six Nations in Québec. Documents in archives say there were. Also, if it hadn't been for the Six Nations, there was no way for the four thousand English to beat nine thousand French in an open field, European style, when said English hadn't beaten the French in 150 years. According to the documents, the English had noted the extreme fear the French had developed of the Iroquois. This was caused mainly by the parents who cautioned their children to behave or "les Iroquois will get you!" The French youth grew up with great fear of the Iroquois. The British used this to their advantage on several occasions, especially at the siege of Fort Louisbourg, when they threatened to turn all prisoners over to the Iroquois if the fort did not surrender. It did.

At Québec City, the English and the French lines marched towards each other, with the Iroquois right behind the English, out of sight. At a signal, the British executed a maneuver which opened holes in their line through which rushed the terrifying Iroquois with terrific yells and war whoops. The English added to the din with their own yells. Imagine the consternation of the poor French soldiers. One moment there were British soldiers marching against them, greatly outnumbered by the French, who for a long time had always whipped them. They felt secure indeed. Suddenly, the British had turned into ferocious, howling Iroquois plunging down upon them. The sudden appearance of their dreaded foe was shocking, and fear took over. The poor fellows dropped their guns, so they could flee the faster. The "battle" took twenty minutes. Mopping up operations in the city took the rest of the day. Les Iroquois were recognized as the greatest guerrilla fighters on Earth. On the warpath, there were none more ferocious. (At this point, let's stop and pat ourselves on the back. After all, that's our grandfathers we're discussing). The fighting which preceded the fall of Québec, in which four strategic French forts were taken, was mainly done by the Six Nations warriors, with token help from the British, who were as afraid of the French as the French were of the Iroquois.

The motive of the British for taking all the credit was to get around the Treaty of Alliance made with the Six Nations Confederacy. A joint military conquest by partners of an alliance would mean splitting up the conquered land between the partners. The British wanted all the land. The Indians had no lawyers to argue the point. The British played in dumb luck from start to finish.

There is another type of warfare waged on the native Onkwehón:we ever since the white man hit this continent. It is waged against the minds of the Natives. This type of warfare is every bit as dirty and deadly as the ones with guns. The casualties are the drunks, dope addicts and suicides. The casualty rate is high. There are Indians walking around dazed and confused, suffering from identity conflict. This is one of the wars the modern 1979 warriors have to fight. To fight any kind of war, one needs courage, gumption, knowledge of the enemy and strategic planning. The biggest single requirement is that people with fighting spirit not become casualties of psychological warfare. How does one acquire fighting spirit? Only 10 percent of any population shall fight for their rights. How can you develop fighting spirit in the other 90 percent?

Our ancestors discovered the secret long ago. All their men were great warriors—100 percent. How did they do it? Were they naturally all great warriors, or were they developed? They must have been developed, because, at present, we who have inherited their blood are also heirs to that 10 percent population fighting spirit. One method that has come to us is the War Dance. Our ancestors brought up the spirit of the people with the War Dance, even of those who did not dance. The Iroquois War Dance is a great performance. It is even used as medicine. Since it works, it should be performed at every opportunity.

The Iroquois say that the Sioux invented the War Dance, and it was called *Wasáse*, the name by which they knew the Sioux. The dance spread all over America. After the people became "civilized and Christian", the War Dance fell into disuse. As time ambled on, many Onkwehón:we dropped out of Christianity, went back to their own customs and beliefs and became known as traditionals. They revived many ceremonies and customs long forgotten. One of these is the War Dance. Many elders among the traditionals frowned upon the performance of the War Dance. They point out that there is no war, and that Indians shouldn't go to war in any event, as their land had been seized by foreigners from Europe. What would they be fighting for? While this seems logical and moral, it's only half true. The elders are so tough, they don't realize there is a war being waged against the Indians, and its effects in racism and oppression run rampant in Indian America.

The present-day Mohawk traditionals are fond of spirited Indian dances. Especially the War Dance. Ten years ago, Mohawk girls took part in the War Dance at social dances. It incurred the wrath of many elders, chiefs and clan mothers. War was men's business. The girls countered by pointing out that in the future conflicts and struggles, they shall take part in the fighting with guns, so they have the right to take part in the War Dance.

The elders prevailed, and for some years the War Dance was again in disuse. Then Ganienkeh happened. One of the rules for taking part in that land repossession was that each participant be armed—men, women and children. All were given lessons in gun classes and in shooting.

During the occupation at Moss Lake, some vigilantes started shooting into the camp. When the Indians fired back, two white people were hit. The district attorney of Herkimer County took out a search warrant to be served by three hundred well-armed state troopers with orders to disarm the Warrior Society and to look for evidence. A federal mediator came to the gate and stated that he was able to arrange a safe conduct out of the camp for the women and children. The women decided in their meeting to stand by their men and fight it out. Here, their prediction came true. Girls had become Warrior Girls. They were now equal partners in the armed

Figure 01 Louis Karoniaktajeh Hall, *The Unity Flag*, n.d.

Figure 02 Louis Karoniaktajeh Hall, *Warrior,* n.d.
Louis Karoniaktajeh Hall Foundation, photo by Christine Guest.

Figure 03 Louis Karoniaktajeh Hall, *The Indian Flag*, 1990.
Louis Karoniaktajeh Hall Foundation, photo by Christine Guest.

Figure 04 Louis Karoniaktajeh Hall, *Self-Portrait*, n.d.
Louis Karoniaktajeh Hall Foundation, photo by Christine Guest.

Figure 05 Louis Karoniaktajeh Hall, *Self-Portrait (at 49, holier than ever—Louis Hall)*, 1967.
Louis Karoniaktajeh Hall Foundation, photo by Christine Guest.

Figure 06 Louis Karoniaktajeh Hall, *Statue of Captivity*, 1991.
Louis Karoniaktajeh Hall Foundation, photo by Christine Guest.

Figure 07 Louis Karoniaktajeh Hall, *Indian Statue of Liberty*, c. 1970s.
Louis Karoniaktajeh Hall Foundation, photo by Christine Guest.

ADODARHO

Figure 08 Louis Karoniaktajeh Hall, *Adodarho*, n.d.
Louis Karoniaktajeh Hall Foundation, photo by Christine Guest.
On Adodarho, spelled Thadodáho in this book, see Timeline "Time Immemorial—Kaianerehkó:wa".

THE GREATEST AMERICAN

DEGANAWIDA

FOUNDED THE HISTORIC
KANONSONNIONWE
CONFEDERACY OF THE IROQUOIS

He devised the world's first national constitution, created the world's first people's republic and established the greatest government on earth. He wanted all the Indian nations to join but was able to get only Five Nations. United, they became the greatest military power in America. Never conquered in war, the Iroquois lost their lands in peacetime by fraud, swindles and sad to say, religion.

Louis Hall

Figure 09 Louis Karoniaktajeh Hall, *Deganawida, the Greatest American*, n.d.
Louis Karoniaktajeh Hall Foundation, photo by Christine Guest.
On Deganawida, see Timeline "Time Immemorial—Kaianerehkó:wa".

Implementing Deganawida's great plan of uniting in alliance all the Indian nations under the Great Law Gayane-rekowa, all nations and chiefs equal in power. Apply the original, proven Iroquois systems of government and co-operative economy. Each nation to use its own <u>national</u> Indian religion.

Louis Hall

Figure 10 Louis Karoniaktajeh Hall, *Multinational Iroquois Confederacy*, n.d. Louis Karoniaktajeh Hall Foundation, photo by Christine Guest.

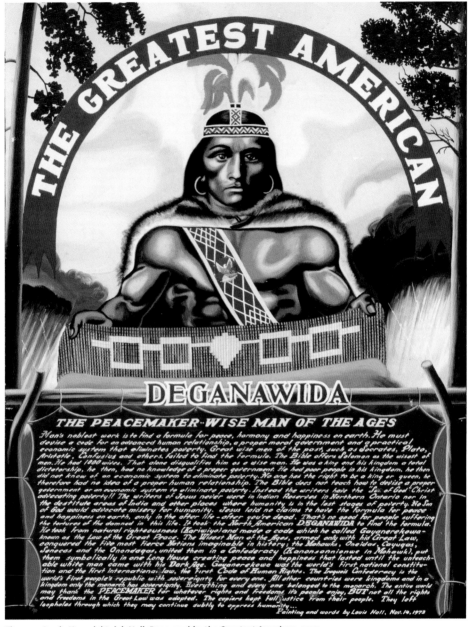

Figure 11 Louis Karoniaktajeh Hall, *Deganawida, the Greatest American*, 1973.
Louis Karoniaktajeh Hall Foundation, photo by Christine Guest.

Figure 12 Louis Karoniaktajeh Hall, *Rotiyaner Headdress*, n.d.
Louis Karoniaktajeh Hall Foundation, photo by Christine Guest.
On *Rotiyaner*, spelled *Roiá:ner* in the book, see Glossary, "Roiá:ner".

Figure 13 Louis Karoniaktajeh Hall, *Ahsarekowa War Chief*, 1973.
Louis Karoniaktajeh Hall Foundation, photo by Christine Guest.
On *Ahsarekowa*, spelled *A'share'kó:wa* in the book, see Glossary, "Aión:wes".

Figure 14 Louis Karoniaktajeh Hall, *Ganienkehaka Kanakerasera*, n.d.
Louis Karoniaktajeh Hall Foundation, photo by Christine Guest.
The term *Kanakerasera*, often translated as *people* or *nation*, refers to being *embedded* or *planted in the ground*.

Figure 15 Louis Karoniaktajeh Hall, *Worlds' First Peoples' Republic*, n.d.
Louis Karoniaktajeh Hall Foundation, photo by Christine Guest.

Figure 16-1 Louis Karoniaktajeh Hall, *Union of Indian Warrior Societies*, n.d.
Louis Karoniaktajeh Hall Foundation, photo by Christine Guest.

Figure 16-2 Louis Karoniaktajeh Hall, *The Sleeping Lion*, 1987.
Louis Karoniaktajeh Hall Foundation, photo by Christine Guest.

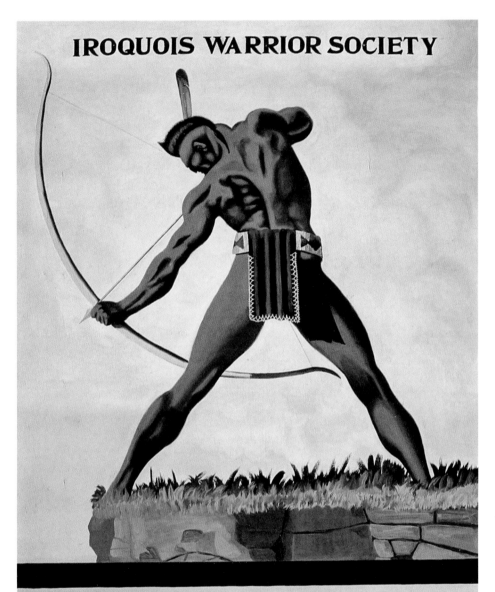

IROQUOIS WARRIOR SOCIETY

DEGANAWIDA's Great Plan for a Union of all Indian Nations in America with Equality for all nations and chiefs was subverted after he was gone by elitist Chiefs who wanted equality for only Five Nations. We now urge an Alliance of all Warrior Societies in America with all Warrior Societies and War Chiefs equal in Power, Voice, Status and to offer the position of Supreme War Chief to the Creator as was done by Deganawida at the formation of the Iroquois Confederacy when they tried to elect him Grand Chief. GOAL: that the Indian people of today may realize the Great Plan of Deganawida. The single feather worn by the warrior above denotes "all of one mind".

Louis Hall

Figure 17 Louis Karoniaktajeh Hall, *Iroquois Warrior Society*, n.d.
Louis Karoniaktajeh Hall Foundation, photo by Christine Guest.

Figure 18 Louis Karoniaktajeh Hall, *The Flute Player*, c. 1976.
Louis Karoniaktajeh Hall Foundation, photo by Christine Guest.

Figure 19 Louis Karoniaktajeh Hall, *Endurance*, c.1953–1963.
Louis Karoniaktajeh Hall Foundation, photo by Christine Guest.

Figure 20 Louis Karoniaktajeh Hall, *White Man's House of Nonsense*, n.d.
Louis Karoniaktajeh Hall Foundation, photo by Christine Guest.

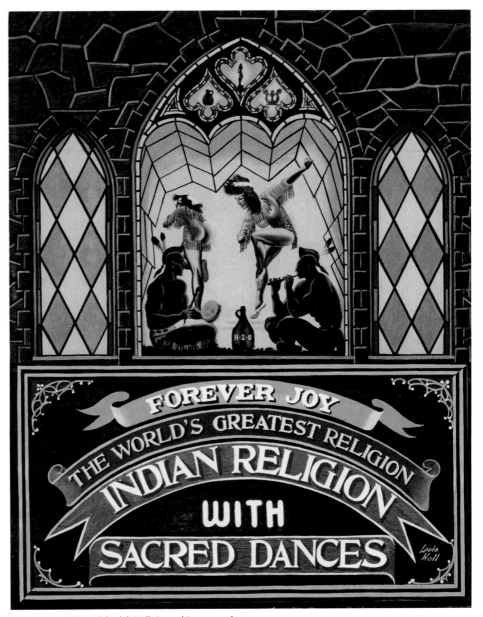

Figure 21 Louis Karoniaktajeh Hall, *Sacred Dances*, n.d.
Louis Karoniaktajeh Hall Foundation, photo by Christine Guest.

Figure 22 Louis Karoniaktajeh Hall, *Holder of Heaven, Toroniawakon*, 1962.
Louis Karoniaktajeh Hall Foundation, photo by Christine Guest.
Toroniawakon, sometimes spelled Tharonhiawagon and meaning *Sky-grasper*
or *Sky-holder*, is a Rotinonhsión:ni mythological figure often understood to
be the grandson of the Skywoman, Aatensic. In some stories Toroniawakon
is described as the "good brother", opposed to the "evil brother" Tawiscaron,
meaning *Flint*. See Glossary, "A'nowarà:ke".

Figure 23 Louis Karoniaktajeh Hall, *Inhumanity Award*, n.d.
Louis Karoniaktajeh Hall Foundation, photo by Christine Guest.

Figure 24 Louis Karoniaktajeh Hall, *Lacrosse Player*, n.d.
Louis Karoniaktajeh Hall Foundation, photo by Christine Guest.

SUN DANCE

Figure 25 Louis Karoniaktajeh Hall, *Sun Dance*, n.d.
Louis Karoniaktajeh Hall Foundation, photo by Christine Guest.

A party of 200 Mohawks, led by Peter Rice of Caughnawaga, erected the steelwork of New York's "eighth wonder of the world", the majestic 102-story 1472-foot high Empire State Building on Fifth Avenue, finishing one year ahead of schedule.

Louis Hall

Figure 26 Louis Karoniaktajeh Hall, *Empire State Building*, 1974.
Louis Karoniaktajeh Hall Foundation, photo by Christine Guest.

Figure 27 Louis Karoniaktajeh Hall, *Mohawks on the Nile—1884*, 1961.
Louis Karoniaktajeh Hall Foundation, photo by Christine Guest.
See Timeline, "1884 Nile Expedition".

Figure 28-1 Louis Karoniaktajeh Hall, *Tkaniatarens Niagara Falls*, n.d.
Louis Karoniaktajeh Hall Foundation, photo by Christine Guest.

Figure 28-2 Louis Karoniaktajeh Hall, *Red Sky*, n.d.
Louis Karoniaktajeh Hall Foundation, photo by Christine Guest.

Figure 29 Louis Karoniaktajeh Hall, *Odiyaner*, n.d.
Louis Karoniaktajeh Hall Foundation, photo by Christine Guest.
On *Odiyaner*, spelled *Iakoiá:ner* in this book, see Glossary, "Iakoiá:ner".

Figure 30 Louis Karoniaktajeh Hall, *Master Head Shrinkers of America*, n.d.
Louis Karoniaktajeh Hall Foundation, photo by Christine Guest.

Figure 31 Louis Karoniaktajeh Hall, *Maple Leaf Forever—Mohawk Version—*, n.d. Louis Karoniaktajeh Hall Foundation, photo by Christine Guest.

KANENTO PAUL DIABO

Figure 32 Louis Karoniaktajeh Hall, *Kanento Paul Diabo*, n.d.
Louis Karoniaktajeh Hall Foundation, photo by Christine Guest.
See Timeline, "1928 Border Crossing Victory"

Figure 33 Louis Karoniaktajeh Hall, *American Indian Movement*, 1973.
Louis Karoniaktajeh Hall Foundation, photo by Christine Guest.
On the solidarity between the Mohawk Warrior Society and AIM (American Indian Movement), see
"Tekarontakeh interview", section "The Rotihsken'rakéhte' and AIM".

Figure 34 Louis Karoniaktajeh Hall, *Progress—1965—Holy Indoctrinal Reactance*, 1965. Louis Karoniaktajeh Hall Foundation, photo by Christine Guest.

Figure 35 Louis Karoniaktajeh Hall, *Big Sister Is Watching You*, c. 1985.
Louis Karoniaktajeh Hall Foundation, photo by Christine Guest.

Figure 36 Louis Karoniaktajeh Hall, *Couple*, n.d.
Louis Karoniaktajeh Hall Foundation, photo by Christine Guest.

Figure 37 Louis Karoniaktajeh Hall, *Kahentinetha*, c. 1965–1970.
Louis Karoniaktajeh Hall Foundation, photo by Christine Guest.

NEHIYAWAK

OJIBWA

BODÉWADMI

Wahta ▼

ODAAWAA

TIONONTATI

MAMACEQTAW

Oneida of Wisconsin ■ • Kanatà:ke

CHONNONTON

MISI-ZAAGIIN⸱

Thatinatón:ni •

Ohswé:ken •

OTHÂKÎWA

Tekahiónhake

▼

HO-CHUNK

MESHKWAKIHUG

Oneida of the Thames ■

Tsi Kanatáher

MASCOUTEN

Tken'taresónsn

Chautauqu

Tiohsahróntion •

O'nionkserì:ke •

ILLINIWEK

MYAAMIAKI

KIIKAAPOA

Kinzua

ERIECHRONO

Tsi Kahionhó:kon

MIAMI

Teiohswathénion

Kenhtà:ke

SHAAWANWAKI

Kanontowá:nen •

PEEYANKIHŠIA

Ohi:yo

YESAÑ

• Tiohná:wate'

Seneca-Cayuga of Oklahoma ←

ANIGIDUWAGI

Ohnawiìò:ke

T⸱

Figures 38–39 Rotinonhsión:ni Place Names Map.
Conception by Philippe Blouin; graphic design by Mathieu Delhorbe; words by Karonhiio Delaronde and Rebekah Ingram; revised by Kahentinetha, Karennatha and Akwiratékha'. Refer to the "Place Names and Peoples' Names" section in this book for translations of Indigenous words.

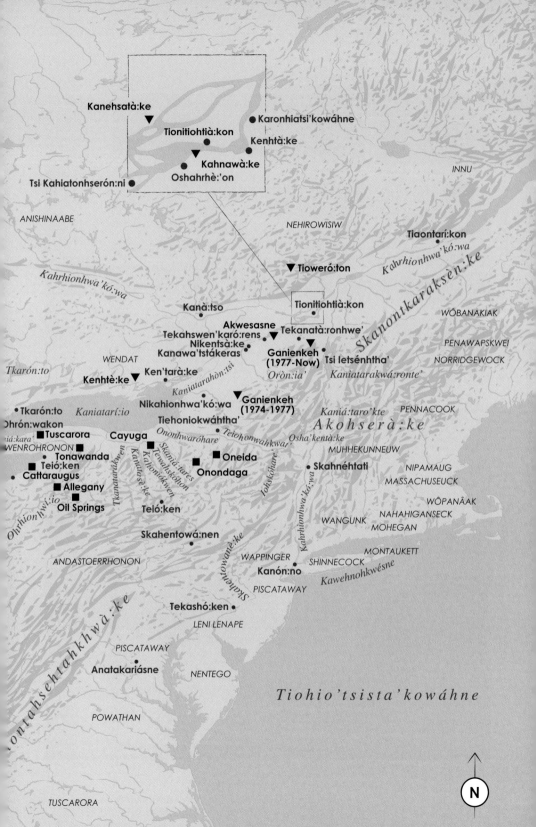

Kanehsatà:ke

Karonhiatsi'kowáhne

Tionitiohtià:kon

Kenhtà:ke

Kahnawà:ke

Oshahrhè:'on

Tsi Kahiatonhserón:ni

INNU

ANISHINAABE

NEHIROWISIW

Tiaontarí:kon

Kahrhionhwa'kó:wa

Tioweró:ton

Skanontkaraksèn:ke

Kahrhionhwa'kó:wa

Kanà:tso

Tionitiohtià:kon

WÔBANAKIAK

Akwesasne

Tekanatà:ronhwe'

Tekahswen'karó:rens

PENAWAPSKWEI

Nikentsà:ke

Ganienkeh

Tsi Ietsénhtha'

NORRIDGEWOCK

Kanawa'tstákeras

(1977-Now)

WENDAT

Ken'tarà:ke

Oròn:ia'

Kaniatarakwá:ronte'

Tkarón:to

Kaniatarahòn:tsi

Kenhtè:ke

PENNACOOK

Nikahionhwa'kó:wa

Ganienkeh

Kaniá:taro'kte

Tkarón:to

Kaniatarí:io

(1974-1977)

Akohserà:ke

Dhrón:wakon

Tiehoniokwáhtha'

Osha'kentà:ke

iá:kara'

Tuscarora

Cayuga

Ononhwaróhare

Teiohonwahkwa'

MUHHEKUNNEUW

WENROHRONON

Tonawanda

Skanà:tares

Skahnéhtati

NIPAMAUG

Teió:ken

Tewahskéhon

Oneida

MASSACHUSEUCK

Cattaraugus

Onondaga

WÔPANÂAK

Allegany

Teió:ken

NAHAHIGANSECK

Oil Springs

MÔHEGAN

Ohrhionhwí:io

WANGUNK

Kahrhionhwa'kó:wa

Skahentowá:nen

MONTAUKETT

ANDASTOERRHONON

WAPPINGER

SHINNECOCK

Kanón:no

Kawehnohkwésne

PISCATAWAY

Tekashó:ken

LENI LENAPE

PISCATAWAY

Anatakariásne

NENTEGO

Tiohio'tsista'kowáhne

POWATHAN

TUSCARORA

N

Figure 40 Louis Karoniáktajeh Hall, with some of his paintings at his home in Kahnawà:ke, c. 1965. Lmleclaire. CC BY-SA 4.0.

Figure 41 *Kakwirakeron, Holding a Two Row Wampum Replica.*
Crystal Courier, March 8, 1978. Courtesy of the Einhorn Collection, Newberry Library.

Figure 42 Kahentinetha, forcibly removed by Cornwall police officers, Akwesasne Bridge Blockade, December 18, 1968.
AP Wirephoto and Paul Seesequasis.
See Timeline, "1968 Akwesasne International Bridge Blockade".

Figure 43 Ganienkeh, 1974. From left to right: Junior Jacobs, Eric McComber, Kakwirakeron. Onkwawénna Raotitióhkwa Language and Cultural Center.

Figure 44 Kanasaraken, in Akwesasne, c. 1970.
Maria van Kints, founder of the Netherlands Association for North American Indians (NANAI), reproduced with the permission of her son, Leo Van Kints.

Figure 45 Tekarontakeh, c. 1990.
Alec MacLead, *Acts of Defiance*, 1992. ©National Film Board of Canada.

Figure 46 Ateronhiatakon and Karoniaktajeh, 1990.
Darcy Henton/*Toronto Star* via Getty Images.

Figure 47 *Ganienkeh—13 May 1974*. Poster by the Native American Solidarity Committee and Amherst Cultural Workers Collective, 1976.
Gift of the American Friends of the V&A, by Leslie, Judith and Gabri Schreyer and Alice Schreyer Batko. Courtesy Bob Winston Papers, Robert S. Cox Special Collections and University Archives Research Center, UMass Amherst Libraries.

Figure 48 Sakoeitah James Gray, *Women's Warrior Flag*.
The late warrior Sakoeitah designed this flag as an homage to Karoniaktajeh's warrior flag in honor of his own daughter, the late Iewaras Gray.

camp. They now, in reality, had the right to take part in the War Dance. The district attorney withdrew his search warrant. They had spies in the camp who reported the numbers of fighting men and women and their high morale and even eagerness for the coming action.

During the Iroquois War Dance, the dancers let down their hair, relax and let themselves go. They dance with abandon. They yell and whoop. All their hang-ups, inhibitions and fears are washed away. It helps the young and old. It's a psychological dance. Let's use this mighty preventative in our fight against the psychological war waged against us. Let's all do the War Dance tonight. Let's shatter the night with our wild yells and war whoops, with female yells in equal volume. Let's permit our fighting spirit to soar once again.

Thank you, O Great Sioux Nation, for inventing the War Dance. Thank you, O Mighty Iroquois ancestors, for making the War Dance exciting, wild and beautiful.

This Thing Called Peace

The most important things in the world are peace and happiness. Their requisites are food, shelter, clothing (temperate zone, not needed in the tropics), proper human relationship, order (peace-keeping) and an economic system which eliminates poverty. One is not at peace when one is not happy. There are those who are happy when they are not at peace. These are the oppressors and war profiteers. They have no use for peace.

People all over the world are concerned about the elusiveness of peace. There are many promoters of peace. They urge all the people to follow them in the ways of peace. There are thousands of religions which proclaim peace. They have followers. Some of the great religions have hundreds of millions of followers. In spite of all this peacemaking, there is a singular lack of peace in the world. There are those who talk of peace in the world. There are those who talk of peace and make profits in the billions out of war and other kinds of strife. There is a universal cry for peace, but not everyone in the world is interested in peace. Not all will follow the promoter of peace.

It would seem that nature created certain peaceful people and others who will be rapacious and ravenous. They shall prey on their fellow men. A study of nature reveals that all humans are born greedy, but many grow out of it. What makes it hard to grow out of a greedy nature is the white man's culture of possession, centered around what he has, what he can get and the means by which to get it. All his institutions, from education to government, are based on possession. Indian culture is known as the culture of the human. The ancient Red man sought to glorify the human, physically, mentally and morally. There was no competition in this culture, which made its advancement in technology very slow. The competition in the white man's culture is frenzied, even panicked, which, while it has made it possible for the white man to make great advances in technology, makes peace impossible. The culture of possession makes greed compulsive.

The culture of the human makes the Onkwehón:we receptive to peace overtures. It also makes them easy victims of the tricky practitioners of the culture of possession. The Onkwehón:we respond instinctively to peace proposals. They are a pushover to the peace promoter, bona fide or rogue. The clue to the solution of the problem of peace is right there. The Onkwehón:we want peace. To make anyone do what you want them to do, you have to make them want to do it. The idea is to make the unpeaceful want peace. Since so many white people also want peace, the work is comparatively "simplified". You now have to go after those who do not want peace. The problem is they don't need peace. They have the "free world" by the tail. For them, it's not profitable to have peace. The thing to do is to make them want peace. Simple, sez you. To billions of others, it's a mystery, but to you it's as clear as glass.

There are those who advise us that the only way to achieve peace is by peaceful means, to approach the peace destroyers with words dripping with honey and show them the error of their ways. In accents sweet, tell them that profits are not everything. It's more profitable to have peace than to have huge profits, disregarding the fact that it's huge profits that make them happy. It's their unhappiness they're concerned about, not yours. Indians have been using this method for the last two centuries. Despite the sweet approach, they've been losing more land, rights and people. Yes, many of our people are joining the white race. White may seem a sickly and sterile color, but it doesn't stop their aggressiveness. If all Indians join them, that's the end of the Red race. The situation may be nature's way of ridding the Indian race of its weaklings.

Starting with individuals, who has any peace? We have seen that the meek, mild and humble people are the most trampled upon, because they don't fight back. What a sweet set-up for bullies! It doesn't pay to bully the strong and fighting people. One can receive more than one gives. It's the strong who get any peace. It's fear. Fear of retribution. That's how the peace destroying bullies of mankind are. They're only peaceful when they're afraid not to be. You don't have to worry about the naturally peaceful people. They don't want trouble.

Now we know who are the enemies of peace. They are in control of the "free and unfree" governments of the world. They are over-rich and overfed, and they overpay themselves. They themselves are not necessarily in the governments. They are in control by way of the money market. As long as they're in control, there'll never be peace. Indians have approached the tycoon-controlled governments with their grievances. The Indians are motivated by the highest of motives—peace. The governments are motivated by the basest of motives—profits by exploitation of people. It's not profitable to grant the Indians peace, for the Indians are no threat to the peace of the profiteers. It's profitable to grant peace to Indians only when the Indians are a threat to the profiteers' peace. No sweet words can make governments honor the solemn international treaties they made with Indians. Why does the "great white father" speak so patronizingly to Indians? Because *the Indians have no bargaining power.*

The US government even funds a school for medicine men (spiritual advisors) to keep Indians from having bargaining power. Said spiritual advisors advise young spirited Indians, "Don't do anything to make the white man mad. He's too strong". Spiritual advisors do their best to kill the fighting spirit of young Indians with their voices of doom and pessimism. They urge spiritual ceremonies and to wait for the Creator to do their work for them.

On the positive side, Warrior Societies are being revived in various places all over the continent. They are learning ways to obtain bargaining power. Uncle Sam is strong alright. Less strong is Canada and Mexico, but they too feel just as secure from the Indians. Is this feeling of security valid? Just as a chain is only as strong as its weakest link, Uncle Sam and these other countries have many weak links. So much so, that they are actually at the mercy of the Indians or any other potential enemy. It's not any secret. Many people in the US are in turmoil over it. To indulge their profits' weakness, all the nuclear nations have installations which are actually monsters that can destroy their makers. All the opposition needs to do is sabotage these plants to start a reign of terror worse than the Inquisition, which took six hundred years to destroy three hundred million infidels and heretics. This is giving away no secret, as millions of people in the US are aware of it and are fighting to get all nuclear installations dismantled. If they want a professional opinion, the governments should ask their war department, "What can Warrior Societies do?" They'll be told the Warrior Societies can do plenty.

Yes, the oppressive governments have to be good to Indians now. Restoring some of the dispossessed land back to the Indians is in the category of being good, so the Indians can grow their own food, provide their own livelihood, have their own style of proven governments, their own education, justice, housing, etc. These, boys and girls, are the prospects in the near future. All Indians have to do is work at it.

To Believe or to Know

Religion is a delicate subject. One wrong word, and one makes enemies. Many are comforted by spiritual ceremonies. Others have less or no need for comfort. Each has an equal right to practice more or to practice less religion. In the past, the deeply religious have been known to force their religion on others. Many terrible deeds in history were done in the cause of religion. Though it's a controversial subject, because of its effects on people, who are expected to base their future on religious interpretations, it should be studied and discussed.

Nothing is more insulting to a man than to cast doubt on his beliefs. You insult his intelligence. Yet what does the word *belief* mean? Dogmas and doctrines are beliefs taught as being true. Belief means to accept as true or real, with or without certainty. Faith is belief without proof. To believe means to think, suppose or assume without really knowing. There are millions of agnostics in the world who are ready to accept as facts the doctrine of the virgin birth and ascension to heaven by Jesus Christ or that he ever even lived, if they are given proof. Agnostics are ready to accept as true the existence of hell, devils, angels, purgatory, if these can be proven. As no proof has been forthcoming, they have stayed agnostics.

For example, nobody can prove the existence of hell, but a lot of people believe in it. They accept it as true without knowing. In brief, one can believe in what one doesn't know. Belief is not knowledge. When one sees a fact before him or has evidence to support the existence of such a fact, then it is not necessary to believe. One knows. Many innocent men have been hanged because the judge and jury believed them guilty without really knowing. It's one of the reasons the death penalty was revoked in many places. Belief can get you hanged. Knowledge can save you. Belief without knowledge can cause a lot of trouble.

Religion teaches that when a person dies the soul leaves the body. The soul then is bodiless. It shall not experience the same sensations as does the body. It shall not know hunger, thirst, sickness, pain or death. It requires a nervous system to transmit these sensations. The creation of hell, then, is a divine mistake, for the souls cast into it cannot feel the heat, since they cannot experience pain. Of course, it's only a belief that God created hell, not knowledge.

Regarding the religion of our ancestors, I can only refer to the Iroquois system. The people gather together for Thanksgiving Festivals on nine different occasions during the year, when they give thanks for various favours of nature, such as the new year, running of the maple sap (first food of the year), new growth of herbal medicines, planting time (Seed Festival), Strawberry (first fruit of the year), Beans (first garden product), Green Corn and the Harvest Festival. The people do not petition or pray for more but give thanks for what they received.

Praying is like telling God (Creator) what to do. People who pray believe that God doesn't know how to conduct his Godhood, so they tell him. Not only that, they tell him over and over again. God's dumb, see! Can't understand anything the first time. Gotta tell him a lot of times. It shows a lack of confidence in the Divinity. Isn't He bound to think: "What's the matter with those cats. Do they think I'm stupid or something? Giving me the same words over and over! How would they like it if somebody did that to them?" The best prayer is a way of life and acts, not sweet words, which aren't going to fool anybody, much less the good Lord. If the Creator made heaven and Earth and all the wondrous words of nature, then He is so intelligent you'll never sweet talk your way to paradise. You will have to be good and kind towards each other. Defend and protect the life given to you. Defend and protect the people who have been given to you as your people You and your people have been given an area of land by the Creator, so take good care of it. Let no other people usurp your land and your authority. If the land has been lost, then fight to get it back for you and your people. Or do you expect God to get it back for you, to then only have someone else come and take it away from you again, because you can't learn how to hang on to what's been given to you? Friends, Romans and fellow Mohawks, the reality of history tells us we're on our own. We are born with a brain, intellect, energy, fighting spirit, hands and feet—all the equipment needed to do the noble work or the dirty work we expect God to do for us. Yes, sir! Action not words is the best prayer.

There is a gimmick used by many religions to fool the Lord. It's a way of going to paleface heaven without doing good deeds and being a good person. One may commit the foulest deeds and yet obtain forgiveness. This is the confession and repentance rituals—to be done frequently. It's a temporary repentance. In between repentances, one may be an utter fiend and do the most depraved acts and yet go to heaven, provided he goes to confession and does the repentance ritual. This system makes it possible for great criminals to be members of great religions, and when they get their comeuppance, they are given $100,000 religious funerals, with impressive eulogies. They are sure to go to heaven, because they repented after every evil deed. The temporary repentance ritual is an open invitation to become liars, crooks, thieves, murderers and criminals of every description, the offenders feeling that they'll get the same reward in heaven as really good people who never did any bad deed. People who had no thought of doing wrong or committing "sins" are greatly encouraged to do so by the temporary repentance ritual. This is a failing on the part of great religions. They also omit to tell the faithful that though the Creator may forgive them, the law doesn't, and they may find themselves in jail. Next time you commit murder, tell the judge and jury you have repented, and God has forgiven you, so they have no right to punish you.

A study of prisons reveals that very few agnostics and atheists are inmates. It must be that when they were children their parents also told them that stealing, lying and crookedness are wrong and shouldn't be done but did not tell them to repent if they should happen to do it. They just told them not to do it. Having seen that temporary repentance doesn't make bad people good, and that it encourages good people to relax their morals and even become evil, it behoves us to recommend that great religions abolish the temporary repentance. It's no good. Stop making hypocrites out of good people.

Everyone can make a mistake. "How did I do a stupid thing like that?" He makes up his mind to do it again, and he doesn't. That's repentance. He makes no big production of it by standing before a congregation telling how, as the Creator is his witness and judge, he is repenting his sins. He does not do this repentance again and again to show what a big spiritual and religious person he is. It is not repentance if one does again and again what one has repented. Repentance means to never do it again. The ritual should be called by some other name, such as "periodic boasting".

No religion makes any claim to have the formula for peace and happiness on Earth, only after you're dead. It makes no special effort to find ways and means to acquire the knowledge. One of the greatest scourges of mankind is poverty. There is a way to eliminate poverty, wars, fear (instead of inducing it, which has been the way of European religions), hate, envy, worry and other conditions which plague mankind. That's by creating conditions which erase them. Proper moral governments and a practical, worthy economic system can create the right environment for the achievement of advanced human relationships. Thus, may peace and happiness be proclaimed. We made a circle and have come back to the Great Law.

By Blood and by Law

One is born a Mohawk, Oneida, Onondaga, Cayuga, Seneca or Tuscarora. One is any of these by blood. The Six Nations Confederacy was brought together by law—the Kaianerehkó:wa. Therefore, one is a Six Nations person by law. A baby is named in a ceremony and ordained into the Six Nations Confederacy.

There are rules and regulations which govern membership in any nation. People who violate certain laws disqualify themselves and lose their citizenship in a nation. A man who was born an Englishman can lose his English citizenship by violating English citizenship law. Though he is still English by blood, he is no longer an Englishman by law.[4] Violation of Wampum 58 of the Great Law alienates a person from the Six Nations Confederacy and its territory. A further meaning of this is that if at any time any one of the confederate chiefs chooses to submit to the law of a foreign power, he is no longer in but is out of the confederacy. Persons of this class shall be called *they have alienated themselves*. Likewise, such persons who submit to laws of foreign nations shall forfeit all birthrights and claims on the Six Nations Confederacy and territory.

The Indian Act of Canada and the US federal Indian law fall into the "laws of foreign nations" category, because one was legislated in the Parliament of Canada and the other by the US federal government. A Mohawk or any of the others of the Six Nations who accepts and follows these foreign-made laws is an alienated person and is no longer a Six Nations person. He becomes an alien by his act of following Canada's Indian Act or US federal Indian law. He indicated rejection and renouncement of his citizenship in the Six Nations Confederacy and acceptance of the Indian Act or US federal Indian law by voting in their elections. The same thing happens when an American citizen votes in Canada's elections. He becomes a Canadian citizen and British subject and loses his US citizenship. This goes for any citizen of any nation in the world. It is a provision in international law that copies the Kaianerehkó:wa—the Great Law.[5]

There is also the case of the Indian Act band councilors at Kahnawà:ke who want to become condoled Mohawk chiefs without bothering to be reinstated. They also propose to continue being band councilors besides. In fact, they want the grand council of the Six Nations to participate in violating Wampum 58 of the Great Law. If all the members of the Six Nations Confederacy were to vote in the band council election of the Indian Act or in the elections of the US federal Indian law, that would be the end of the Six Nations Confederacy by virtue of Wampum 58 and international law. They would dissolve the Six Nations and also the individual nations. They would become junior citizens of Canada or the US, where they would still be called "bands" and "tribes". Going further, if the Six Nations were to vote in Canadian or US federal elections, they would become full-fledged citizens of Canada or the US, with all the rights, privileges and protection of the first-class citizens (try and get it).

There are elected council people who think they are also Six Nations people. That's like being citizens of two nations.[6] There are also white people who keep them confused. In a meeting of white people on Indians in Ottawa about a dozen years ago, organized by the Unitarian Church, the white people present were astounded to learn that besides being Canadian citizens, they were also British subjects. They didn't believe the Indian who told them (me). They had to get it from a lawyer who was present to explain. It took him about five minutes. They were shocked. So it's not only Indians who don't know what they are. Many white people don't either.

There are Mohawks and other Indians who were alienated through no fault of their own. As babies they were taken to a white man's church and turned into imitation white people. As grown-ups they asked to be reinstated in the Six Nations Confederacy. They had to go through a ceremony, just as white people go through a ceremony when taking the oath of allegiance to the US or Canada, etc. A reinstating Mohawk is required to hold the Pledge Wampum in his hand, which means that he shall protect and defend the land, the people and the constitution (Great Law), which

contains, besides the law, the culture, customs and religion of the Six
Nations Confederacy. In brief, he re-enters the canoe of the Two Row
Wampum. It will be recalled that the Five Nations (at the time) made an
agreement with the Dutch, and later with the British, that they shall not
legislate to one another, and they shall fight a common foe. It was called
a Treaty of Alliance and it was commemorated by the Two Row Wampum,
whereby each shall follow a parallel path, the white man in his vessel, in
which he shall have his laws, customs, religion, etc., and the Iroquois in
his canoe, wherein he shall have his laws, religion, customs, etc. The two
shall never join each other but shall travel together in peace and harmony.
The English did not try to force their religion on the Iroquois. The French
did, and that's how so many European religions abound in Kahnawà:ke,
Akwesasne and Kanehsatà:ke.

The Great Law, the Kaianerehkó:wa, orders certain spiritual obser-
vances during the course of the year, besides naming the babies, marriage
ceremonies and funeral rites. Thus, the Great Law binds the government
and religion together. That is why a reinstating Mohawk is required to
drop all other religious affiliations he may have to be accepted. When
this unmeek and unhumble writer, along with two others, applied to the
local longhouse for reinstatement into the Six Nations, we were told we'd
have to quit the white man's religion. That wasn't hard, for we had already
dropped out, said white man's dogmas and doctrines having stopped
making sense to us.

The Great Law imposes no terrible religious dogmas and doctrines,
such as hell, devils, purgatory and multitudes of mostly illogical sins.
There is nothing in the Great Law about temporary repentance to make
hypocrites out of people. To show appreciation and thanks for the bounties of nature, the people perform various sacred dances, which are more
fun than fruitful. The purpose of dancing is to show happiness for the
favours of nature. Judging by the beaming faces, the system works. The
people go home happy. The Indian religion doesn't ask much. All it asks
is to show happiness.

European religion demands mortification of the flesh and spirit.
Some of the practices imposed on the religious during the Dark and
Middle Ages were very depressing and morbid, such as burning witches
and heretics at the stake, torture at the rack, the iron maiden, etc. When the
Jesuit priests were sentenced to death by the tribunal of war chiefs, they
asked to be burnt at the stake slowly! The Iroquois method of executing

traitors and spies was by a blow on the head with a war club. According to the European religion, one who is burnt at the stake goes straight to heaven and becomes a saint. What a terrible doctrine to teach the faithful! For a while, the Iroquois felt obligated to burn their enemies in order to cleanse them of their sins, so they could go to heaven. That also stopped making sense, and they quit it.

A lot of Christianized Indians have no wish to be nor are they able to be reinstated in the Six Nations Confederacy. It requires strength, understanding and knowledge of the subjects involved. Also needed is a strong sense of duty towards the survival of the Indian race and nations.

The Handsome Lake Code was added to the Iroquois system in the early 1800s. It consists of dogmas and doctrines, such as hell, devils, angels, purgatory, limbo, sins, temporary repentance, etc., which were adopted from Christianity with a bit of Judaism thrown in. The Kahnawà:ke Mohawks who were reinstated in the Six Nations Confederacy were once Catholics and had lost faith in such unprovable doctrines. When the reinstated Mohawks refused to follow the old dogmas and doctrines they had renounced, it became a matter of dispute and controversy in the Six Nations, which was resolved at the grand council when it was decided that anyone who didn't want to follow the Handsome Lake Code didn't have to. While other religions permitted their followers the right to defend themselves and to kill in self-defense, it's a sad circumstance that the Handsome Lake followers would allow themselves to be killed without raising a hand in self-defense. When asked about it, a chief who is a follower of Handsome Lake Code said, "That's when we shall be meeting our Maker". They had buried their weapons, and with them their fighting spirit. It's something like a death wish. It is noted that when a people loses its fighting spirit, it also loses its will to live, and its population declines until it is no more. The much-revered Hopi Nation, the Peace People, numbered more than a hundred thousand a hundred years ago. Thirty years ago, they were down to twenty thousand. Now they number seven thousand. They too refuse to fight, not only for their lives but also for their rights. A follower of a death wish doctrine cannot be a warrior. He would not have the fighting spirit so necessary for survival as a race of nations. Burying the weapons is only practical when everybody in the world does it, and they're certainly not about to copy any such example. It wouldn't be safe, and it's against the first law of nation—self-preservation.

Posters—An Important Device for Survival

Posters of Ganienkeh. The pen is mightier than the sword. Posters can help traditional Indians working towards regaining lost sovereignty and self-sufficiency. Make copies and distribute them. Make additions to the posters, if needed. If you have ideas for posters, make them! Brains and actions are needed for Native American survival.

Tom Paine saved the American Revolution time and again by writing leaflets, which were distributed all over the colonies.[7] With words he helped the colonials regain their faith in their revolution. They had given up. His words made deserters go back to the front and fight again. Inspiring words and art posters have aroused men and women in the past to great performances. Our race stands in danger of extinction by being absorbed by another race. Even the masses of the white people themselves are in danger from their own greedy masters. It is time for Native American people with the knack, talent and ability, whether in writing or in art, to use it for a great cause: to win restitution and restorations of land, sovereignty and economic independence.

Scalp Ripoff

The civilized art of scalping was introduced to America by Europeans, when bounties were put on the head of Native Americans, who were the first victims. Headhunters complained of the loads of decomposing Indian heads they had to carry long distances to the paymasters. The authorities relented and ordered that only scalps be taken. They offered $50 for the scalps of men and $35 for the women and children, the women while still alive, to make better wigs. Bounties were in effect for up to 150 years. The Onkwehón:we fought back and took a few scalps themselves.

What Is a Conquest?

White men say the Indians' land is now theirs, no matter how they got it. It's not stealing, they say; it's a conquest. According to the dictionary, a *conquest* is *winning a war over an enemy*. In the case of Onkwehón:wekeh (America), the Onkwehón:we (Indians) didn't know they were in a war or that they were an enemy. They were just slaughtered. It surely was an illegal war and an illegal "conquest".

Actually, a conquest is a big organized gang of men with felony, plunder, looting and murder in their hearts, out to ravage other people's lands and possessions, no different from a gang of robbers looting a bank and killing people while they're at it. One is glorified, and the other is condemned. It depends on who planned the caper. While the Iroquois were never conquered, they lost their lands by fraud, politics and, sad to say, religion. Thievery and deceit are also approved forms of conquest, if not as glamorous as John Dillinger conquering a bank. It's no comfort to the victims of conquests that the proud conquerors get their comeuppance sooner or later. There have been quite a number, among them were Alex the Great, Big Julie (Julius Caesar), Attila. Ah, here was a rough and ready ripping plunderer! When the people of a country couldn't provide food for this half million men, they ate the people. There was Napoleon and, last but not least, Hitler. They created empires, but no empire ever lasted. The people who were conquered arose and flung out the conquerors.

Invasion

Armed intrusion into Onkwehón:wekeh (America) by self-righteous Europeans, carriers of contagious Dark Ages diseases, started epidemics among the Onkwehón:we (Indians), resulting in the death of 90 percent of Native Americans. Through a thousand years of the Dark and Middle Ages, the Europeans had built up an immunity to diseases caused by lack of personal hygiene. Bathing was a sin and against the religion of Europe. By force of arms, the polluted invaders tried to finish off the weakened Natives, whose present-day descendants represent the dazed and confused "survival of the fittest". Highly infectious "manifest destiny" went all over the world and diseased the Native people into subjection and created empires which are now gone. Opinion has it that without the mighty and pestilential ally, contagious epidemics, there would have been no European conquest in America. Native nations of the world have regained their lands. The only Native nations still in subjection are the Onkwehón:we, but the time is coming soon when they too shall regain their rightful heritage.

Civilization

Refined and approved corruption. State of advanced technology and low human relationship. Primitive white men beat each other over the head with wooden clubs; civilization enabled them to do it with iron. Modern civilization turned mankind into packs of wolverines in sheep's clothing. Called it "majority rule", ruled by a clever minority of super rich. Polluted the land, water, air and minds, including their own. Stole Indian land in the name of God. Let God take the blame. Kill all the Indians who resist and those who don't. "Civilization" is advancing towards an unknown destiny, and the rulers don't give a damn, as long as the profits keep coming. Is civilization bound towards self-destruction? Only the masses shall be destroyed. The super rich have safe hideaways.

Tribe or Nation

A tribe is the primitive man's attempt at a social order. The nation is the finished product. In ancient times, a family and their relatives got together and organized themselves into a band for self-protection. That is the tribe. Later, the tribes, or families, got together and coalesced into nations.

One definition of *tribe*: a derogatory term meaning *primitive and low-class people*—in brief, an insulting expression.

When the Europeans came to America, they made treaties with the Native Americans and, in doing so, recognized the Indians as nations. Only nations can make treaties. International law says that a nation once recognized as a nation remains a nation until it dissolves itself. No nation may dissolve another nation. The US action in 1871, reducing whole Indian nations to mere tribes, is illegal according to international law.

For the white race, the nation is a recent concept. When the Red and white races met, all the countries in Europe were kingdoms. In a kingdom, only the monarch has sovereignty. Everything and everyone belong to the king. A true nation is where the authority flows upward from the people to the installed leaders, as in the case of the Six Nations "Iroquois" Confederacy, also known as the longhouse, the world's first people's republic and the first to make a national constitution, a state far ahead of any then known.

The Iroquois Confederacy never accepted the reduced tribal status but always stands on its international rights as a union of nations and insists that the US honor the treaties their ancestors signed with the Six Nations Confederacy.

Indian Reserve or Indian Territory

Definition of *Indian reserve*: (US) *government land set aside for use by Indians*; (Canada) *crown land set aside for use by Indians*. Note that no ownership of the land is accorded to the Indians. The governments "reserve" the right to assume rule over the Indians. Definition of *territory*: *the land and waters under the jurisdiction of a nation, ruler, etc.*

This is one of the causes of the Ganienkeh Territory repossession: the right of the Indian nation to exercise its *sovereignty* in its own land and waters, a right confirmed in the 1794 treaty between the Six Nations Confederacy and the United States. It is a right guaranteed to everyone in the world but denied the American Indian.

No nation on Earth should be so deprived it has to exist on a reservation. Germany and Japan were defeated completely and unconditionally in 1945. Were they placed on reservations? No, that would be inhuman!

Behold! O, Oppressor,
We have just begun to fight!

Indian Police

Indian police physically enforce the will and laws of the oppressors on their own people—with billy clubs, mace and guns.

Indian police are people destroyed as Indians, casualties of the psychological warfare waged on the Indian people. Indian police are used by dominant society to harass the Indian people, especially those fighting for national and racial survival. Many Indian leaders were murdered by Indian police, notably Sitting Bull, among others.

There was a time when the Injun rez needed only one cop, called the village constable.

Cop means *constable on patrol*. About a dozen years ago in Kahnawà:ke, somebody got the bright idea there should be a police force. "Progress", they let us know. Like a city. Funny thing, with the advent of the police force came the crime, dope racketeering, protection rackets, muggings and even prostitution they proudly tell of. Methinks, the *dominant society* (it means *bossy*) had something to do with this. It's not hard to think this, because the Injuns themselves are not paying the salary of the police force and the firekeepers... beg your pardon, the fire department. Oh, yes, there's a fire department in Kahnawà:ke. It's a brother of the police department. Before the fire department was organized, we used to have a fire once or twice a year. Right after organizing, the firemen went out two or three times a week. We used to save buildings with the bucket brigade. Now, it's a fireman's business, so they burn right down to the ground.

Injuns are told that the Indian police force is for their protection and that they enforce Indian law. The Indian Act was legislated by the Canadian government. It was not made by Indians, so it cannot be Indian law.

The band council says it's their police. The federal and provincial governments split the policemen's salary 60 percent and 40 percent, so it must be their police force. Whoever pays the police is the boss.

The bossy society brings all this white man's progress onto Injun reservations to prepare the Onkwehón:we for the projected municipalization of the Indian reserves.[8] Some Indians don't believe this. They don't think the government can do such a thing to them. Besides that, it's Crown land, they say. They used to say, it's "Indian land". Now that the final dispossession comes hovering over the horizon, they don't think they can cope. So they want to pass the buck. Canada's Order in Council Queen Elizabeth II won't allow anything to happen to Indian reservations. White man had promised it was going to be reserved land forever, where life would pass like a pleasant dream. It has been a nightmare at times, but it's the last inch of land and last blade of grass. According to the indications, the reservations in the Province of Québec shall be hit first.

In July 1979, getting nowhere with the Canadian government, 350 disillusioned band council chiefs from all parts of Canada were delegated to go to England to meet Canada's senior tribe and its Queen.[9] The "uniqueness" (overused word) of the situation inspired the following immortal, unique words:

> The Great White Mother
> We Injun Chiefs from Canada are come
> To Merry Olde England's ancient Kingdom,
> To visit Our Protectress in her fortress.
> We beg reception by Her Royal Highness
> The Queen, Our Great Good Queen Bess.
> How! O Magnificence and Majesty!
> O Greatest Mortal we ever did see!
> Grant thy Red Sons the precious boon
> Of thy protection from perils coming soon!
> Save! oh save us from René Lévesque,
> Ripping conqueror and plunderer of Québec.
> Conspires he to grab ever Indian Reservation,
> Thy Crown Lands under thy mighty protection.
> Deliver us from the BNA patriation.
> Save us, they wretches, from racial extirpation!"
> Her Majesty sat and pondered a while,

As befits a Sovereign, smiling a sad smile.
At length she spoke, ah! what golden accent!
Honey dripping tones of music from heaven sent.
"Arise! mine Indian Sons and poor noble wretches,
I, too, have to lick their boots, the sons of bitches!
To hang on to mine precious Queendomhood.
Alas! I may be the last of the Great White Mamas.
Propose they to put me on a pension!
And my palace turn into a tourist attraction!
Great Britain, say they, can't afford a Queen.
'Tis now Little Britain, a might has been.
Say I, bad cess on the whole bloody mess,
A bad day has fallen on Your Good queen Bess.
Am I about to join thee in dark despair,
Mine golden throne tottering in evil disrepair.
Let us, dear Red Children, weep together
And dream of other great times that were!"
On this scene of wretchedness, misery and woe,
Let us ponder the wisdom and lessons of long ago.

At the time of this writing (1979), there were reports that Queen Elizabeth II of Little Britain had refused to meet with the dissident chiefs of the Indian Act of Canada. Her reason being that it is an internal matter of Canada. That's what Indians get for fooling around with the tribal status. When they were nations, it would have been an international matter.

Excerpt from a treaty between the United States and the Six Nations, from the 1794 Canandaigua Treaty.[10]

> *Article VII.* Lest the firm peace and friendship now established should be interrupted by the misconduct of individuals, the United States and the Six Nations agree that for injuries done by individuals on either side, no private revenge or retaliation shall take place, but instead thereof complaint shall be made by the party injured to the other or by the Six Nations or any of them to the President of the United States, or the Superintendent by him appointed, and by the Superintendent or other person appointed by the President to the principal chiefs of the Six Nations, or the nation to which

the offender belongs,—and such prudent measures shall then be pursued as shall be necessary to preserve our peace and friendship unbroken.

We shall resist by every
means any aggression,
any violation of the treaties,
any disturbance of our people
in the free use and enjoyment
of our land, any
usurpation of our
sovereignty, any encroachment
and oppression. We
pledge that the noise will be
heard from one end of the
world to the other.

The above is a copy of a five-and-a-half-foot by three-and-a-half-foot canvas sign posted on the side of the communications building at the entrance of Ganienkeh Territory. Part of the text was taken from Article IV of the 1794 Canandaigua Treaty, in which the United States agreed that it will never claim any of the land within the Six Nations Territory nor disturb the people of the Six Nations in the free use and enjoyment of their land.

This treaty confirms the sovereignty and national independence of the Six Nations Confederacy. Neither the US nor any other country can sue the Mohawk Nation or any of the others of the Six Nations and take them to their courts without their consent. It's known as sovereign immunity. We try any crimes committed in our territory. It's up to us to take care of anything that happens in our territory. We don't call in the police of another nation. Doing that would place us under the jurisdiction and authority of that said other nation, contrary to the rights of nations.

When we were sued by the New York State in the matter of the Moss Lake land repossession, we refused to go to court on the above grounds. The state's case was dismissed several times as a result. In the case of the shootouts with vigilantes, we refused to allow state troopers into the repossessed Ganienkeh Territory on the grounds of Article VII of the 1794 treaty. According to the said treaty, disputes shall be resolved by negotiation between the United States and the Six Nations Confederacy.

The Moss Lake situation became so frustrating to the opponents of our land repossession that they resorted to "dramatic" action. On Sunday, May 9, 1976, an opposition group called Confused Persons of Central Adirondacks (COPCA) staged a protest demonstration against Indians at the gate of the repossessed land of Ganienkeh, sometimes called "Mohawk Mountain Stronghold". A protest demonstration is nothing new. It happens all the time. Indians demonstrate in different parts of America over one point or another, usually injustice, oppression, racism and land disputes. The unusual thing about the COPCA demonstration was that this time it was a company of white people demonstrating against Indians.

Demonstrations are staged by people protesting against wrongs committed against them by an entrenched power. This is the only way open to them to voice their grievances. It's a case of one set of people having more power than another and taking advantage of its superior position to exploit the other. By staging this demonstration, the people of COPCA (rich land and property owners) took the position that the Native Americans at Moss Lake are an entrenched power.

They say advertising pays. Big business invests huge sums of money in billboards and signs. It brings in the money. Posters on social situations can bring in the people. Many Indians don't know what this struggle is all about. Many Indians are not aware of their human rights. They think being oppressed is a natural way of life. They think there's no other way for Indians to live. It is the duty of those who know to disseminate much-needed information. Many Indians want to do something but have no information on how to proceed. Other Indians need only be awakened and made aware of their true destiny. Some have never even heard that living is more than just being pushed around by foreign colonizers. They don't know they have the right to decide their own destiny.

Being oppressed for so long, the Indians have lost all concept of who they should be, what they should have and how to get it. They have been trained to follow "dominant society" around and once in a while say, "Boss! you're wonderful!" They've been told to turn the other cheek if struck, making it that much easier for the oppressor. The next blow is always harder. They are taught to be meek and humble, so they won't fight for their lands and rights—that their unmeek and unhumble oppressors may inherit their Earth without any trouble.

Indians are piously told that all authority is from God and must be obeyed, so the foreign colonizers assumed authority and expected the

Native Americans to obey said assumed and usurped authority. Some Indians are surprised to learn that this cultural development called "country" is a right guaranteed to everyone on Earth by the United Nations. Many Indians are surprised to learn that their ancestors had countries and governments, and that one of these, the Six Nations Iroquois government, was so far ahead of its time that it took the "dominant society" more than two hundred years to understand the people's republic. Also surprising is the fact that the so-called "advanced civilization" has yet to adopt all the freedoms in the Kaianerehkó:wa, the national constitution of the Six Nations Confederacy, from which the US Constitution was copied. After the copiers were done, it took seven Philadelphia lawyers to interpret it. This is how this civilized people developed loopholes in their constitution, enabling themselves to dictate.

This is just a bit of a wealth of information that should be available to Indian fighters for human rights. Word posters and picture posters should be everywhere. These should be billboards and outdoor signs telling Indians of their rights. The Chinese have the right idea. Photos of their cities and towns show word posters and billboards of information necessary for all to know. This is a social trick that Indians would do well to copy.

While not all Indians can be fighters, it is still necessary for the peaceful and the fearful to know the facts of the Indian situation, so that they can be silent supporters of the fighters. There are many good, hard-working Indians who cannot become involved in any trouble, controversies or come to possible grips with the law. Hardworking people are said to be the backbone of a nation and are absolutely indispensable in the perpetuation of the Native society in the future. There has to be a balance of opposites. Only 10 percent of any population can stand up and fight for their rights. It's no shame to be among the 90 percent who are too fearful to be involved in any possible controversies, confrontations, contentions or even bloodshed. The Creator made more timid people than heroes. Information is necessary for all Indians to absorb.

Activists shall have to become missionaries for the cause. Since it's impossible and impractical to personally see every Native American, posters, billboards, signs, charts and tracts should be made available wherever Indians may be, so they'll learn their rights.

Akwesasne was given the occasion to fight for its rights as a member of the Mohawk Nation. According to treaty agreements, the Six Nations people have sovereign immunity. They cannot be sued or summoned to any US court unless they consent. The 1794 Canandaigua Treaty provides the procedure to follow in the event of physical or civil offense being committed by either side.

A US federally funded program employing the Young Adults Conservation Corps got busy cutting trees on a private property, without asking permission or even notifying the "owners". One of the owners, Chief Kanasaraken (Loran Thompson), stopped the cutting and confiscated the tools until some kind of settlement would be worked out. It gave the puppet tribal council a chance to get at the traditional Mohawks. At first, they agreed to a meeting to discuss the matter of the intrusion on private property. Then they were incited by someone to lay charges of grand larceny days ahead of the scheduled meeting. Five Indian police and four state troopers descended on the residence of Kanasaraken and assaulted him and an old woman with billy clubs and dragged him off to a white man's jail. He was later released pending a hearing. The aged woman was taken to the hospital.[11]

Posters at Akwesasne: Fort Kanasaraken
Second stronghold established by the Kanien'kehá:ka in two hundred years. First, at Moss Lake's famous Mohawk Mountain Stronghold in 1974, where the Six Nations' jurisdiction, sovereignty and national independence were enforced by the Warrior Society. The Two Row Wampum, the 1794 Canandaigua Treaty and the Great Law regained respect and honor in white governments and Ganienkeh relations due to action programs by fighting men and women.

Fort Kanasaraken is the first such move on a reservation where the Mohawks face not only white man's entrenched authority but also their satellite Indians seemingly sworn to help destroy their own people.

> HELP LIBERATE AKWESASNE
> Help Akwesasne regain its territory status.
> Start by calling it a TERRITORY now!
> LONG LIVE THE WARRIOR SOCIETY!

> Traditional Indians are nationalists. "Dominant Society"
> is trying to stop nationalism all over
> Indian America. They use Indians who don't understand

nationalism to fight their own people who
are fighting for national survival.
Indians against Indians again. Tribal Councils and followers,
YOU ARE BEING USED!

At this point in time, other Mohawks have been added to the list of indictments. Said indictees refuse to go to court on the grounds of sovereign immunity as confirmed by the 1794 Canandaigua Treaty. They intend that the treaty shall be respected and honored at Akwesasne. They intend to fight it out with guns if necessary. Bunkers were erected surrounding the home of Kanasaraken, manned by the Warrior Society, men and women.

Why Why Why

Many Indians may have wondered why Indians were called "savage and brutish men, little better than wild beasts—subhuman nomads—Wild beasts in the path of civilization". John Smith, who was saved by Pocahontas, urged that the "viperous brood" (Indians) be enslaved, though he admits they saved Jamestown from starvation (some gratitude). Finally, when every white man was convinced by the propaganda that Indians were like animals, and that they should be hunted down like animals, bounties were offered for their scalps, just as if they were wolves. So much so that in the far western frontier in the nineteenth century, Indian flesh was eaten like game by white people, who were the first to condemn cannibalism.

When a people intend to destroy other people (or animals), they attribute the worst qualities to those they wish to destroy. In the case of Indians, the reason for their destruction was to get their land. They spread the worst rumours, the worst lies, calumnies and malicious slanders, so that the Indians would be extremely hated and despised, and the headhunters would feel justified in hunting down the Indians as if they were the worst kind of animals.

The settlers thought it would take only a matter of months to destroy all the Indians. How many generations of Indian people were on the run continuously to save themselves for 150 years? A lot of Indians went to the far north to evade the dreaded foe, the hunters of the Indians. There are Indians still in the wilderness whom nobody ever sees. They make sure no one but their own ever sees them. Theirs is a culture of hiding. They are the most elusive of game. They still think they're hunted. Maybe they are.

If Indians are human wolves, then the white man must be a leopard, the most cruel of hunters, who kills even when he doesn't need the food. *Indian menace* and *Indian peril* were the terms for Indians in the days of yore. What's more menacing these days than the nuclear menace? Indian slaughter was called the "inexorable march of civilization displacing savage hunters", even if their civilized killers were more savage. "Primitive hunters" meant people who killed for food. Civilized hunters means people who kill for fun. "Indians didn't develop the land". There are three million acres in Ganienkeh Territory not being used, and we want them back. We can certainly use them. To live on.

Although agriculturists were far beyond the abilities of the Europeans, the Native Americans were subjected to importunities by the white invaders to be like them, *civilized*, which shows that many white people don't know the meaning of the word. It has been said that certain Indian nations copied European "civilization", notably the Cherokees, who adopted a constitution like that of the US (which was adopted from the Iroquois constitution). The Cherokees published books and a newspaper in their own language, with Sequoyah supplying the alphabet.[12]

"A census taken among them in 1825 showed that they owned 33 grist mills, 13 sawmills, 1 powder mill, 69 blacksmith shops, 2 tan yards, 762 looms, 2,486 spinning wheels, 172 wagons, 2,923 plows, 7,683 horses, 22,531 black cattle, 46,732 swine and 2,566 sheep. This adaptation to white concepts of progress, urged upon them by Jefferson, did not save but rather accelerated demands for their expulsion" (from *The Indian in American History* by Virgil J. Vogel).[13] The Cherokees, along with other Eastern Indians, were removed to Oklahoma and all their possessions seized. Their substantial homes were grabbed by greedy white settlers.

According to the same source, Europe makes many false claims. "Indians had no conception of the wheel.... Aztecs put wheels on children's toys. They had no beasts of burden to put the principle to better use". Europe borrowed its wheel, its alphabet, numerals, domesticated plants and animals from Semitic people of Asia. Gunpowder, compass and printing press were inventions of Oriental people. The Mayans of Mexico had a superior calendar and understood the zero before Europe did. Indians domesticated more than forty plants, of which corn is the outstanding example, because it does not and cannot grow wild. In some respects, they excelled in medicine and surgery, e.g., trepanation (cutting through bones in the head to remove tumors, etc.) and knew the properties of drugs like coca (from whence cocaine), cinchona (from whence quinine), curare, cascara sagrada and many more. They alone discovered rubber.... Indians north of Mexico used about 150 medicines which were later included in the United States Pharmacopoeia and the National Formulary, and the Indians of Latin America contributed about fifty more. Accounts of explorers from Cartier on are filled with tributes to the Indians' medical skill, which was considered by many to excel that of Europe at that time. Mayan astronomy, mathematics and architecture, the skillful metalwork and other arts of the Aztecs and Incas, the domestication of the turkey, Muscovy duck, honeybee, alpaca, llama and guinea pig; the roads, communications, scientific land use and political organization of the Incas, the invention of paper and the weaving of cotton cloth in Mexico. North American Indians mined and worked copper, lead, mica and coal. They discovered oil and made salt by evaporation. North American Indians planted corn, squash, beans, pumpkins, tobacco, sunflowers and drug plants (medicine). Central and South American Indians mined gold, silver, tin, platinum and jade. The white men smoke the Indians' tobacco and eat their foods: the tapioca of the Amazon, the beans, avocado, pineapples, chocolate, peppers and vanilla of Mexico, the tomatoes, potatoes and peanuts of Peru, the cranberries, squashes and pecans of North America, the pemmican of the Plains Indians. From the Mexican Indians, the white man got his chewing gum tamales, chili and tortillas and from the US Indians, hominy, succotash, corn pone and popcorn. Other Indian inventions are the canoe, kayak, pirogue, cigar, hammock, toboggan, snowshoes, cradleboard, rubber, pipe, cigarettes and lacrosse.

Hear Ye!

In a news interview, a leader of the tribal council proudly said: "We are United States citizens", which means they are legally no longer Indians, but naturalized Americans of Indian descent. If they prefer to legally be white people, what are they doing on an Indian "reservation"?

Akwesasne's traditional people are citizens of the Mohawk Nation of the Six Nations Confederacy, the world's first people's republic, the first to devise the national constitution, "the greatest political society ever devised by man.... I think no institutional achievement of mankind exceeds it in either wisdom or intelligence" (*Indians of the Americas* by John Collier).[14]

Paleface brainwashing reaps big success. Makes Injuns think it's progress to renounce the greatest for a pale imitation. Make Injuns into imitation paleface. Some paleface good. Help Injun. Others make Injuns into fools, drunks, dope fiends, cause them to commit suicide or become tribal councilors and talk nonsense for the rest of their lives.

Here's some more:

> Uncle Sam did, in the Canandaigua Treaty of 1794, "engage never to claim any of the land within the Six Nations territory nor disturb the people of the Six Nations or their Indians friends residing thereon in the free use and enjoyment thereof" (part of Article IV). The United States is once again violating this treaty, intruding into private property and disturbing the people of the Six Nations in Akwesasne, in the free use and enjoyment of the land; arresting those who protested this violation of treaty agreements.
>
> Where, oh where, is the white man's famous honor and integrity? Is it nonexistent? Is howling civilization the fate of mankind? Know ye, O Oppressor, that Indians are sick and tired of oppression and shall, henceforth, fight by every means.
> *And We Have Just Begun To Fight!*

We used to wonder why the Mohawks didn't sign the treaties the Six Nations made with the US. Barbara Graymont, in her book *Iroquois in the American Revolution* tells us why.[15] She wondered how her country could do such a thing! She was amazed when she was conducting her research for the book and came across the fact that the US makers of the 1768 Fort Stanwix Treaty wouldn't let the Mohawks read the treaty, and that is why they wouldn't sign it.[16] There were things in it they didn't want the Indians to see. There were Indians who signed it, but not one of them was a chief. That's what the Indians get for allowing the white man to do all the composing. When the treaties were read out, the Indians heard only the good things they included, and the things they wouldn't like were not mentioned. That was for later, like now. They are now saying that Article VII of the Canandaigua Treaty of 1794 gives Congress the right to grant New York State jurisdiction over all Indian reservations in the state. So, you see, boys and girls, that's what they didn't want to show the Indians in those long gone days. Of course, the Injuns could turn the reservations into territories, which is as it should be. No nation should be so deprived it has to exist in a reservation.

Extinction

There is a book with the unintriguing title *The Uses of the Past,* by Professor Herbert J. Muller, which deals with history and why great civilizations of the past collapsed and became extinct.[17] It took him ten years of research to track down the events that led to the decline and fall of the classical Greek civilization, the great Roman Empire and other great civilizations of the ages.

There is a parallel in present-day events and those of the bygone eras which should give the modern Onkwehón:we pause for reflection. Professor Muller gives four major reasons why these powerful institutions wilted and died away. Surely, they did not expect to die away. Who wants to die? It takes a psychological condition to make a person wish to die and commit suicide. That whole nations and a part of a race can disappear from the face of the Earth without being slaughtered is intriguing. It can even be frightening. That millions of classical Greeks, millions of Romans and other powerful nations can be abolished so that not a drop of blood is left is a sobering thought indeed. How can the native Onkwehón:we of the stolen continent of America, in this greatly reduced condition, resist and win against the threat known as extinction? Not only can whole peoples get into certain conditions, do certain things, ignore warnings, neglect duties and laugh at the wise, which can and will destroy them completely and extirpate them from the face of the Earth, but there is the added threat from outside interests at work to achieve such an end to unwanted nations' races. Life is indeed full of traps, natural and manmade, for the unwary. Even the careful can become careless and go, baby, go! Seemingly of small moment, the four reasons are:

1. loss of language;
2. "outgrew" the rules and regulations that made them great;
3. economic system deteriorated after the people became great;
4. spies and traitors.

1. Loss of Language

According to the book, no one in Greece today speaks the language of the classical Greek era. The people who live in Greece today do not have an ounce of Greek blood. There are no Romans today. The people who live now in the center of ancient Rome do not speak the language of the Romans. Likewise, there are no Persians today. No one speaks the language of Persia, now called Iran. Loss of language is a big step towards extinction. There is a parallel here among the Onkwehón:we. Most of the people do not speak their own national language. Among the people of the Six Nations Confederacy, called "Iroquois" by the French and Kanonhsionni'ón:we by themselves three hundred years ago, the language has been broken up into dialects. The people themselves have changed the name of the Six Nations Confederacy to Haudenosaunee, from the broken Seneca dialect, instead of Kanonhsionni'ón:we from the original language.

The white man can say that the Iroquois made themselves extinct, buried even their own names. If they are not the Kanonhsionni'ón:we, then they are not the people known as the great and mighty Iroquois. It inspired the judge to say there are no more Mohawks, in connection with the Akwesasne dispute. Yet the Mohawks speak the original Iroquois language. Fortunately, as mentioned above, the Mohawks resisted the language breakup. Linguists are amazed at the pureness of the Mohawk language. They say it is certainly not a dialect. The others of the Six Nations can draw back from this big step towards extinction by relearning the language of their ancestors. It's not lost. The Mohawks speak it. According to linguists, when a language breaks, the first sound to go is R. It turns into L. Then the L goes. It is also noticeable that the last sound a child masters when he begins to speak is the R. For a while he says "thlee" for "three". When a people breaks up its language, it seems to go backwards to its childhood. Is the broken dialect "baby talk"? The last thoughts of a dying person are also what his first thoughts were. Does that actually mean that when a language breaks, the people are preparing to die out? Knowing this the people can save themselves by relearning their ancient language.

2. Rules and Regulations

Rules and regulations that made ancient civilizations great were ignored after the people became great. Corruption became the rule. The people took the second big step towards extinction. To start the Six Nations along the same path, someone put a taboo on reading the Great Law. So, now, the people don't know when they are violating it. Fortunately, most Mohawks put no stock in taboos and will read anything, including the Great Law. It is the law in effect in Ganienkeh. We believe that the taboo is a conspiracy to put the Six Nations on a greased skid to extinction. Indians on reservations are forced to follow laws made by the US and Canadian governments. A big step towards extinction.

3. Economy

When the ancient civilizations became great, their spirit of cooperation relaxed in the matter of the economy of the people. It became everyone for himself. Some people became super rich, while the masses became poor. Sound familiar? Our ancestors used the cooperative farm community economic system adopted by present-day Mennonites, Amish, Hutterites and other well-off groups. Only Ganienkeh, among the Six Nations, is using the ancient system and working towards economic self-sufficiency. Careless economics is the third big step towards extinction.

4. Spies and Traitors

Great civilizations of the past ignored their spies and traitors. "They can't hurt us", said they, while the spies and traitors hacked away at the very foundations of their existence. When the great civilizations collapsed, the spies and traitors also became extinct, along with the people they helped to destroy.

Spies and traitors abound on Indian reservations. Indians say, "How can they hurt us? We have nothing left to lose". There is something Indians still have. Their existence. If they do not stop their spies and traitors, they will go the way of lost civilizations. Oblivion. The Indian informers, spies and traitors are many, because no one does anything about it. It's a safe occupation. The fact that traitors are the lowest things on Earth and most shameful of humans doesn't mean a thing to them. *Honor, loyalty* and *integrity* are just words that have no meaning. Their destiny is to destroy their own people, as they are themselves destroyed as Indians. Nature's first law, *self-preservation*, is ignored at the peril of the people's existence. It is the last big step towards extinction.

The book notes that only people who struggle survive, and their population increases. The people who stop struggling decrease and eventually die out. The effects are said to be psychological. According to the book, the meek and humble, who only want to be peaceful, decrease in number. The aggressive and greedy increase, rule and overpopulate the Earth. The solution has to be the happy medium between two extremes. Get some spunk and fighting spirit into the meek and humble. Indoctrinate the overly aggressive and overly greedy and make them wear chastity belts. Anything to check the population explosion.

As a race, Injuns are small in numbers. Most are browbeaten into meekness and humility. Many die young. Many are on welfare, which kills initiative and fighting spirit. Welfare is an effective aid in the program to make Injuns extinct. What must they do to avoid the easy road to extinction? Injuns must change their style. Instead of meekness and humility, Injuns shall have to stand on their hind legs and fight for their rights. They must struggle to create their own economy. They should not continue to depend on the white man's precarious economy, which has a bad habit of collapsing every once in a while, and then many Indians starve to death. Working for the white man is depending on his economy. To ensure continued existence, Injuns should grow their own food, make their own bread, etc. Injuns should produce their own cloth to make their own clothes. Make their own styles. Now, there's a thought! Something for the imaginative young designers. Injuns should cut their own lumber and make their dwellings, according to their own architecture. Or make it of stone. Plenty of stone around. Help each other. One of the ways of survival.

Many Injuns do not think they're headed towards extinction. The extinct Greeks and Romans thought the same way. Intelligent Injuns have their work cut out to save their people, some of whom don't want to be saved. The US and Canadian governments have a policy of assimilation for Indians. It means legal extinction. There are Indians who are already US or Canadian citizens. They have committed racial and national suicide. Naturalized Americans or Canadians of Indian descent. No longer legally Indians. That's extinction, man! In time, according to white man's calculations, there won't even be any sign that once upon a time a race of Indians did exist. This plan must be resisted and fought until the battle is won. The Great Law provides that once a battle is joined, it must not stop until the people have won.

Fighting against All Odds

Uncle Sam doesn't mind admitting his army lost the battle of Little Big Horn, because the US army of 266 men were outnumbered by the Cheyenne and Sioux who were gathered for a spiritual ceremony.[18] They suspended the ceremony while they knocked off General Custer and his Custeristas. The Injuns were engaged in the Creator's business when attacked, and that's bad medicine. Like attacking people who were at worship in church.

There are at least three battles with Injuns Uncle Sam doesn't like to talk about. This happened in the 1812 War.[19] There were only two thousand English troops to defend 1,900 miles of frontier, as the British were busy with Napoleon in Europe. Every available English soldier was on the old continent with other European armies trying to conquer the conqueror Napoleon. Canada was actually defenseless, and what an opportunity for the US to conquer Canada. The United States sent a ten-thousand-man army into Upper Canada and a seven-thousand-man force into Lower Canada. These latter troops were marching on Montréal and had a day to go to reach Kahnawà:ke, embarkation point for the Island of Montréal. There was a wharf on the Kahnawà:ke Injun reserve where the newfangled steamers, called packets, took aboard horses and buggies and later even trains bound for Montréal, until the Victoria and CPR bridges were built in 1860 and 1885[20] respectively. It was calculated that a whole week was required to ferry the army and equipment across the Saint Lawrence River. Meanwhile, the army would occupy the Kahnawà:ke village and, according to customs, when an army invades another country, they would take over the homes, turn out the people, sleep in their beds, eat their food and rape the women.

The Injuns of Kahnawà:ke did not appreciate this kind of attention from the "dominant society", even if it was Canada's big brother Uncle Sam. During the night before the seven-thousand-man army reached Kahnawà:ke, six hundred Injuns quietly left the town and like shadows slipped into positions in the woods along the highway near Châteauguay. The army of conquest marched into the ambush in the morning. The would-be rapists of Injun women were cut down in the flower of their fighting days. Less than half returned to the US faster than they had come. They reported that there was an Injun behind every tree, and there were millions of trees. The Injuns captured huge horses, wagons and other army equipment. Having no use for artillery they turned those over to the defenders of Montréal: Oh yeah! Salaberry and his three hundred men were stationed down the road waiting for the US army and took the credit for the victory, without firing a shot. The Injuns of Kahnawà:ke took on odds of more than eleven to one and won.

In Upper Canada, the Americans crossed into what is now known as Ontario and into Canada's history book: Did eight hundred dead men stop ten thousand troops? Well, sir, it seems that a thousand warriors from Ohswé:ken ambushed the Americans and drove them back across the border and, in doing so, picked up a bad habit from the paleface. The Mohawks took credit for the victory, even though there were other Injuns present. Since the victory was unheralded, as was the credit-taking, it has fallen upon deaf ears.

At Beaver Dams, likewise in "Ontario", the Kahnawà:ke warriors wiped up the forest with the invaders.[21] Fitzgibbons said all the fighting was done by the Injuns and not a shot was fired by the white soldiers. Ten thousand troops vs. a thousand warriors is ten to one odds. Again, the "tigers of the forest" prevailed. Canada was saved by the Injuns in the 1812 War.

Great odds are against the Injuns in the psychological war waged against them. The strong shall survive. They shall have to struggle and fight for it. In the physical struggle, a strange statistic emerged in 1945, following the end of World War II. The "most dangerous man in the world" was unmasked.[22] Forgot his name after thirty-five years. He said, "Give me one thousand men and I can bring down to its knees any country of the world no matter how powerful". He was also the one who said that a "man fighting in a certain way is equal to a thousand men". Let's analyze that. A chain is as strong as its weakest link. Every country is like a chain with weak links. They build nuclear power installations, which provide inviting targets for potential enemies, foreign and domestic. The more installations the merrier. These installations can be destroyed, and the released radiation fallout would itself destroy millions of people without further effort by the enemy—a sort of a bonus. More technology means more weak points for the powerful countries. A fighter can now take on odds up to a million to one and win.

Statistically, a lesson may be learned in René Lévesque's lament in the Province of Québec.[23] Lévesque's plan for Québec's separation from the rest was the peaceful and legal way—the referendum. It requires more than 50 percent of the people to win. A violent overthrow, such as a revolution, requires 10 percent of the people, even less. By coincidence, in every cause believed in by a certain number of people, only 10 percent shall fight for it. Ninety percent of the people are not able to be involved in controversies, confrontations (especially armed) or in any kind of possible trouble. They are called the *sheep*.

Some Definitions

Angels: fabulous celestial beings whose space suits are superior to those of the astronaut Earthlings, who can only go to the moon or claim to.
Civilization: 1. refined corruption; 2. progression from using wooden clubs to rule the people to using metal firearms besides the wooden clubs.

Columbus: first white man to rob and slaughter Indians. To keep his memory alive, they set a day aside to celebrate his crime and the example he set for future robbers.

Democracy: a government of, by and for the people under majority rule directed by a rich clever minority.

Economy: a system of wealth management whereby the super rich get richer and the poor go on welfare.

Education: teaching the children of dumb parents who cannot teach their own children. Parents gladly pay to evade this duty. The establishment gladly provides the schools, as it gives them a chance to brainwash the kids.

Government: a system of ruling or misruling, directing or misdirecting, a country so the mighty may prevail.

Heaven: an abode in outer space full of joy and happiness under the control of—you guessed it—the white man. He decides who goes there. Its celestial reaches are dotted with Indian reservations, where the good Indians who obeyed the white man here below go, and where they enjoy daily heavenly encroachments by paleface saints, the same crooks who disposed of us here in the name of God. Pearly thrones for Columbus, the Pizzaro brothers, Kit Carson, etc. To make the Indians feel at home and not miss the good life here below, there is daily violation of the treaties.

Indian reserve: (new definition) land set aside for use by Indians and surrounded by thieves.

Indian treaties: paper tigers that eat up both the Indians and their land.

Mock chiefs: system of chiefs on Indian reservations devised by the colonizers from Europe, such as Canada's band council chiefs and the US tribal council chiefs. The purpose of mock chiefs is to bury the system devised by Indians, such as the traditional system.

Pagan: one who doesn't believe in what the "good" claim to believe.

Policeman: a caveman with a club.

Religion: one of many systems of worshiping God, gods or goddesses. Unorganized natural religion doesn't cost a cent. Organized needs money in fabulous amounts.

Rhetoric: beating around the bush.

Saint: one who gives up the pleasures of this world in order to enjoy them in paleface heaven. Oh, he'll be a devil up there.

Sin: that which is forbidden by the faithful but enjoyed by their masters. "Don't do what I do, do what I tell you to do".

Sinner: one who enjoys openly what the good enjoy in secret.

Taxation: one-sided communism. You share your money with the super rich who are in control.

Truth: reality and facts providing they do not conflict with one's own reality and facts. "Revealed truth" was spread by the fire and sword, and anyone who doubted was fit only to be burnt at the stake. The greatest truth is that most people don't know the truth about most truths.

Unique: an overworked word in connection with Native Americans. It's white man's way of telling the Indians, "You're alone, baby, you're alone".

USA: usurpia, a land invaded and stolen by foreign colonizers who usurped the authority from Native people.

Usurpials: white people who boss Indians around.

Welfare: bribe to the poor. Destroys the recipient's initiative and fighting spirit. Helps keep the super rich in control.

Summarizing the Injun Situation

1. We did not come from Asia. We originated in this land and are Indigenous to the soil of Onkwehón:wekeh (America).

2. We are Onkwehón:we, not Indians. An Indian is a native of India.

3. According to the dictionary, a *savage* is a *primitive, barbarous, cruel and brutal person.* We can never hope to equal the Europeans in the savage manner this land was stolen from us.

4. They called us "tribes" but recognized us as nations when they made treaties with us, for only nations can make treaties.

5. We have the right to our own area of land for our territory where we can exercise our own system of government and economy according to our customs and traditions. No other nation or power has the right to deprive us of our nationality, our lands or the right to regulate our own lives.

6. We lived a million years without being told what to do by foreigners.

7. We have been given a life to live, and it is our duty to protect this life and the lives of our people who may be less able. It is

our duty to stop anyone who tries to destroy us individually or our people as a whole. It is the first law of nature, and the nations which ignored this law are now extinct.

8. As warriors, it is our right, privilege and duty to fight for the most important things in life, and these include survival as a distinct people and a race of nations. We have the right not to disappear into any melting pot devised by foreign people which has been designed to destroy races and nationalities.

9. If the Creator made all the people of the world, then he wants them to be as he created them, and so we must fight by every means to remain Onkwehón:we and not be a part of a mongrel mixture in any melting pot.

10. We have more right to have a country in our own land (America) than do the Europeans, who say they were fugitives from European oppression and, once established here, introduced their own brand of oppression.

To regain their place among the sovereign nations of mankind, the Native American must fight for it.

A Law of Nature
According to lessons of history, people who
give up the struggle decrease in number,
die out and become extinct.

People who continue to struggle, increase in
number, grow strong and achieve survival.

Forever Life the Onkwehonwe!
Warrior Society
Rugged men and exotic women, arise!
Take thy sleepless enemy by surprise.
America, foreign raped and usurped, is ours!
America, once as wide and free as woodland flowers.
Our mother, polluted and by strangers blighted
Calls to us, her children, who lay uprooted.
We, the oppressed, like our mother, man damned
and to a like fate, by the foreigner condemned,

Hear the call! Hear the whisper: "Revenge-Revenge!"

Hear the wind and the trees echo the word "Revenge".

Even the rocks and the creeks murmur "Revenge-Revenge!"

Let every man, woman and child awake!

Let us all Red men arise and the shackles break!

Let us once again stand on our two feet and fight!

With knowledge and power can make things right.

Let us the Vision of Dekanawida realize.

Let us this Great Ancestor honor and revitalize!

Be his Great Law our voice, will and strength.

Be his name known and shouted the entire length

Of this Red man's great Land of America.

Hear every Red American Native shout, "Eureka!"

From every mountain top, prairie and sylvan retreat.

Hear the distant beat as every warrior's on his feet!

Men and women of the warrior Society,

On thou and thou alone await thy destiny.

There's a right and wrong way to fight.

Power is great and knowledge makes might.

Man! in certain and clever way move thou

And ten thousand men equal thou!

Great are thy rewards, honor shall be thy fate.

Take back what is thine and gone'll be thy hate!

Courage, men! and it's thine, peace and country.

Long Live the Warrior Society!

Notes

1   The Bering Land Bridge theory holds that North American Aboriginal peoples crossed the ice bridge linking the Asian continent to Alaska between 12,000 and 15,000 years ago. Presenting Indigenous peoples as fairly recent immigrants, this theory was recently challenged by archeological evidence suggesting that humans may have occupied the continent much earlier in history, potentially following the coast by boat instead of crossing by foot. In 2007, 23,000-year-old fossilized human footprints were discovered in the White Sands National Park, suggesting that humans were on the continent before the dates consistent with the Bering Land Bridge theory. In 2017, archeologists discovered animal bones showing markings of human or Neanderthal origin that were no less than 130,000 years old.

2   See Timeline, "1970 Akwesasne Islands reoccupied".

3   See Timeline, "1754–1763 French and Indian War."

4 In fact, a British citizen can only have his or her citizenship revoked if he or she is also the citizen of another nation.

5 While this statement is inaccurate for Canada and the United States, which allow dual citizens to vote in two different countries, more than fifty nations do not recognize dual citizenship, including India, China, Japan and Ukraine.

6 While dual citizenship exists in many countries, there are no examples of dual citizenship within two countries that are embedded in each other, as is the case for the Iroquois Confederacy with regard to Canada and the United States.

7 Thomas Paine (1737–1809) wrote several revolutionary pamphlets advocating the independence of the United States, the most famous being *Common Sense*, published anonymously in 1776; see Thomas Paine, "Common Sense", in *The Writings of Thomas Paine*, ed. Moncure Daniel Conway (New York: G.P. Putnam's Sons, 1894), accessed April 28, 2022, https://oll.libertyfund.org/page/1776-paine-common-sense-pamphlet.

8 See Timeline, "1969 White Paper".

9 When the Canadian constitution was about to be "patriated" from the United Kingdom to Canada in 1982, Indigenous peoples were concerned that they would lose rights warranted by their nation-to-nation relationship with the British crown. In the ensuing wave of protests, approximately one thousand Indigenous people traveled across Canada by train as part of the Indian Constitutional Express, to raise awareness about their rights, while others went to the United Nations headquarters in New York City and to the UK, where they notably presented their concerns before the House of Lords. These efforts resulted in Article 35, which acknowledges the sovereignty of Indigenous peoples on their unceded territories.

10 See Timeline, "1794 Canandaigua Treaty".

11 See Timeline, "1979 Fort Kanasaraken".

12 Sequoyah (1770–1843) was a Cherokee intellectual and diplomat famous for having invented an innovative syllabary for Cherokee language, which was officially adopted in 1825.

13 Virgil J. Vogel, *The Indian in American History* (Amherst, MA: Integrated Education Associates, 1968).

14 John Collier, *Indians of the Americas* (New York: W.W. Norton & Company, 1947).

15 Barbara Graymont, *The Iroquois in the American Revolution* (Syracuse, NY: Syracuse University Press, 1972).

16 See Timeline, "1768 Fort Stanwix Treaty".

17 Herbert J. Muller, *The Uses of the Past: Profiles of Former Societies* (Oxford: Oxford University Press, 1952).

18 See Timeline, "1877 Chief Joseph".

19 See Timeline, "1812–1815 War of 1812".

20 The Victoria Jubilee Bridge, the first bridge connecting Montréal to its south shore, was inaugurated on August 25, 1860. Many Mohawks worked on its construction. The Saint-Laurent Railway Bridge was built between 1885 and 1887, allowing trains from the Canadian Pacific Railway (CPR) to cross from Kahnawà:ke to LaSalle, on the island of Montréal.

21 On June 24, 1813, American Troops were ambushed by Indigenous warriors near Queenston, Ontario; see Timeline, "1812–1815 War of 1812".

22 Karoniaktajeh likely refers to the US Army general Douglas MacArthur. He was called "the most dangerous man in America" by Franklin D. Roosevelt when he

was the governor of New York, fearing that MacArthur would become the president of the United States. However, during the Korean War MacArthur's keenness to extend the conflict to China, including through nuclear attacks, against the advice of his superiors, pushed President Truman to remove him from command.

23   Québec prime minister René Lévesque led the nationalist Parti Québécois when it took power in the province in 1976, and then held a referendum on the sovereignty of Québec in 1980, which was lost.

Rebuilding the Iroquois Confederacy

The seeds of decay were planted before the Iroquois Confederacy became great and famous. The Five Nations had joined in an alliance under the guidance of the great founder Dekanawida, who wanted all the Native nations in America to be members of the alliance which became known as the Iroquois Confederacy. He wanted all nations to be equal in power, influence and legal authority. He had no plans for a super nation or nations to lord it over other nations. Dekanawida wanted all the Rotiianérshon (chiefs) to be equal in power. He had no wish to see a single individual elected as a grand or supreme chief, as such a position only leads to errors and corruption. He got the original five nations of the confederacy to offer up the position of "grand chief" to the Creator who does not err, cannot be corrupted and does not die.

The Kaianerehkó:wa, the Great Law, began with thirty articles or wampums formulated by Dekanawida himself. Other laws were added "to the rafters" by the grand councils in the following centuries, as needed. It took five years for Dekanawida and Hiawatha (a transplanted Onondaga, who left his nation because of persecutions suffered by his family and joined the Mohawks, who recognized his special abilities and made him one of the Bear Clan chiefs) to gather and join into alliance the first five nations. Convinced they'd do fine, Dekanawida set out to gather more nations to join his great alliance. He was never seen again. It is believed that he came upon evil people and was killed. Deprived of his counsel and sound guidance, the people of the original five nations were not ready to act with good judgment when the outside nations came to join the alliance. Instead of making them equals, they put them in a subordinate state, without a voice in the grand council. They came in "on the cradleboard", meaning they were treated like children and not allowed to develop their potential. In time, there were twenty-eight of these dependent nations in the Iroquois Protectorate of Indian Nations. The five nations became overlords of the twenty-eight subordinate nations, not what Dekanawida had in mind at all. The Five Nations grand council even added "a law to the rafters" that any adoption of a nation or nations shall be temporary only, subject to certain conditions, and they shall have no voice in grand councils or any authority. When Dekanawida left to gather in more nations, he certainly did not want to bring them in "on the cradleboard" but as equals. As a consequence, when foreign European invaders arrived, they had only a Five Nation Confederacy to face instead of thirty-three, which would have been the case had they given the twenty-eight protectorate nations equality. The French invaders saw the protectorate situation and used the twenty-eight protectorate nations as a tool to overcome the Iroquois. For twenty-five years, the French, with the help of their missionaries, coaxed and incited the dependent Indian nations, telling them, "They treat you like children. You have no voice in their council", until the protectorate Indians agreed to attack their protectors.

Fortunately for the Iroquois, their own agents warned them in time. Conspirators can't keep anything secret for twenty-five years. Weeks before the expected attack, and while still in wintertime, the Iroquois turned on their lightning war, a strategy which found its way into all books of war in military academies. In 1940, Hitler admitted he got his idea of the Blitzkrieg (which means *lightning war*) from the Iroquois. More than a century of warfare followed, at the end of which time the French had lost all their landholdings in North America, the protectorate nations were all gone, but the Iroquois, bleeding and staggering, were still roaring and defiant. All this happened because some elitist grand council chiefs wanted equality for only five nations. It's not inconceivable that otherwise one hundred or even two hundred nations of Indians would now be members of the Iroquois Confederacy, a mighty alliance of Indians in America.

Lording it over other Indian nations did the Iroquois no good. Not having the Peacemaker Dekanawida around to help make great decisions, the elitist chiefs could only see themselves as masters over all. Even at this late stage of the game, they still have this superiority complex. At a grand council in Onondaga in 1976, representatives of two outside Indian nations made an appearance on a mission of joining in some kind of alliance with the Six Nations (one of them the Tuscarora, not having equality).

The two visiting groups are the leading Indian nations in their areas. One was representing the Sioux Nation from the west and the others were Chippewa from Ontario. When word got around about their mission, the Onondaga Handsome Lake preacher Huron Miller, sitting against the well, became very enthusiastic: "Great! We'll put them under our wings", he said. Larry Red Shirt of the Sioux said: "But we don't want to come in on the cradleboard". The elitist grand council chiefs would have it no other way. The Sioux and Chippewa delegates didn't return. "Putting them under our wings" implies the protectorate nonsense once again. How can the elitist grand council protect anyone when it can't even protect itself? It can only pretend to protect or defend, for it has buried its weapons and its fighting spirit and can only dream of the glories of the past. At this late date, Indians all over America can do wonders by following the Great Plan of Dekanawida, by joining all American Indian nations in one big alliance or confederacy, all the nations to be equal in power, influence and legal authority. Had the original Five Nations Iroquois Confederacy followed Dekanawida's Great Plan, there would now be a confederacy of two hundred or more nations. What kept the Iroquois down were their elitist chiefs who wanted equality for only five nations and subsection for all the others. It's up to the Iroquois people of the present who see and understand the problem to do something about it while there is still time.

To understand the problem, it is necessary to dredge up some of the events of the past and expose them for the people to see and understand, so they can see what to do about it. At the end of the American Revolution, the Iroquois still had enough military power to force the new US republic to sue for peace in 1784. After the famous hit and run Sullivan raid of 1779, which killed thirty-three Senecas, the enthusiastic reports said the Seneca population was decimated, which means a tenth of the population had been killed.[1] The Seneca total population couldn't have been only 330. Sullivan reported destroying certain towns he never even went near. The following year, 1780, the Iroquois went on a rampage of their own, cleaning out three huge areas, Ohio being one of them. This was the last military action by the Iroquois in the United States and would have split the new US in half if the United States had not been able to get the Indians to agree to the 1781 Treaty of Peace.[2]

In 1797, Governor Morris of New Jersey State asked the Seneca Nation to hold a council. He was too old to make the trip himself, so he delegated his son to perform the simple chore of buying five million acres of Seneca land. Morris junior couldn't get all the Seneca chiefs to agree, so in the evening he broke open the whiskey barrel, and a party went on.[3] By morning everyone was so boozy and happy that the governor's son very easily persuaded the Seneca to part with the five million acres for $100,000. Even Red Jacket was as drunk as a lord.[4] So was Handsome Lake, whose name appears fourth on the list of signatures on the agreement. When they sobered up and realized what they had done, they swore off booze. The Senecas are very proud of this abstinence, even if it lasted less than two years. In 1799, the Senecas went on the now famous spring hunt. When they returned, they had no meat, no furs and no money, but everyone was gloriously drunk. They had fallen off the wagon. They sobered up one by one. There was one who kept on drinking whisky, and that one was Handsome Lake. He stopped when he collapsed from the DTs. He came back to the land of the living after four days (not four years). The first person he saw was his nephew Henry O'Beale, Cornplanter's son. Cornplanter was Handsome Lake's half brother.[5] When Handsome Lake's father died, his mother married a white man, and Cornplanter was the happy little result. Cornplanter grew up and married a white woman, and they had three boys, one of whom was Henry, who was only a quarter Seneca but 100 percent Quaker. He was always trying to convert his uncle. Here he was at his famous uncle's bedside listening to his complaints: "Snakes, snakes, all sizes, all colors wrapping themselves around me. It was horrible!"

Henry said, "Don't tell anybody you saw snakes. Tell them you saw angels, and they took you to a place of everlasting fires and torments, where all drunks shall go when they die".

The idea was so novel the old drunk decided to help his nephew start a new religion. He preached against alcohol while tippling every chance he got. According to the story, old Handsome was so fascinated by the new religion that he saw a way of dealing with his critics. According to the nephew, the Christian church burns heretics and witches at the stake. Since the critics didn't believe him they were, therefore, heretics. The first was a woman he charged as a witch, because she had calluses on her hands (from working with a hoe in her garden). Either he forgot or Henry neglected to explain that witchhunters stuck needles into calluses and if the subject suffered no pain, that was her witch mark, and, therefore, she was a witch. Handsome Lake merely said, "You've got calluses, and so you're a witch!" The woman said, "If you did some work in your garden you'd have calluses too". Handsome Lake ordered his followers to kill her, and so buried her in her own garden. Two other critics followed the fate of the first.

The fourth intended victim was to be Red Jacket, the most sarcastic of Handsome Lake's critics. During a chief's council, Handsome Lake had broken out into a sermon and had suddenly become confused. He turned to his nephew Henry, sitting close by. He asked Henry, "What was it the angels said?" Red Jacket, sitting across the house, asked, "If the angels spoke to you, how is it it's your nephew who knows what the angels said?" That earned the death penalty for Red Jacket. The chief's council stepped in and stopped Handsome Lake's elimination of rivals. Red Jacket was the best orator they had ever had, and they weren't about to allow him to be terminated by a boozy prophet. Handsome Lake charged Red Jacket with witchcraft. The chiefs' council was held to hear Red Jacket's defense. Red Jacket spoke for a couple of hours in his own defense, describing how there cannot be any witches, and that even the white man's church no longer burnt witches at the stake, having come to disbelieve such things. There is even a painting of the famous trial by a noted painter of the day showing the council in session and Red Jacket in full regalia defending himself.[6] The Seneca council decided there would be no more executions of witches.

Then came the missing babies case. While working in the fields, the women hung cradleboards on branches of trees cut off for that purpose. A baby turned up missing. The next day another baby disappeared. The next day, a guard cleverly hid himself. There came a shadow through the woods who, looking furtively around, grabbed one of the cradleboards and started off with it. He didn't get far before he was grabbed and over-powered. It was Handsome Lake. They banished him from the Seneca country like they would anyone convicted of murder. He was ostracized everywhere he went. He ended up in Onondaga. They didn't want him there either, but he promised to make them the greatest of the Six Nations if they allowed him to stay. The Onondagas must have been at a low ebb in their self-estimation. Anyway, they had to be pretty naive, hypnotized or drunk to believe that a baby snatcher could make them the greatest of the Six Nations, but the Onondagas allowed him to stay, even let him live in the loft of the longhouse while he worked the miracle of making them the greatest.

He was followed into the woods, where he made friends with snakes, letting them wrap themselves around him. He explained that it was neces-sary to do this to get the power to make them the greatest of the Six

Nations. In between power-making exercises, he would visit the red-light district in nearby Syracuse and arrive back home dizzy and staggering from all the loving cups of joy he had imbibed. In today's language, he was living it up. The longhouse in Onondaga achieved a curious aroma, and while the power maker was absent, one of the men climbed into the loft. The first thing he saw was an arm hanging from a nail on a rafter. Then there were other arms and legs. At the end of the loft was a crate, which was duly noted to contain several squirming snakes. In a sober moment the prophet was confronted for an explanation. The holy power maker reminded them how hard it was to make them the greatest and that he had to do the hardest things to get the power necessary to accomplish his goal and not to worry, he was getting there. Then the power maker became very sick. He had achieved a power dose at the houses of joy in Syracuse that it was his habit to visit. He had all the venerable diseases they had to offer. The poor fellow rotted before he died. No one could go near him. The toughest rolled him in his blanket and carted him to the swamp, where they buried him, hoping the curative mud would stop the diseases from spreading into an epidemic. Then, they burned down the longhouse and built another one, which is now presently known as the "old one". Thus passed away a famous religion maker, time 1815.

Meanwhile, the nephew Henry O'Beale was busy spreading the new gospel. Five years after the death of Handsome Lake, Henry had the Handsome Lake Code completely organized. Copying from the Quaker Code, Henry wrote the Handsome Lake Code complete with the "repentance ritual" which makes it possible to go to heaven after committing the most revolting sins or crimes just by repenting every time. Going along with the peaceful nature of the Quaker Code, Henry instructed his Seneca cousins to bury their weapons and never again to fire them at anyone. The Senecas got caught up in the religious fever, buried their weapons and told the world they'd never fight again. They actually thought the whole world would copy their example. All it did was to encourage the white settlers to pour all over their lands, since it was now safe. The Handsome Lake religious fever spread to some others of the Six Nations. The Tuscarora, already Christian, didn't need another Christian religion to add to the confusion. Some of the Oneidas, Onondagas and Cayugas, being close to the Senecas, got caught up in the frenzy. The Mohawks of Kahnawà:ke, Akwesasne and Kanehsatà:ke had been prisoners of war of the French who converted them by force to Roman Catholicism more than a century before the time of the Handsome Lake Code. In 1716, after four forced migrations, the Mohawks arrived at the present site of Kahnawà:ke. That same year, the Reverend Jesuits decided to move several hundred (dissenters?) to the Lac-des-Deux-Montagnes, where a village called Kanehsatà:ke was established. Starting in 1754 and up to 1759, the Reverend Fathers removed half of the remaining Mohawks seventy-five miles up the river to where the partridge drums and called the new town Akwesasne. We later found out the Mohawks had refused to remain serfs (who work for nothing) and were talking of national independence and sovereignty (sound familiar?). Anyway, the big increase in Mohawk numbers made the French nervous and the Reverend Jesuits felt it was necessary to divide the Mohawks, by then prisoners of war for over a hundred years, to keep them conquered. All the Mohawks should get together again. They divide the people to conquer them. Stands to reason the people should stay together. The free Mohawks living in Mohawk River Valley left the territory in 1783 because of the Revolutionary War. It wasn't until 1922, when they asked to be reinstated in the Six Nations Confederacy, that the Handsome Lake Code arrived at the three divided Mohawk towns. The condoling chiefs from Ohswé:ken made the acceptance of the Handsome Lake Code one of the conditions for being reinstated. Not knowing the facts of the case, the Mohawks of Akwesasne, Kahnawà:ke and Kanehsatà:ke accepted. When it became apparent that the Handsome Lake Code was a violation of the Great Law, the Mohawks of Kahnawà:ke, Kanehsatà:ke and half of Akwesasne repudiated the Handsome Lake code.

Not one of the existing Iroquois nations in 1820 had any idea of the results of accepting the Handsome Lake Code. Present-day followers of the Handsome Lake Code are convinced they have the answer to the problems of the world. Even if the presumed solutions violate some laws in the Iroquois Constitution, also known as the Great Law. They have some well-trained speakers who promote the system they regard as the hope of the future. In all their speeches, they use the Two Row Wampum Treaty as an example of our ancestors' intellect. In that treaty, both the white man and the Red man agreed never to legislate for each other and to keep their laws, governments, religions and customs in their respective vessels, the ship, in the case of the white man, and the canoe, in the case of the Indian. The speakers fail to tell their audiences that Handsome Lake reached into the white man's vessel and took out the white man's religion and adopted it as his own. Doctrines such as hell, devils, angels, purgatory, etc. adopted by Handsome Lake are unprovable Christian beliefs, and until they are proved they shall not be regarded as a knowledge system. They would be better left in the white man's ship, since they never did the white man any good morally or spiritually, only financially and politically. Of course, followers of Handsome Lake may not think that taking the white man's religion out of his ship violates the Two Row Wampum treaty. Also, taking the white man's law as a code means taking "a body of laws of a nation". Since the Handsome Lake Code was copied from the Quaker Code, it is a white man's law. It would be much better if we didn't boast about the Two Row Wampum treaty.

Besides violating the Two Row Wampum treaty, the Handsome Lake Code also violates Wampum 25 and Wampum 58 of the Iroquois Constitution (Great Law). In 1820, the Great Law was not in written form. The people had to hear it recited from the wampums every five years. As a result, they did not know the law. Can anyone around remember anything recited five years ago? Such as 117 articles of law? The promoters (Henry O'Beale and followers) were just as ignorant of the law as the people they were leading down the garden path. The present controversy is a result of ignorance. The Great Law is now in written form, but the leadership of the Handsome Lake Code does not allow the followers to read it. It's a form of induced ignorance.[7]

Wampum 25 of the Great Law provides:

> If a Chief of the League should seek to establish any authority independent of the Jurisdiction of the League of the Great Peace, which is the Five Nations (at the time the law was made), he shall be warned three times in an open council, first by the women relatives, second by the men relatives and finally by the Chiefs of the Nation to which he belongs. If the offending chief is still persistent, he shall be dismissed (deposed) by the War Chief of his nation for refusing to conform to the laws of the Great Peace. His nation shall then install the candidate nominated by the female name holders of his family (clan).

The Handsome Lake Code was established as an authority independent of the jurisdiction of the Great Law. All chiefs who practice the Handsome Lake Code are guilty of the violation of Wampum 25 and can be deposed if they do not heed the three warnings and continue to practice this foreign code.

Wampum 58 of the Great Law provides in part:

A further meaning of this is that if at any time any one of the Chiefs of the League choose to submit to the law of a foreign people, he is no longer in but out of the League, and persons of this class shall be called *they have alienated themselves* (*Tehonatonkóhton*). Likewise, such persons who submit to laws of foreign nations shall forfeit all birthrights and claims of the Five Nations Confederacy and territory.

In submitting to the Handsome Lake Code (law of foreign people), the Six Nations people who are Handsome Lake followers thereby alienate themselves from the Iroquois Confederacy and territory. There is no necessity for the three warnings in this case. The Great Law was created for the people's protection and to keep them together in unity. There must have been a lot of confusion and misunderstanding in Handsome Lake's time. In spite of such wise men as Red Jacket and others, the Handsome Lake Code was able to rend asunder the peaceful unity of the confederacy like no other force has been able to. What wars couldn't do, white man's religion easily did, and it doesn't stop there. It seems that it did not occur to anyone at the time that a serious violation of the Great Law was being committed. That may be due to the fact that the Great Law was recorded in an unwritten language, the wampums. We now see it in written form, so we can point out any law that is being violated. The Handsome Lake promoters were quick with their own law (or taboo), which forbids the reading of the Great Law in its written form. One must wait to hear it recited orally every five years. How can we remember all that the man said? Or did the man remember to say all the laws? It requires a tremendous memory on the part of the reciter and his audience. No wonder the Handsome Lake followers do not know the law! And they are forbidden to read the Great Law. They are also forbidden to mention the name Dekanawida! It looks like a conspiracy to do away with all traces of the Peacemaker and his works. They are only permitted to mention the name of Handsome Lake. Some conspiracy is afoot to put the Iroquois people in a daze and brainwash them into dissolving the great Iroquois Confederacy. They are doing away with the Great Law. It's a forbidden book. They have buried their weapons. They are trying to abolish the war chief and his men (Warrior Society). The followers of the Handsome Lake Code deposed and abolished the centuries-old institution of the war chief. Who's going to depose an errant chief now? They announced that there is no more Warrior Society (the people's power).

It is the duty of all the Iroquois people who are faithful to the Great Law to straighten out the followers of the Handsome Lake Code. It is the duty of the Iroquois people to remove the intruding code, which is usurping the place of the Great Law. To any ideas or fears that the removal of the Handsome Lake Code means the cancellation of all ceremonies and rituals of the longhouse, it must be impressed on the interested parties that these ceremonies and rituals were in existence and in use hundreds of years before the Handsome Lake Code arrived on the scene. The only ritual to give up is the "repentance" ritual, which came with the intruding code and permits that any sin or crimes no matter how grievous can be committed and will be forgiven just by repenting each time. It is an open invitation to any good person to do any evil, since it's so easy to be forgiven. It simply doesn't make sense. In the Mohawk definition of *repent*, it means that the repenter makes the pledge that, as the Creator is his witness, what he did he will never do again. That he keeps repenting shows that he keeps breaking his pledge over and over again. This, of course, is an insult to the Creator, who is his witness. The people are better off without this insulting repentance ritual. The dictionary defines *repent* as *to feel sorry*, without any pledge never to do it again. *Sakatatehriwá:sten* in Mohawk means *I am sorry. Sakatathré:wahte'* means *I repent and pledge never to do it again.* The word *repent* does not mean in Mohawk what it means in English.[8]

Burying the weapons doesn't seem like much of a sacrifice. Peace-minded folks will tell you that the world would know peace if all the world would only bury all its weapons. Peace by peaceful means. Doesn't it seem so logical? In two world wars, they only got peace after killing nine million people in the first and fifty-six million in the second.[9] Why didn't they bury their weapons instead? They'll tell you they couldn't have gotten the peace without the weapons. If there were no weapons, they'd have fought with bare bands, which no doubt they did the first time they came to clash. In any event, it's the strong who get peace. What happens when one or a whole nation buries its weapons? In the case of the Handsome Lake folks, it became easier for the white settlers to take over their lands. Without even thinking about it, the good folks also bury their fighting spirit. What's wrong with that? It seems that the world is such that life is a struggle and one needs fighting spirit to cope with life and life's struggles. A ten-year study was made on the causes of national extinctions, such as those suffered by the classical Greeks, Romans, Phoenicians, Persians and other great civilizations once numbering in the millions and now all gone. The professor came up with four great causes of extinction: 1. loss of language; 2. disregarding the laws that made them great; 3. disregarding the economic system that made them strong and great; 4. doing nothing about their spies and traitors. The greatest single cause was "giving up the struggle". People who gave up the struggle decreased in number, grew weak, died out and became extinct. People who continued to struggle increased in number, grew strong and survived.

To explain these strange acts of life, let's take the Onondagas and the Mohawks as examples. The Onondagas, once more numerous than the Mohawks, accepted the Handsome Lake Code and lost their original Iroquois language, which is still spoken by the Mohawks, and now the Onondagas speak a "dialect", which is said to be "a language reduced to baby talk", have buried their weapons and their fighting spirit and have given up the struggle. Ten years ago, their number was given at nine hundred, and, this year, their number is said to be down to five hundred. The Mohawks still speak the original Iroquois language and did not bury their weapons and fighting spirit. They did not give up the struggle, and their numbers exceed fifty thousand.

To one who is not slated for extinction, it may seem easy to stop the slide to extinction. Not only are the Onondagas decreasing, to reverse the trend, the potential victims would be required to change their lifestyle. They would have to start struggling. The first thing to realize is that the extinct civilizations did not think they were slated for extinction. They did nothing about their decreasing numbers. They did not think they would become extinct. The fact that there were millions of them, and they did, should be a cause for reflection. The writer heard an Onondaga chief say that the Creator will not permit the Indian people to be destroyed. According to him, God will save the Indians. There are extinct Indian nations. God did not save them. God helps those who help themselves. So unless the people themselves do something about their precarious position, they are sure to disappear. The way to save themselves is right there in front of everyone. While it seems easy to one who is not in that precarious position, it may be a monumental task for the potential victims. They shall have to change their lives around. Since the results are worthwhile, let's get right down to it.

The first order of business would be to unbury their weapons and their fighting spirit. Let the people revive their Warrior Society and restore the war chief. Doing this much makes a big difference. There is an immediate lifting of the spirit. The will to live and to regain springs back to life.

> No. 1: relearn the original Iroquois language. The Mohawks still speak it and will be glad to teach it.
>
> No. 2: reactivate and reassert the Great Law. It is the law made for Indians by Indians. The Handsome Lake Code is a law made by white people, for it's a copy of the Quaker Code. Give it back to the Quakers, along with the unreasonable repentance ritual which makes the "repenter" think he can commit the worst evil and get away with it just by repenting.
>
> No. 3: revive the cooperative economic system used by our ancestors and in use today at Ganienkeh.
>
> No. 4: do something about the spies and traitors. They hack away at the very existence of the people, and they are one of the four main causes of the extinction of great civilizations of the past.

The Great Law is the only law in use in Ganienkeh, the only place in America where the Indians have full control and authority. It was established by the Mohawk Warrior Society, which shows what the Warrior Society can do. It shows why the Warrior Societies should be revived by the Indian nations. The Onondagas and other Indian nations in danger of extinction shall have to become like the Mohawks: struggle, fight and win.

The Lessons We Have Learned Up to This Point

1. Our ancestors should have followed Dekanawida's great plan to make all American Indian nations equal in power, voice and authority in the Iroquois Confederacy instead of having an ego-indulging elite group of just five nations lording it over other nations. The Iroquois Confederacy had a chance to create a mighty union of Indian nations in control of all of America, and the European invaders would not have been able to gain a foothold on Red man's land. It is not too late to organize a huge confederacy or republic of Indian nations like that envisioned by Dekanawida, the greatest American. It represents a big challenge to the abilities of the present-day true Americans, the Red race.

2. The ancestors should have made the Great Law more available to be learned and studied so the violations of the law, such as the usurpation of the authority of the Great Law by the white man's Quaker Code, which masqueraded as the Handsome Lake Code, could have been avoided.

3. Every nation on Earth has armed forces for defense and protection. All the nations of the future multinational confederacy shall revive well-trained powerful Warrior Societies, and all war chiefs shall be equal in power and authority. The most important requirements of the people of mankind have been the government, the law, the economic system and religion. Some may place them in a different order.

How About an Indian Republic? (1984 Idea)

To the Indian Nations of North America, Greetings:

The word "unity" has been worked to death. At this stage of our experience with the benedictions from Europe, which are now legislating our national demise and finally carrying out the legal genocide of the Red race, we are now considered to be in a completely weakened state and ripe for extinction.

Let's all of us Indians in America organize. No, I'm not trying to make you laugh! True, the Indians have tried to organize many times in the past. The reason this time is different: the legislatures of Sir Caucasian are deliberating on our national and racial demise. They shall pass an order in council declaring us dead, nationally and racially. They shall declare that we have joined their nations and are no longer legally Indians. They shall proclaim that the Indian race is no more, and that the nations of that race have joined the white race.

There are Indians who want this. They want to commit racial and national suicide. Anyone who commits suicide, whether physical or national, is of unsound mind. He no longer has the instinct of self-preservation for his physical or national life, which is a part of his mental equipment. Those of us who are of sound mind have no wish to become extinct. We wish to see our race live on. We also are of sound mind and have no wish to join another nation or race. Let's strive to be equal to any other race or nation, but not by joining another race. Let us create a Republic of Indian Nations, sovereign and independent, on this great Red man's land of ours. We know that our great ancestor Dekanawida did create a Republic of Indian Nations. He wanted all the Indian nations to be members as equal partners. He was able to gather only five nations in his time. He left the gathering of nations for his successors to continue. They did gather Indian nations, but not as equal partners. Instead, they created an empire of protectorate nations, which was not the aim, purpose and intention of our great founder. Did any empire ever last? The weakness of an empire is in the subject nations. The Iroquois empire went the way of all empires, to destruction. If the subject nations had been given equality what a mighty republic it would be today! The subject nations of the Iroquois protectorate were incited by clever missionaries to attack their protectors. It took a quarter of a century of urging and cajoling to make them take such a drastic step. The Iroquois Confederacy, to save itself, had to fight the people it was protecting. The war lasted more than a hundred years, by which time the protectorate Indian nations had mostly become extinct, the French instigators had lost their land possessions in Canada, and the great Iroquois Confederacy, though reduced and weakened, was still fighting and struggling. Let's not make the same mistake. Let's make a republic of equal Indians nations. All Indians need each other to survive.

The present-day Iroquois Confederacy is no longer a great powerful League of Indian Nations. To compound its weakness, it was conned into accepting the Handsome Lake religion, which features unprovable white man's doctrines, such as hell, devils and other vague mysteries. It also had to bury its weapons in the mistaken, misled and deluded belief that Uncle Sam would protect it. In all treaties, Sir Caucasian always engages to protect the Indian party of the treaty but never really does any protecting. Those are just empty words. The Iroquois ended up having to protect the English colonies. Not all the Six Nations fell for the "burying the weapons" trick. Many centuries before Handsome Lake, there was burying of weapons but only among the five original nations. The occasion was the formation of the Five Nations Confederacy. They pledged never to make war on each other again, but if they were attacked by enemies they would ally themselves to fight together to repel invaders. This latter-day act of "burying the weapons" is different. It's not to stop fighting among themselves but to never fight again, even if attacked. They would allow themselves to be shot down without defending themselves. It's a death wish religion. There's a white man's hand in this business somewhere. No longer needing Iroquois protection, white men now want the Iroquois to be so weak they'll wish and will themselves into oblivion.

The Mohawk Nation has an organized Warrior Society to defend and protect the people. The Oneidas at the thirty-two-acre territory at Oneida, New York, have revived their Warrior Society. The Tuscarora have revived their Warrior Society. The Six Nations people who follow the Handsome Lake Code are not allowed to have a Warrior Society or to fight in self-defense. When asked what they would do if attacked, an Onondaga chief said, "That's when we'll meet our Maker", meaning they'll not even fight to defend their lives. When the Onondagas had trouble on their highway, they had to call up the Mohawks and Tuscarora to do their fighting.[10] Once protectors of nations, they now need protection themselves. The Iroquois have the strongest of the Indian treaties with the United States: "The United States engages never to disturb the people of the Six Nations in the free use and enjoyment thereof [land]".[11] In spite of this treaty, the US went ahead and disturbed the Six Nations people by constructing the Kinzua Dam,[12] as well as making counties of the Seneca Nation land and the US side of Akwesasne, and the people can't put up a fight (besides protesting), because it's against the new Handsome Lake religion, which forbids fighting.

The Mohawk Nation is the most powerful of the Iroquois Confederacy. It has not buried its weapons. With so many Indian nations on the uprise and ready to fight for their lives, their lands and their survival, it is possible for these emerging Indian nations to ally themselves with the Mohawk Nation, the Oneidas and the Tuscarora (others of the Six Nations may want to be involved in this great work, if they can break away from the weakening influence of the Handsome Lake Code) on an equal footing and create a new Republic of Indian Nations. Being of sound mind, the emerging Indian nations did not bury their weapons and can organize their Warrior Societies. An alliance of all Indian nations on an equal basis would have pleased the greatest American, Dekanawida, because that's what he wanted. The founder of the greatest political society ever devised by man, the Iroquois Confederacy, preached peace among all Indian nations through law (the Great Law). He also preached peace through the power achieved by many nations allied together. So let's gather the Indian nations together and make a treaty of alliance among them all. Let all the people of said Indian nations hold the Pledge Wampum and solemnly declare to defend and protect the people of each member nation and pledge to follow and defend the Great Law, the Kaianerehkó:wa, mankind's first and greatest national constitution. It made the Iroquois powerful and great while they followed it. It shall make the new Republic of Indian Nations strong. Indians need power.

It is generally acknowledged that the government devised by Dekanawida is the most practical, intelligent and moral. It's the best guide to follow. It's natural for people to want to change laws and systems only to discover later that the new laws and system they devised are not so good after all. It's best to use a proven system which has stood for ages, such as the Great Law. Wampums 74 to 77 were legislated after Dekanawida was long gone. They begin with: "When any alien nation (no white people were around at the time) or individual is admitted into the League, the admission shall be understood only to be a temporary one". Wampums 74 to 77 are the flaw of the Great Law. They do not reflect the purpose and the intention of the founder Dekanawida and, as before stated, led to the downfall of the Iroquois Empire of Protectorate Nations. The end result is the weakness of the confederacy today.

Whenever the grand council or any individual national council of the Iroquois Confederacy pass an issue or make a decision the people in general regard as a bad decision, harmful and injurious to the nation or nations, the people in general may hold a people's council and decide that the chief's decision should be recalled, and the grand council or the individual nation's council shall be required to reconvene their councils and recall their errant decision and agree with the people's council decision, as, after all, the Iroquois government is a people's government. In order to implement Dekanawida's Plan of a great confederacy of all Indian nations, all equal in power, Wampums 74, 75, 76 and 77 shall have to be revoked by the people's council and stricken from the Great Law and different laws substituted, whereby new member nations shall be admitted and given equality with the other nations. The people's council has the power to do this (or to even depose all the chiefs if necessary). All the new member nations are required to do is to follow the Great Law, which also makes it possible not to have too many laws, which is the universal complaint among nations these days. The government and law of the Great Peacemaker Dekanawida is hereby recommended to any projected Republic of Indian Nations.

The white man says he has the best form of government. He calls it the government of the majority. It has been said that the majority of the world are fools, and that the wise and intelligent are in the minority. This makes the majority government a government of fools. But sez thou: the majority of the world is controlled by a clever minority of oppressive exploiters, which makes the majority government actually a minority government, and so it's a government of both fools and the clever exploiters, with the latter running the show. The standing army is an arm of the government trained to protect and defend the system, not the people. The government uses the people, for the army men are of the people. The government creates laws designed to defend and protect the government from the people, and police departments are established to enforce the laws, again using some of the people whom they first alienated by indoctrination from the other people, to protect the system from them. The exploited people are required to pay taxes in enormous amounts to pay the costs of these institutions, the government, the standing army and the sitting police departments. The white man's majority government is really not a government for all the people but for the super rich who are in control. The same super rich are also in control of the "free world". It seems reasonable to expect a world revolution in the not too distant future.

The Nation's Economy Is Important

The economic system used by the Iroquois was known as the cooperative community system. Everyone shared in the work. They helped each other. Since it was not a competitive system, there was no super rich and no poor. There was no tension, frenzy, panic, envy, jealousy and hate. There was some private enterprise. If the entrepreneur didn't make out, he merely joined the cooperative.

The white man's economic system features the competitive spirit. It is a constant and never-ending struggle to get ahead. There are rich and super rich. The failures in this system find themselves in the streets scrounging in garbage cans for something to eat. Even doctors, lawyers and other professional people have come upon evil times and become street people. It can happen to anyone under capitalism. There is no publicity when a street person dies of starvation. It's a shame on the country's economic system. Millions of people are living in the streets of the richest country on Earth, the US.

The white man has other economic systems, such as communism, where the production and distribution is shared equally by the people. The communist countries were communists for a few years before the fascists stepped in and took over. Fascism is an economic system where the government is the boss of production and distribution. According to the dictionary, *capitalism* means the *economic system in which the means of production and distribution are privately owned and operated for profit.*

Small enterprises are also allowed. When the production and distribution are turned into cash, the government steps in and takes the cash in the form of excessive and exorbitant taxation. Capitalism, then, is fascism in subtle disguise. So, the cooperative economic community is the safest system for Indian nations to use.

What Is the Warrior Society?

The Great Law, the Kaianerehkó:wa, called them the *war chief and his men*. The term *Warrior Society* was supplied by the white man. The term seems to fit nicely. The Great Law has definite functions for the war chief and his men. They are charged with the defense and protection of the people. Their duties take many forms. Keeping the peace, teaching, public speaking, repossessing lost lands and human rights, taking care of confrontations, settling dangerous disputes and international negotiations and doing all kinds of work to promote the welfare of the people.

The Rotiianérshon of the national council are chiefs of peace and are chosen for their wisdom and intelligence to legislate laws and make decisions on political issues. They have to be mild, calm and peaceful types in order to make just laws. It's against the Great Law for a Roiá:ner to participate in a disturbance or conflict, as taking care of such is the function of the war chief and his men. In the event of war, if a Roiá:ner wishes to take part in the struggle, he must first depose himself from the chieftainship in the national council, go in as a simple warrior and take orders from the war chief. After the war is over, if he is physically intact and well, he may resume his duties as a peace chief.

There have been objections by some well-meaning Indians against having a Warrior Society. "There is no war", they say. Nothing could be further from the truth. There has been constant psychological warfare waged against the Natives of America right from the start of the European occupation of the Red man's land, and it's as deadly as the one with guns. It's war against the minds of the people, and the casualties are the drug addicts, drunks and suicides, which are at the highest among the Indians. The Europeans went on an all-out drive to give the Natives an inferiority complex, which destroys the personality of the people. Oppression is an act of war against the people. Legislating the Indians into extinction by way of assimilation is an act of war against the Indians. Legal extermination of the Indians as a distinct people is an act of aggression. Genocide as practiced against the Indians is an act of war, and the Indians must act in self-defense. The answer is the Warrior Society, whose task force is charged with finding ways to protect the people from every form of aggression being waged against them.

The traditional peace chiefs, Rotiianérshon, as well as Canada's Indian Act band council, are not oriented to strife and confrontational violence. They are politicians and not military people. This is why the Great Law has peaceful functions for them. The war chief by nature and training is fit to deal with violence and aggression. The Warrior Society is trained to deal with every kind of emergency, from invasion to childbirth. A modern phenomenon in the Warrior Society is the presence of girls and older women within its ranks. The distaff side has taken to the study of weapons of war and has become expert in their use.

The Warrior Society is actually the power of the people in action. The Indian struggle for survival has many sides. One of the most important is to counteract the psychological warfare inflicted on the Indian people. This calls for talented men and women (yes, women have an important place in the Warrior Society) to speak publicly and write tracts describing the rights of the people and the best ways to fight for survival. It's called propaganda, and it's important in any warfare, psychological or physical. Words of encouragement and pep talks are a big help. There are Indians walking around dazed and confused, suffering from identity conflict as a result of the psychological warfare. To fight any kind of war, one needs courage, gumption, knowledge of the enemy and strategic planning. The biggest single requirement is *fighting spirit*. People with fighting spirit shall not become casualties of psychological warfare. Only 10 percent of any population will actively fight for their rights. How does one acquire fighting spirit? Our ancestors discovered the secret long ago. All their men were great warriors—100 percent. How did they do it? Were they naturally all great warriors, or were they developed? They must have been developed, because, at present, we who inherited their blood are also heir to that 10 percent population fighting spirit. One method that has come down to us is the War Dance. Our ancestors raised the spirit of the people by the War Dance, even of those who did not dance. Since it works, it should be performed at every opportunity. Publicity is another important work of the Warrior Society. Artists have the job of making word and picture posters, signs and billboards giving all kinds of useful information to the general public. Whenever and as often as necessary a press conference should be held to acquaint the general public everywhere with any important developments among Indians, so that any action by Indians shall be clear and understandable to all. Many friends and support groups were made that way.

The Warrior Society is a big entity in the life of an Indian nation, just as an army is important to all other nations of the world. Not having an army is unthinkable to any nation. They would be speedily overcome. In any international dispute, no nation has a chance in negotiations if it hasn't got defense and protection. It would be negotiating from a position of weakness. Likewise, one of these days, Indian nations shall find themselves engaged in a matter of life and death negotiations with white man's governments, and if they have no bargaining power, they're licked right from the start. They shall be forced to make concessions and back down on their demands. The government may even refuse to negotiate. It only negotiates when its peace is in danger. An Indian nation with no Warrior Society presents no threat to the white man's peace. In the negotiations which shall arise and when the survival dispute becomes hot, the Warrior Society is going to be the bargaining power. To have bargaining power, the negotiating nations shall not only have the power to make peace, which anybody can do, even the weakest, since they can do nothing else, but the negotiating nations should also have the ability to destroy the peace of the opposition. That's bargaining power. How can the Warrior Society destroy the peace of any opposing nation no matter how powerful it may be? That's in the realm of strategy not open to discussion here. Nations negotiate to achieve peace—usually only temporary. Hostilities stop for a while. No peace ever lasted forever.

People tell us the only way to peace for Indians is through peaceful means. The Indians are urged to approach the peace-destroying white man with honey-dripping tones to talk to him and make him a better white man and his government a better government. Unknown to each other, all Indian groups have been doing this for the last two hundred years. This is frustrating to the good folks who are doing it the good way, the Creator's way to achieve peace, justice and a good life. It should be so obvious to anyone with a grain of righteousness that peace through peaceful means is the good and only way. But it doesn't work. Why? Who has and enjoys any peace? We have seen that the meek, mild and humble people are the most trampled upon. They don't want to hurt anybody. They don't want any trouble. They are peaceful, but they don't have or enjoy any peace. They do not, cannot and shall not fight back against any injustice or oppression. What a sweet setup for bullies! These same bullies do not bully the strong and fighting people. They may get more than they can give. It's the strong who get any peace. The peace-destroying bullies are only peaceful when the strong are around. The world is that way. Only fear is respected. Fear inspired by the strong.

Indian nations without a Warrior Society are in a weak position. They are also fear-ridden. People in fear are often very vocal and infect others with their fear. Fear is so infectious that there is a record of two Indian nations so fear-ridden that they committed suicide after killing off their young to evade the Spanish who slaughtered twelve million Native Americans in the first twenty years of their "crusade" in America. People in fear inspire no respect, only pity mixed with contempt. They are ripe for extinction, for only those who struggle grow strong and survive. Indians who do not have a Warrior Society and do not struggle decrease in number, die out and become extinct—lessons of history. When an Indian nation revives its Warrior Society, there is an immediate change. The nation immediately feels stronger. Hope for future survival is renewed. Their struggle is no longer weak. Their strength grows every day. This is reflected in their spirit and speech. They become impressive. They soon inspire uncertainty in their oppressors. They then inspire some fear and respect—hence bargaining power. The Warrior Society works closely with the council of Rotiianérshon and has much to negotiate for. The most important is to regain enough land to enable them to live by their own efforts and exercise their own traditional government and society. For example, the land of Kahnawà:ke and the Seigniory is not the extent of the Mohawk land. There are nine million acres in New York State and Vermont. It extends into the Province of Québec from the Canada-US border, up to and including Montréal. All Indians should work to regain whatever they can of their total areas. Indians should strive to achieve a state no less than a *republic*, as the term is defined in the white man's dictionary.

The Procedure of Rebuilding

According to Wampum 59 of the Great Law, the people's council has the most power and the last say. They may thus:

1. Convene the People's Council. Make public the violations of Wampum 25 and Wampum 58 of the Great Law—Handsome Lake Code, a violation of the Great Law. Guilty chiefs should

be deposed and banished along with other people who are also guilty. The guilty can save themselves by declaring solemnly on the Pledge Wampum to defend, protect and follow the Iroquois Constitution (Great Law) and not to ever disobey the Great Law again.

2. The people's council should install and swear in (hold Pledge Wampum) new chiefs who are loyal to the Great Law. Their first act in council should be to repeal Wampums 74 to 77 and to enact new laws permitting new member nations into the Iroquois Confederacy as equal partners, voice and authority, who shall make the necessary pledge on the wampum to follow the Great Law and to defend and protect each and every member nation.

3. The second act in council should be to make the Tuscarora Nation a full partner in the Iroquois Confederacy. Presently it makes up the sixth nation, but because of Wampums 74 to 77 was not given equality.

The above are suggestions by the writer to help out in the work of removing the deplorable conditions and sad state of affairs. May the superior minds in the Six Nations and among other Indian nations come to the fore with more suggestions.

The whole idea must first be presented to the people of the Iroquois Confederacy with the explanation that it was originally the plan of the founder of the confederacy himself, Dekanawida. The plan was diverted after the founder went missing. He did not return with more nations to join the alliance of Indian nations. It is necessary for the people of the Six Nations to revoke Wampums 74 to 77 to open up the Iroquois alliance for other Indian nations to join. There are many things, all important, for all the involved nations to consider, such as the type of government for Indian nations to follow. The system of government devised by Dekanawida himself is the greatest ever made. To fully understand and appreciate the system, the Great Law should often be read completely.

The type of religion to be practiced by the projected huge confederacy of Indian nations is important. It has to be a national religion, for it is a force for unity and national survival. Some Indians are members of various white man's Christian sects. Christianity is an international religion and does not inspire unity and national survival. In two world wars,

Catholics and Protestants slaughtered Catholics and Protestants by the millions—nine million in the World War I and fifty-six million in World War II.[13] *Catholic* means *universal*, so it is international, and not a power for unity and national survival. The Handsome Lake Code being a copy of the white man's Quaker faith is in this category. Anyway, no evidence can be produced to prove the existence of hell, devils, purgatory, etc., etc. If the white man cannot prove what he is saying, then he is not telling the truth. If he is not telling the truth, then he is telling lies.

Dekanawida urged the Indian nations to continue practicing their own national religions, and it is even more necessary for Indians now. Look at the Jews who have survived three thousand years of inhuman persecution and give due credit to their national religion for their survival. Many of them do not believe in any kind of religion but are members of the Jewish religion, because it's a force for unity and survival. Indians should do the same. Join their national religion, even if they don't believe in any kind of religion. It's the most important route to unity and survival. And don't worry about the soul; it cannot suffer, weaken or die. If there is punishment for evil deeds done in this life, then there is no escape by being members of the most exalted religions on Earth. Some of the worst criminals in history were members and even leaders of great religions. They say Hitler was the most terrible human in all history, and he was a Roman Catholic. When it seemed certain he wasn't going to win the war, he was excommunicated by the Church. When it was safe, baby, when it was safe. No one was going to irritate Adolf while he had the most destructive force in the world in his hands. If there is a God up there in heaven, and he can see all and knows all, and you're a good person, what have you got to worry about? Your religion doesn't have to be enormous and fantastically rich to be good. In fact, the fabulous wealth of the world's great churches defeats their own purposes. They're more concerned with garnering "filthy riches" than with garnering filthy sinners.

Since white man's religions are a failure, and the people they have "made better" are no better than they were when white man's religion began, we do now urge all Indians to drop out of white man's churches and return to their own natural national religions. If an Indian nation wishing to join the projected alliance of Indian nations has lost its own national religion and wishes to adopt one, the Mohawks or any of the others would gladly demonstrate the Thanksgiving Festivals, marriage ceremonies, baby naming, funeral rites, etc.

Economic System

The Iroquois, as well as other Indian nations, used the cooperative economic system. The system was copied by the Amish, Mennonites and other groups. They succeeded in developing some well-off and well-run economic communities. These are restrictive religious groups, but there are other cooperative communities in the south that do not practice any religion at all but who are equally as well-off and as well-run as the restrictive religious ones. The "free world" boasts of its democratic capitalist economic system. The US claims to be the richest country of all—the "Breadbasket of the World"—yet, fifty million live at the subsistence level: seven million in Canada. Millions live in the city streets in the US and thousands in Canada. They scrounge in garbage cans for something to eat, while the government dumps shiploads of wheat into the Pacific Ocean— "overproduction". They should dump the wheat on city streets so the street people can make their own bread. It takes only a month of eating nothing to starve to death. When one victim goes, another takes his place. There is no end to this procession of people who failed in this much-vaunted capitalist economic system. We wonder if the communist countries have millions of people starving to death on their city streets. It seems that no matter what type of "ism" the people attach to their government, the fascists take over. In communism, the theory is that the production and distribution is shared equally by all the people. They had that for a few short years, and then the fascists took over. In fascism, the production, distribution and everything else is the special privilege of the government alone. Capitalism permits private ownership of resources, personal profits from business, etc. In capitalist democracy, the government waits until the production and distribution are turned into money to come out and take the money by exorbitant taxation. It's called a quiet and subtle fascism.

Yes, the route to go for Indians is the cooperative economic system which our ancestors followed. It benefits everyone.

The first grand councils were held in the open air, outdoors. In time, they thought of council houses but did not think of a grand council longhouse. It is now time to think of it. It has to be a huge council house that belongs to all the nations, and it has to be large enough to seat the chiefs of a hundred-plus nations and accommodate the people's gallery, so said building must be extendable. To be big, one must think big. The cost of the building should be shared by all the member nations. According to the Great Law, such a council house would have to be in Onondaga Territory, because it's in a central location, with only the grand councils to be held there. All the nations have their own national longhouses to hold their own individual national councils. In the event that for some reason it cannot be built in Onondaga Territory, then a second choice would be Ohswé:ken Territory, which has held Six Nations grand councils for a great number of years. If Ohswé:ken has become unsuitable, then the place where the Great Law is supreme, Ganienkeh Territory, may be agreeable to all.

Let us now leave it all in the hands of the people of the Iroquois Confederacy, the projected hundred-plus nations confederacy of the future.

Notes

1   See Timeline, "1779 Sullivan-Clinton Expedition". It is estimated that the Iroquois lost half of their population in the wake of the American War of Independence.

2   The American War of Independence was practically over when British Army General Cornwallis surrendered, in Yorktown, on October 17, 1781, although it ended officially only with the signature of the Treaty of Paris in 1783.

3   In August 1797, Robert Morris, who was the superintendent of finance of the United States, sent his son Thomas Morris to accompany various government representatives and land-holding businessmen in negotiations that would lead to the Treaty of Big Tree, where the Seneca were forced to relinquish their rights to 3.5 million acres of their traditional homeland and were left with only two hundred thousand acres of land. In 1788, the Phelps and Gorham purchase had already cost the Seneca six million acres of land, half a million acres of which would eventually be purchased by Robert Morris himself.

4   Red Jacket (1756–1830) was a Seneca spokesperson from the Wolf Clan. His talents as an orator were well known, as testified to by his Indigenous name, Segoyewatha, meaning *he keeps them awake*. An intense rivalry emerged between Red Jacket and both Joseph Brant and Cornplanter.

5   Seneca leader Cornplanter (1740–1836) was also known as John O'Beale, sometimes written O'Bail or Abeel—his Indigenous name being Kaiiontwa'kon. By contrast with most Iroquois nations that fought alongside the British, except for the Oneida, Cornplanter's Seneca warriors sided with the Americans during the Revolutionary War, as they would in the War of 1812.

6   John Mix Stanley, *The Trial of Red Jacket*, 1869.

7   See Timeline, "1916 First Published Version of the Kaianerehkó:wa".

8   See "Enskerihwakwatá:ko'", in the "Skakwatakwen—Concept Glossary."

9   Contemporary estimates suggest twenty million deaths during World War I, half of which were civilians, while around sixty million people, including forty-five million civilians, were killed during World War II.

10   See Timeline, "1971 Highway 81 Protest".

11   See Timeline, "1794 Canandaigua Treaty".

12   See Timeline, "1965 Kinzua Dam".

13   See note 9 above.

PART VI
Appendices

———

This section provides tools for understanding the context and meaning of the Indigenous knowledge shared in this book. Spanning over five hundred years of recorded history, the "Mohawk Warrior History Timeline" recounts a selection of landmark events in the evolution of Rotinonhsión:ni resistance, from the first contacts with Europeans to contemporary struggles, bolstering a genealogical understanding of the Warrior Society and providing a chronological narrative of its historical evolution. The "Skakwatakwen—Concept Glossary" suggests English translations and contextualized explanations for the Indigenous words and notions found in this book, as well as other important concepts. This lexicon is based on the explanations provided by Tekarontakeh, whose intricate knowledge of the "old words" of his native tongue is acknowledged throughout the Rotinonhsión:ni Confederacy, indicating alternative etymological interpretations from other native speakers when necessary. This is followed by a list of traditional Rotinonhsión:ni festivals and Native names for the confederacy's nations. Finally, the "Place Names and Peoples' Names" section reveals the geographic location of past and current Rotinonhsión:ni territories, utilizing the Indigenous Mohawk terms for place names, giving an idea as to the extent of the Rotinonhsión:ni's historical presence and alliance networks on the territory. Resisting colonial conceptions of bordered spaces, this map does not delimit these territories into mutually exclusive zones but, rather, shows an open space textured by the topographic and oceanographic features of the land.

Mohawk Warrior History Timeline

Time Immemorial—the Kaianerehkó:wa

According to the story, a bloody war was raging among the five neigh-bouring Iroquoian-speaking nations in ancient times, spearheaded by death-worshipping snake-haired Onondaga chief Thadodáho, the *Entangled*. A man called Dekanawida living in the vicinity of then Wendat Tyendinaga heard about the turmoil ripping Iroquoia apart and under-took to travel there and help his neighbours make peace. Dekanawida was thereafter known as the *Peacemaker*. On his way, he encountered two allies. First, he met Jigonhsasee, *she who is a new face*, a woman who lived along the path where warriors traveled, and who offered them shel-ter regardless of their allegiance. Jigonhsasee imparted to Dekanawida the women's perspective, which led him to entrust women with the crucial roles of both selecting the Rotiianérshon and being caretakers of the land. Second, Dekanawida met a young Kanien'kehá:ka (accord-ing to some, also partly Onondaga) chief, Ayonwentha (Hiawatha), who was experiencing deep grief after losing his wife and daughters during the previously mentioned war. Dekanawida's words of condolence to Hiawatha—inviting him to clear his eyes, ears and throat to overcome his sorrow—would provide the basis for ending the civil war through the establishment of the Kaianerehkó:wa. Together, they all set out to convince the five warring nations to stop their fighting and bundle their arrows together into an unbreakable alliance. After the Kanien'kehá:ka first joined the peace, all the other Iroquois nations accepted it, until only the Onondaga and their leader Thadodáho were left to convince. Thadodáho was told that if he joined the alliance, he would become the Rotinonhsión:ni Confederacy's great chief, vested with the privilege of hosting grand councils in Onondaga, and would have a final say in any decision. However, this privilege was annulled by the fact that for a decision to be made a strict consensus had to be reached between each and every one of the forty-nine matrilineal families represented by their Rotiianérshon. Hiawatha combed the snakes out of Thadodáho hair, and words of condolence were spoken to allow him to overcome his anger. Distributing the Rotiianérshon within the longhouse between three sides—the elder brothers, the younger brothers and the firekeepers—the Kaianerehkó:wa became an intricate system of decentralized and consensual decision-making protocols, comprising 117 articles enclosed in wampum belts. The women retained a powerful role in this system, as they both selected the Rotiianérshon and could depose them with the help of the warriors if they were found to be violating the Kaianerehkó:wa. Their constitution allowed the Rotinonhsión:ni to become a powerful confederacy, extending the rafters of its never-ending longhouse to all nations who desired to join their alliance.

1534—First Contact between French and Iroquoian Peoples

During his first voyage into the Saint Lawrence River Valley, French explorer Jacques Cartier met the Saint Lawrence Iroquoians and Stadacona (Québec City) chief Donnacona, whose traditional medicine rescued Cartier's crew from scurvy. Ignoring Donnacona's warnings, Cartier pushed further downstream to an Iroquoian village he understood to be "Hochelaga", where today stands so-called Montréal. Cartier reacted to Donnacona's discontent by capturing ten prisoners, including Donnacona and his sons, bringing them to meet King François I, in France. Donnacona and the other Iroquoian captives died in Europe.

1603—Samuel de Champlain

Nearly seventy years after Jacques Cartier, a second French explorer, Samuel de Champlain, entered the Saint Lawrence River. The previous Iroquoian inhabitants of what would become Montréal were no longer there. Historians often suggest that these original inhabitants were not related to the actual Iroquois Confederacy, but Indigenous oral tradition suggests that the Saint Lawrence Iroquoians had simply temporarily moved to other parts of their territory, in accordance with the semi-sedentary ecological patterns practiced in this region, where villages were abandoned every fifteen to thirty years to let the land replenish, before returning a few generations later.

1608—Establishment of Québec City

Samuel de Champlain established the French settlement of Québec.

1609—Samuel de Champlain Kills Iroquois Chiefs

Accompanying Wendat, Innu and Anishinaabe warriors down the Richelieu River, Samuel de Champlain stumbled on an Iroquois party and fired his arquebus at them, killing at least three chiefs. French-Iroquois relations never recovered from the violence of this first encounter.

1613—Two Row Wampum

First exchanged with Dutch settlers in the early seventeenth century, the Teiohá:te wampum belt displays two parallel purple lines on a white background, symbolizing a river where the Indigenous people's canoe and the settler people's ship sail side by side. As an alliance belt, it suggests that both parties can only advance in the same direction if they refrain from encroaching on each other's path—thus, precluding both assimilation policies and cultural appropriation. It requests that the Europeans keep their culture, language and laws aboard their own ship, which is said to be docked to Turtle Island through a hemp chain (and later, an iron chain for the French, a silver one for the British and a gold one for the Americans). In this sense, the Teiohá:te allowed Europeans to stay in the waterways, provided they did not take roots on the land. Yet the Kaianerehkó:wa people also consider the Teiohá:te to be a wider diplomatic principle, understood as the "law of the land", applying beyond relations with settlers to relations between and among Indigenous nations, genders, social groups and even non-human beings. Advocating reciprocity and respect of difference in all relationships, this law of the land was extended to Europeans when they were first encountered. Although its date is contested by some historians, the 1613 Tawagonchi Treaty between the Rotinonhsión:ni and Dutch merchant Jacob Eelckens is often considered as the origin of the Teiohá:te.

1640–1701—The Beaver Wars

Beginning in the 1640s, war broke between the French—alongside their Anishinaabe, Wendat (Huron) and other Indigenous allies—and the Rotinonhsión:ni, backed by the English, to gain control of the beaver pelt trade routes connecting the Great Lakes to the Saint Lawrence and Hudson River Valleys. In addition to economic motives, demographic losses due to war and epidemics within Indigenous communities were also a determinant factor in what historians called the "mourning wars", where captives were taken back to communities to replace deceased family members. The large scale of these adoptions, integrating thousands of captives into Rotinonhsión:ni society, transformed many of their villages into multinational settlements: Jesuit Gabriel Lalemant estimated that only 20 percent of their inhabitants were of Iroquois origin in 1660, while Paul Le Jeune counted no less than eleven ethnic groups in Seneca villages. Within the course of a few years, adoptees would become equally fervent Rotinonhsión:ni warriors, taking back captives in their turn, while also bolstering the confederacy's diplomatic capacity with their new cultural input. Some peoples, like the Wendat, were almost entirely wiped out during these wars, as large portions of their population were absorbed by the Rotinonhsión:ni.

1642—Establishment of Montréal
Paul Chomedey de Maisonneuve established Ville-Marie, which would become Montréal, as a provocation against the Rotinonhsión:ni, whose presence in the Saint Lawrence and Ottawa River Valleys was threatening French occupation. Maisonneuve wanted to establish a utopian town where the French would live alongside Christianized Indigenous inhabitants, thus securing the latter's support.

1645—Kiotsaeton Truce
Mohawk leader Kiotsaeton traveled to Trois-Rivières, then the largest commercial outpost in North America, to propose a peace treaty with the French. Standing on the prow of the French ship which escorted him, his body entirely covered in wampum, Kiotsaeton delivered a powerful speech on behalf of the Rotinonhsión:ni league, metaphorically proposing to clear the rocks and obstacles in the Saint Lawrence River to allow free passage between French settlements and Rotinonhsión:ni territories. Kiotsaeton's peace proposal was short-lived, however, as the Rotinonhsión:ni soon discovered that the French had secretly been mapping extant routes to Iroquoia, proving their invasive intentions.

1650–1660—Wendat Dispersion and Integration
Speaking an Iroquoian language and sharing many traditions with the Iroquois, such as building longhouses, the Wendat mainly lived along

the north shores of Lake Ontario and near the Georgian Bay. As their French allies would only give guns to the Wendat if they converted to Christianity, they were bound to suffer important losses when the Rotinonhsión:ni launched a thousand-man-strong attack on them on March 16, 1659. Dispersed from their homeland, many Wendat were sheltered in French Catholic missions, including on the Island of Orleans near Québec City. The Rotinonhsión:ni, and particularly the Mohawks and the Onondaga, approached them, proposing to integrate them into their confederacy and promising to build new homes in their territories to welcome them. Many Wendat accepted the proposal, bolstered the ranks of the Rotinonhsión:ni with their people and added the fresh cultural perspective of the Wendat to that of the Rotinonhsión:ni. Most Wendats adoptees continued to nurture diplomatic relationships with their former kin, as adoption (including of Iroquois captives) was also widespread in their own culture. During the second half of the seventeenth century, Iroquois diplomacy led to a significant expansion of the confederacy's alliance networks. New Rotinonhsión:ni settlements were established on the north shore of Lake Ontario to circumvent French influence in the region. Wenrehronon, Eriechronon, Chonnonton and Shaawanwak territories were conquered, as the Rotinonhsión:ni pushed against the Illiniwek in the west. According to Paul Le Jeune, the Iroquois tongue was understood no less than 1,200 miles away from their homelands, becoming a diplomatic lingua franca of sorts. Iroquois expansion through both diplomatic and military means compelled the French to accept peace in 1701.

1664—New Amsterdam Becomes New York

Without any bloodshed, the colony of New Netherlands surrendered its territory to the English, who threatened them with an impressive armada at the gates of New Amsterdam, thereafter known as New York.

1666—Carignan-Salières Campaign

As Iroquois raids on French and Native allied settlements were successfully securing Rotinonhsión:ni control over the fur trade corridors from the Great Lakes to the Hudson River Valley, the French began conspiring to retaliate against them. In 1665, the French King Louis XIV sent 1,200 fresh troops from the Carignan-Salières Regiment to help the French colony reassert its control over the region. Lieutenant General Alexandre de Prouville (Marquis de Tracy), the Governor de Courcelle, and Jean Talon, the intendant of justice, police and finance were sent to New France on the same boat, which disembarked on September 12, 1665. In the harsh winter of 1666, the first expedition led by de Courcelle failed, as the French were forced to withdraw, outnumbered by the Iroquois. On September 30, 1666, the Marquis de Tracy tried again to lead the Carignan-Salières Regiment into the Mohawk River Valley. Even though the Mohawk had already strategically retreated from their villages, de Tracy adopted a scorched earth policy and burnt all dwellings and crops that could be found, seizing the empty villages in the name of the king of France. This led the Iroquois to sue for peace, and after the treaties signed with the Senecas in May and with the Oneida in July, a third treaty was signed in 1667, allowing French missionaries to move into Iroquois villages.

1667—Establishment of Ken'tà:ke/Kahnawà:ke and Kanehsatà:ke/ La Montagne

The costly Carignan-Salières campaign was followed by a peace treaty between the French and the Iroquois, which would last until the 1680s. Its terms provided for the establishment of the Jesuit Catholic mission of Ken'tà:ke—in present-day La Prairie, on the south shore of Montréal— which welcomed Rotinonhsión:ni families as early as 1667. After several relocations upstream on the Saint Lawrence River (in 1676, 1690, 1696 and 1716), partially because of the erosion of the soil, Ken'tà:ke became *Kahnawà:ke*, meaning *at the rapids*, using the same name as Gandaouagué in the Mohawk River Valley. The French considered these new Catholic Iroquois communities in the Saint Lawrence River Valley as their allies, but, in reality, these communities kept close ties with the Rotinonhsión:ni Confederacy, with whom they exchanged vital intelligence on upcoming raids and collaborated militarily by refusing to attack each other. French Sulpician priests established a new Catholic mission near Mount Royal (in present-day Montréal) and the French settlement of Ville-Marie. At first, a multi-ethnic mission which included many Wendat and Anishinaabe people, this settlement, which became known as Kanehsatà:ke, slowly became predominantly Rotinonhsión:ni. In 1721, Kanehsatà:ke was relocated to the north shore of Montréal, on the Lac-des-Deux-Montagnes, where it still exists today, while two turrets dating from the original Catholic mission of La Montagne are still visible on Sherbrooke Street, in present-day Montréal.

1675–1678—King Philip's War

Fifty-five years after the first English colonists disembarked from the *Mayflower*, their colony of Plymouth would become the site of one of the deadliest wars in the colonial history of North America. While his father Messasoit had nurtured good relations with the *Mayflower* pilgrims, things quickly deteriorated when his son Metacom (called King Philip by the colonists) became the chief of the Wôpanâak (Wampanoag). Colonists regularly violated their alliance, confiscating the Wôpanâak's guns and hanging three of them in 1675. In response to Wôpanâak raids on settler homesteads, New England colonies mustered 1,000 militiamen and 150 Native allies to attack the Nahahiganseck (Narragansett), who had given shelter to their Wôpanâak neighbours, killing 600 Natives in the Great Swamp Fight of December 1675. After Metacom was killed by militiamen on August 12, 1676, the Wôpanâak were defeated, their land confiscated and many of them were enslaved by New England colonists.

1677—The Lenape and Susquehannock Integrate the Rotinonhsión:ni

Peace with the French allowed the Rotinonhsión:ni to concentrate their war efforts southward, fighting their Andastoerrhonon (Susquehannock) neighbours, who were supported by the then English colony of Maryland. As their warriors had dwindled down to a few hundred individuals, the Andastoerrhonon were compelled to surrender to the Iroquois and were included in a Covenant Chain treaty that was reached between the Rotinonhsión:ni and the colonies of Virginia and Maryland. Many Andastoerrhonon resettled among the Mohawks and Oneida, while their own allies, which included the Leni Lenape (Delaware), became tributaries to the Rotinonhsión:ni Confederacy—remaining so until 1753. Although they did not have an equal voice in the confederacy, many individuals from tributary nations eventually became prominent leaders, some even rising to the position of war chief.

1684–La Famine

When the Rotinonhsión:ni were at war with the Illiniwek (Illinois) peoples, taking several hundred captives in 1682, the Illiniwek's French allies decided to retaliate by attacking the Onondaga. However, French governor Antoine Lefèbvre de La Barre's 1684 expedition ended in complete failure, as his soldiers got sick with what is thought to have been a form of influenza as they were traveling to Onondaga. In the ironically named camp of La Famine, on the south shore of Lake Ontario, La Barre had to accept humiliating terms of surrender to Onondaga leader Otreouti (also known by the French as La Grangula—the big mouth), known for his rejection both of French and English hegemony. Nevertheless, La Barre's successor, Jacques-René de Brisay de Denonville, would not abandon the project of invading Iroquoia, writing to the French king that the only option for the survival of New France was "the extermination of the Iroquois".

1687—Denonville's Raid

After the failed 1666 and 1684 raids, the French tried once again to invade Rotinonhsión:ni territory, now targeting the Seneca, whose diplomatic efforts in the Great Lakes region threatened French trade networks. Denonville led more than two thousand French, Canadian and Indigenous troops into Iroquoia. But, as in 1666, Denonville's army, finding already empty villages, resolved to burn them along with the surrounding crops, pillaging graves to steal interred goods and erecting Louis XIV's coats of arms at the entrance of the pre-emptively deserted villages.

1689—Mohawk Raid on Lachine

Following Denonville's incursion into Seneca territory, the French were forced to abandon their western outposts, including Fort Frontenac, which was besieged by the Rotinonhsión:ni. On the morning of August 9, 1689, 1,500 Mohawk warriors took the French by surprise by attacking the settlement of Lachine, near Montréal, killing and capturing at least eighty French settlers. Tensions were high, as the War of the League of Augsburg (1688–1697), a conflict mainly opposing France to the Hapsburg-controlled Holy Roman Empire, which is often cited as the first global war, pushed the English and the French to resume their hostilities in North America. As the French set out to attack the English colony of Albany in January 1690, their Kahnawà:ke and Kanehsatà:ke allies successfully deflected the French raid at Schenectady in order to save the lives of Mohawks living farther south in Albany.

1693—French Raid on Mohawk Country

The French invaded Iroquoia once again, as 625 soldiers led by Governor Louis de Buade, Comte de Frontenac et de Palluau, commonly known as Frontenac, penetrated Mohawk country, burning the towns of Gandaouagué, Canajoharie and Tionondogen. The English, who had known that the invasion was going to happen, failed to inform the Mohawks of the incoming danger. Yet neither the French nor the English knew that at the same time Rotinonhsión:ni delegates were visiting the French's Anishinaabe allies in the Great Lakes to negotiate a separate peace, agreeing to share hunting grounds and trade routes following the principle of "one dish, one spoon".

1696—French Raid on Onondaga

Seeking to circumvent the Rotinonhsión:ni's increasingly successful diplomatic efforts with Anishinaabe peoples around the Great Lakes, French governor Frontenac attempted another incursion into Iroquoia. Yet when his 2,150-man expedition reached the biggest Onondaga village, it was empty. Even though the Oneida had agreed to join the alliance with the French and the Iroquois who were living in Catholic missions around Montréal, a detachment led by Philippe de Rigaud de Vaudreuil was sent to Oneida on the same occasion, destroying all villages and fields on its way.

1697—Treaty of Ryswick

Even though the September 1697 Treaty of Ryswick ended the war between France and England in Europe, the treaty did not include the Iroquois, and the fighting between North American Indigenous nations continued.

1701—Great Peace of Montréal

Despite English efforts at blocking the Iroquois from negotiating their own peace treaty with France, the Rotinonhsión:ni's intensive efforts to secure peace with France's Indigenous allies in the previous decades finally bore fruit. Stopping in Kahnawà:ke on their way, delegates from the Rotinonhsión:ni Confederacy (except the Mohawks, whose represent-atives would arrive later) arrived in Montréal in July 1701 to meet French colonial representatives and more than 1,300 delegates from thirty-nine Indigenous nations to make peace, at a time when Montréal counted only 1,200 inhabitants. Featuring exchanges of prisoners of war and material goods, the peace conference established that the Rotinonhsión:ni would remain neutral if war was to ever break out again between France and England—although the latter were not informed of this decision. The peace talks also allowed the French to build a new western trading post in

Detroit, in exchange for the promise that the Rotinonhsión:ni could freely circulate within and beyond French outposts. The principle under which the peace was concluded was the "one dish, one spoon" tradition shared between both Rotinonhsión:ni and Anishinaabe peoples, which implies an agreement to share hunting grounds across nations. The fifty-seventh Kaión:ni, or wampum, of the Kaianerehkó:wa states that the confederacy chiefs "shall eat together from one bowl the feast of cooked beaver's tail. While they are eating, they are to use no sharp utensils, for if they were to accidentally cut one another bloodshed would follow".

1704—Deerfield Raid

On February 9, 1704, during Queen Anne's War (1701–1713), French troops, accompanied by Wabanaki, Pocumtuc and Saint Lawrence River Valley Iroquois warriors, raided the English settlement of Deerfield, in Massachusetts, killing 47 colonists and taking 112 captives to Montréal. Some died on the way, others were ransomed back to their families, but some were also adopted by the Saint Lawrence River Valley Mohawks, including Eunice Williams, the daughter of Reverend John Williams, who chose to stay with her adopters in spite of her father's attempts to repatriate her. Reverend Williams's account of his own captivity, *The Redeemed Captive*, was widely read when it was published in 1707.

1721—Kanehsatà:ke Moves to the North Shore of Montréal

Most Rotinonhsión:ni and Anishinaabe residents of La Montagne Catholic mission on the island of Montréal moved to a new location on the Lac-des-Deux-Montagnes, where Kanehsatà:ke still sits today. Some of its Anishinaabe, Nipissing and other non-Rotinonhsión:ni inhabitants would stay in Kanehsatà:ke for only a few weeks each year, spending most of their time hunting in the woods. They would end up migrating north towards the Ottawa River Watershed during the nineteenth century.

1722—The Tuscarora Integrate into the Rotinonhsión:ni

The Iroquoian-speaking Tuscarora people had to leave their homeland in present-day North Carolina after being attacked by English colonists in the 1711–1713 war. Taking refuge in Pennsylvania, they formally requested to join the Rotinonhsión:ni Confederacy, which welcomed them as "younger brothers" sponsored by the Oneida. Thereafter, the Five Nations Confederacy became the Six Nations Confederacy.

1754–1763—French and Indian War/Seven Years' War

As an overseas extension of the Seven Years' War raging in Europe, the French and Indian War pitted British colonies against French colonies, along with their respective Indigenous allies on Turtle Island. The neutrality which the Rotinonhsión:ni had generally observed since the Great Peace of Montréal of 1701 crumbled under the pressure of war. Most Rotinonhsión:ni nations allied with the British, save for Oneida and Seneca factions, while the French fought alongside Anishinaabe and Wendat warriors from the Great Lakes and Ohio country. The North American war ended in 1760, following the battle of the Plains of Abraham in Québec City and British General Amherst's conquest of Montréal, but the fighting continued in Europe until the signature of the Treaty of Paris in 1763. With the French driven out of the northeastern part of the continent, the Iroquois could no longer take advantage of colonial rivalries and had to deal with a single colonizer.

1755—Establishment of Akwesasne

In the mid-1750s, about thirty Rotinonhsión:ni families left Kahnawà:ke, where available lands were getting scarce, and migrated seventy miles upstream to a new location along the Saint Lawrence River. Led by John and Zachariah Tarbell, two brothers whose father was an English colonist who had been adopted by the Iroquois in 1707, the Saint Regis Mission of Akwesasne was officially established by French Jesuits in 1755.

1763—The Royal Proclamation

After winning the war against France, George III, the king of Great Britain, feared that Indigenous nations in the west, who were used to dealing with the French, would form a coalition against the British. The Royal Proclamation of 1763 sought to stabilize the relationship between the British Crown and Indigenous nations by formally forbidding colonists from establishing new settlements on the western side of the Appalachian Mountains, considered "Indian territory".

1763–1766—Pontiac's War

After the French and Indian War, British general Jeffery Amherst, known for despising Indigenous peoples, drastically cut back the gifts which the French customarily distributed to Indigenous nations in the west to secure their allegiance, also restricting the sale of firearms and ammunition to Indigenous peoples. Inspired by Lenape (Delaware) spiritual leader Neolin, who prophesied that traditional Indigenous lifestyles would be integrally restored, Odaawaa leader Pontiac created a confederacy regrouping many Indigenous nations around the Great Lakes to drive the British out of the region. Pontiac's warriors seized eight British forts and besieged Fort Detroit and Fort Pitt—where Amherst famously distributed blankets infected with smallpox to spread disease among his Indigenous enemies. British superintendent of Indian affairs William Johnson, who had built his personal mansion in the Mohawk River Valley, had married Molly Brant, the sister of Mohawk leader Joseph Brant, and spent a fortune on gifts for the Rotinonhsión:ni, to make sure that they would not join Pontiac. However, the Seneca keepers of the Rotinonhsión:ni's western door, especially the Mingo Seneca, who had recently migrated to Ohio Country, played a key role in Pontiac's alliance. The insurrection ended in a stalemate, as both parties stood their ground on opposite sides of the Mississippi River. However, the conflict compelled the British to seek stability with western Indigenous nations by limiting the encroachment of British settlers beyond the Appalachian Mountains, much to the settlers' discontent.

1768—Fort Stanwix Treaty

The Fort Stanwix Treaty was signed in 1768, near Rome, New York, between Rotinonhsión:ni chiefs and the British superintendent of Indian affairs William Johnson. As English businessmen were filing compensation claims for the financial losses they sustained due to Pontiac's War, new lands in the west were still being obtained by them for the purposes of financial speculation. More than three thousand participants attended these financial recompensation proceedings, lured by Johnson's reputation for generously distributing gifts. Fraudulently pretending that the attending Rotinonhsión:ni chiefs were landlords over regions that they did not control, Johnson convinced them to relinquish Lenape and Shaawanwaki (Shawnee) lands in Ohio and Kentucky, pushing the boundaries for colonization set by the 1763 Royal Proclamation further west, to the Ohio River. Although individuals from each of the five nations had signed the treaty, the Rotinonhsión:ni Confederacy refused to ratify it, and the Indigenous inhabitants of the concerned regions never recognized its validity.

1773—Boston Tea Party

Disguised as Rotinonhsión:ni warriors, wearing war paint and feathers and chanting war whoops, American patriots and members of the Sons of Liberty dumped tea in the Boston Harbor on December 16, 1773, an event later considered by many historians to be the beginning of the American Revolution.

1775–1783—American War of Independence

More than the French and Indian War, which split the Rotinonhsión:ni nominally but did not result in many fratricidal battles, the American War of Independence caused deep divisions and bloodshed, as most Tuscarora and Oneida communities sided with the Americans, while the other nations joined the British, notably led by Joseph Brant.

1779—Sullivan-Clinton Expedition

In response to the British and Rotinonhsión:ni attacks on American forts and settlements in the west of New York State, the Sullivan-Clinton Expedition raided Iroquoia in 1779, following George Washington's orders that "the country may not be merely overrun, but destroyed". The American troops destroyed forty Rotinonhsión:ni villages in the Finger Lakes Region of New York State. More than five thousand Rotinonhsión:ni escaped to Canada via Fort Niagara. Some resettled around the Bay of Quinte, in Ontario (Tyendinaga) and others at Grand River, also in Ontario (Six Nations of the Grand River, or Ohswé:ken). The central council fire of the confederacy was temporarily transferred from Onondaga to the Seneca village of Buffalo Creek, before moving back to Onondaga, while Rotinonhsión:ni exiled to Canada rekindled a second council fire in Ohswé:ken—a division between two Rotinonhsión:ni Confederacy fires that still exists today.

1784—Haldimand Proclamation

On October 25, 1784, the British governor of the Province of Québec, Frederick Haldimand, allocated 550,000 acres of Mississauga land to Rotinonhsión:ni refugees from the American War of Independence. One thousand eight hundred Mohawks, Cayugas, Onondagas, Lenape, Yesañ (Tutelos) and Tuscaroras moved into this new settlement, Six Nations of the Grand River, near Brantford, Ontario. Even though the "Deed of Gift" originally stipulated that the land could not be sold to British subjects, Mohawk leader Joseph Brant, who had close ties to William Johnson, and whom

Haldimand described as the most "civilized" of all Indians, proceeded to lease and sell large portions of the tract to white settlers and loyalist soldiers. In 1798, the sales were ratified by the British Crown, and the Rotinonhsión:ni lost 380,000 acres of the tract. Joseph Brant used the proceeds from these land transfers to agriculturally modernize Iroquois society and make it competitive in the colonial world, even if it involved acculturation.

1794—Canandaigua Treaty

Signed on November 11, 1794, by fifty Six Nations chiefs and Timothy Pickering, representing George Washington, this treaty formally put an end to the war between the United States and the Rotinonhsión:ni Confederacy. The treaty acknowledged the sovereignty of the Oneida and the remaining Seneca territories in New York State, promising that no settler would be allowed to "claim or disturb" their lands. However, the provisions of this treaty would largely be ignored by the following American governments, and the encroachment of settlers into Rotinonhsión:ni territory would progress steadily throughout the nineteenth century.

1794—Northwest Indian War and Jay Treaty

Signed on November 19, 1794, between the British Crown and the United States of America, the Treaty of Amity, Commerce and Navigation, commonly called the Jay Treaty, stated that the Indigenous peoples whose territory straddled the newly designated border between Canada and the United States of America could cross it freely and could live or conduct trade on either side of the border without being subject to tariffs and border controls. The Jay Treaty put an end to the Northwest Indian War that had been raging since 1785, during which Americans had suffered major defeats against the British-backed "Northwestern Confederacy", which had included Rotinonhsión:ni, Wendat, Shaawanwaki, Lenape, Myaamiaki (Miami), Anishinaabe, Bodéwadmi (Potawatomi), Odaawaa, Ojibwa and other Indigenous groups, until it was defeated by American general "Mad Anthony" Wayne's Legion of the United States during the Battle of Fallen Timbers in 1794.

1796—Seven Nations of Canada

Although there is no documented record of its existence before the mid–eighteenth century, the transnational coalition of Indigenous villages in the Saint Lawrence River Valley known as the Seven Nations of Canada, or

Tsiatak Nihononhwentsá:ke, or Seven Lands, may have taken shape at the turn of the seventeenth to the eighteenth century. The alliance included the Rotinonhsión:ni territories of Akwesasne, Kanehsatà:ke, Kahnawà:ke and Oswegatchie (established in 1749), the Wabanaki villages of Odanak and Wolinak, and the Wendats village of Lorette. Even though their central fire was in Kahnawà:ke, and the Wendats of Lorette had a special status as the "uncles" of the alliance, each village was independent and had its own fire. The French were also allied with the Three Fires Confederacy, regrouping Anishinaabe people living on the north side of the Great Lakes and the Saint Lawrence River, who were in turn allies of the Seven Nations. Diplomatic negotiations between the French and the Three Fires Confederacy were managed by the Anishinaabe of Kanehsatà:ke, while negotiations with the Iroquois Confederacy were handled by the Mohawks of Kahnawà:ke. Although the Seven Nations of Canada were initially allied with the French, their Rotinonhsión:ni members were often reluctant to attack their Iroquois Confederacy kin allied with the British. After the capitulation of the French in Montréal during the French and Indian War, the Great Peace of 1760 officially "buried the hatchet" between the Seven Nations of Canada and the Six Nations Confederacy. On May 31, 1796, the Seven Nations of Canada signed the Treaty of New York with the United States, abandoning all claims to lands in New York State in exchange for monetary compensation. Thereafter, the Seven Nations of Canada would fight alongside the British in conflicts with the Americans, notably during the War of 1812, before it dissolved in the 1860s.

1799—Handsome Lake

Handsome Lake (1735–1815), or Sganyodaiyo, the half-brother of Seneca war chief Cornplanter, was a Seneca religious leader whose 1799 visions, following a depression caused by alcohol, created a new "longhouse religion", mixing Christianity with some elements of traditional Rotinonhsión:ni spirituality. Along with prohibiting drinking and introducing Christian practices, including the confession of sins, Handsome Lake's religion shifted away from the matrilineal economic and political structure of Iroquois society, notably leading to violent witch-hunts against powerful matrons. Insisting, like Joseph Brant, on the necessity of adopting farming instead of hunting, Handsome Lake's ideas were endorsed by President Thomas Jefferson, who saw his religion as a promising sign that Indigenous peoples could eventually make progress towards adopting European lifestyles.

1812–1813—Tecumseh's War

As Pontiac's insurrection fed from the ideas of Neolin, Shaawanwaki leader Tecumseh was inspired by the visions of his brother Tenskwatawa, "the Prophet", who envisioned the downfall of the European way of life on Turtle Island. After fighting against the governor of the Indiana Territory and future president William Henry Harrison during the battle of Fallen Timbers, Tecumseh was shocked by the 1809 Fort Wayne Treaty, in which Harrison got Myaamiaki, Bodéwadmi and Lenape chiefs to surrender three million acres of their land. In response, Tecumseh formed a large coalition of Indigenous nations in the west—including Bodéwadmi, Anishinaabe, Myaamiaki, Shaawanwaki, Odaawaa, Lenape, Dakota, Peeyankihšia (Piankashaw), Ho-Chunk (Winnebago), Othâkîwa (Sauk), Meskwaki (Fox), Kiikaapoa (Kickapoo), Wendat (Huron), Mamaceqtaw (Menominee) and Rotinonhsión:ni warriors—to drive the Americans out of the region. Based in Prophetstown, which attracted no less than three thousand inhabitants after it was established by Tecumseh and his brother at the forks of the Wabash and Tippecanoe rivers, the Indigenous coalition led several raids against encroaching settlers. Tecumseh also traveled south to exhort the Creek—called *Red Sticks* in reference to their two-foot-long war clubs—to resist against the young Georgia State. They were successful until General Andrew Jackson drove them out of their land, forcing them to surrender twenty-one million acres of land in 1814 and to march west on the infamous "Trail of Tears". On November 7, 1811, Harrison took advantage of Tecumseh's absence to attack Prophetstown, which was burnt to the ground after the defeat of Tenskwatawa's warriors at the Battle of Tippecanoe. Tecumseh would continue fighting the Americans by joining the British during the War of 1812, until dying in 1813 during the Battle of the Thames, as the Americans took back control of Detroit from British forces.

1812–1815—War of 1812

As the British were busy fighting Napoleon in Europe, the United States declared war on Great Britain, endeavoring to invade Canada. Most Rotinonhsión:ni living in Canada were compelled to abandon their neutrality to defend their lands against the American invasion. Mohawk warriors notably played an important role during the Battle of Châteauguay in 1813, repelling the much larger American force marching towards Montréal. Another important episode was the Battle of Beaver

Dams, where a Canadian woman, Laura Secord, famously walked twenty miles in the woods to inform Mohawk warriors that the Americans were going to attack. On Christmas Eve, 1814, after the British had imposed a naval blockade and burnt most American government buildings in Washington, the Treaty of Ghent put an end to the war. Both sides considered that they had won the war, and practically no territorial concessions were made.

1828—Mohawk Institute

The Anglican Church opened the Mohawk Institute in 1828, in Brantford, Ontario, near Six Nations of the Grand River. It became Canada's first residential school. In 1834, girls would also be admitted to the school, which would come to be considered a model for assimilating Indigenous people into Euro-Canadian culture. According to the Bagot Commission (1842–1844), the best way for this forcible assimilation to be achieved was to separate Indigenous children from their parents and forbid them to speak their language and practice their culture.

1851—Lewis Henry Morgan

Lawyer Lewis Henry Morgan published what many consider the first book of anthropology, the *League of the Hau-de-no-sau-nee*, in 1851. Fascinated with the Iroquois, Morgan had created a secret society, the Gordian Knot, which sought to establish a specifically American culture by mimicking Indigenous traditions, even though Morgan thought that it was inevitable that Indigenous peoples would be assimilated into European society. This book, which inspired Friedrich Engels's conception of "primitive communism", relied on information Morgan received from Seneca Ely S. Parker, a descendant of Handsome Lake—thus marking the origin of a longstanding conflation between the Kaianerehkó:wa and the Handsome Lake Code. At the time, Ely S. Parker and his Seneca people were struggling against the Ogden Land Company, which was pushing to acquire their lands by corrupting handpicked chiefs.

1852—Kahnawà:ke Railroad

The Lake Saint Louis and Province Line (LSL & PL) was completed in 1852. It transported goods from Lake Champlain to Kahnawà:ke, where a dock was also built to ship the goods to Montréal. Thirteen acres of Kahnawà:ke farmlands were expropriated to build the docking terminal.

1853—French Dauphin Controversy

John H. Hanson published *The Lost Prince*, popularizing Episcopal minister Eleazer Williams's claim that he was the missing French dauphin (pretender to the throne) of France, Louis XVII, the son of Louis XVI and Marie Antoinette, abducted in 1792. While the dauphin Louis-Charles, or Louis XVII, had allegedly died from scrofula in France in June 1795, Kahnawà:ke Mohawk Eleazer Williams had a vision when he saw a picture of Antoine Simon, a French shoemaker and republican partisan who had been designated to watch over Louis XVII after the royal family had been slaughtered by the French revolutionaries. As he recognized Antoine Simon, Eleazer Williams suddenly realized that he was the missing dauphin, adopted by Mohawks after crossing the Atlantic. While historians doubt that Eleazer Williams was really the missing dauphin, the story is still alive in Rotinonhsión:ni oral history, exemplifying the tradition of adopting foreigners.

1858—Seminole Wars

The First Seminole War followed the War of 1812, with American general Andrew Jackson's expeditions against the "Maroon" communities which had formed in Florida, mixing Seminole and African American fugitives. Unable to control this swampy territory, the Spanish Crown had transferred it to the United States in 1821. In 1830, the Indian Removal Act expressed the government's wish to remove the Seminoles from Florida, who in turn responded by increasingly harassing American troops using guerrilla war tactics. In the Second Seminole War of 1835, the longest and most expensive conflict between the United States and Indigenous peoples, the Seminoles were able to inflict seven times more casualties on the American side than they suffered during the Battle of Lake Okeechobee. Lasting from 1855 to 1858, the final Third Seminole War and the threat of starvation forced the Seminoles to leave their territory for Oklahoma. Oral tradition says that many Rotinonhsión:ni warriors joined the Seminoles during these wars.

1876—Indian Act

In 1876, the Canadian Parliament started to implement the "Indian Act to amend and consolidate the laws respecting Indians", which still defines the relationship between the Canadian government and First Nations today. The Indian Act notably determined that Indian reservations were lands set aside by the Crown to be governed by a band council, in defiance of local governance traditions. Representatives from twenty-one Indigenous nations met in Six Nations of the Grand River to reject the Indian Act, which they considered paternalistic and dismissive of earlier treaties, as it had been adopted without any consultation. Further amendments would later be added, including forcing Indian youth to attend school in 1884, criminalizing the West Coast Potlatch ceremony in 1885 and depriving Indigenous women of their Aboriginal status if they married a non-Native man in 1951.

1877—Chief Joseph

On October 5, 1877, Chief Joseph and 418 Nimíipuu (Nez Perce) were arrested by American troops as they were about to cross the Canadian border, after having eluded them for more than a thousand miles. The Nimíipuu were trying to reach the Lakota chief Sitting Bull, who had settled in Saskatchewan after defeating American general Custer at the Battle of Little Bighorn in 1876. Chief Joseph and the Nimíipuu had won no fewer than eighteen battles against two thousand American soldiers before being defeated.

1883—Residential School System

The residential school system, as a network of compulsory boarding schools targeting Indigenous youth, became a nationwide reality in 1883, when three "industrial schools", allegedly teaching agriculture methods that would help Indigenous communities become self-sufficient, were opened in the Prairies. While the first industrial schools were managed by the Anglican and the Wesleyan Methodist Churches, the Catholic Oblates received substantial funding from the Vatican, which allowed them to manage the highest percentage of residential schools throughout Canada. The highest mortality rates in residential schools, over 50 percent in certain institutions, would be reached between 1913 and 1932, during Duncan Campbell Scott's mandate as the Canadian deputy superintendent of the Department of Indian Affairs. In a report, chief medical officer of the federal Departments of the Interior and Indian Affairs Dr. Peter Henderson Bryce described the massive outbreaks of tuberculosis caused by the lack of sanitary measures, as well the outright starvation of children due to the lack of funding. It was deliberately ignored by the government. The last residential school was officially closed in 1996, leaving a century of child abuse and intergenerational trauma in its wake. In 2015, the Truth and Reconciliation Commission declared that by separating children from their families to eradicate Indigenous traditions, the residential school system had committed "cultural genocide". Yet in the summer of 2021, the discovery of 215 unmarked graves in the grounds next to a residential school in Tk'emlúps te Secwépemc territory (Kamloops, British Columbia), followed by thousands of other unmarked graves being found across the country, showed that the genocide was not merely cultural but outright physical as well.

1884—Nile Expedition

Fifty-six Rotinonhsión:ni and other Indigenous people were hired by the British army to pilot the boats that would bring the British expeditionary force up the Nile to Sudan and evacuate their allies as Mahommed Ahmed's rebellion took control of the country. Kahnawà:ke Mohawks were particularly famous for their boating skills, as they were used to navigating vessels through the dangerous Lachine rapids.

1885—North-West Rebellion

This rebellion, led by Louis Riel and Gabriel Dumont, gathered the Métis people of mixed French and Indigenous origin living in the Canadian Prairies settlement of Red River. Canada had just become independent from Great Britain through the 1867 British North America Act, purchasing the Northwest Territories, known as Rupert's Land by the Hudson's Bay Company. Louis Riel and the Red River Métis reacted against Canada's planned encroachment into the Northwest Territories by declaring its independence during an uprising in 1869. Exiled in the United States after the uprising failed, Louis Riel, now enlightened by Christian mysticism, was invited by his partisans to come back to Saskatchewan in 1884 to establish a provisional government. Transported by the brand-new Trans-Canadian Railroad, nine hundred Canadian government troops quelled the rebellion. Despite winning the battle of Fish Creek against all odds (the Canadian troops outnumbered the Métis four to one), on April 24, 1885, the insurgents were finally defeated in the Battle of Batoche on May 15, 1885. Louis Riel was convicted of treason and hanged. Rotinonhsión:ni oral tradition remembers that some of their warriors had been sent to Saskatchewan to crush the rebellion but had changed sides when they understood what was going on. Fighting alongside the Métis, many remained in the region and are currently fighting to be recognized as a Rotinonhsión:ni tribe. Simultaneous with the Métis uprising, the Cree and

Assiniboine peoples of Saskatchewan were facing starvation as the bison populations on which they relied for survival dwindled due to overkilling by settlers. Led by chiefs Poundmaker and Big Bear, they launched a series of raids against Hudson's Bay Company posts, settler towns and army outposts. On April 15, 1885, two hundred Cree warriors raided Fort Pitt, forcing the garrison commander to capitulate. On May 2, 1885, they repeated the exploit at the Battle of Cut Knife, forcing Canadian troops to retreat when their Gatling gun proved ineffective. But lacking ammunition after the Métis' defeat, the Cree and Assiniboine were forced to surrender on July 2, 1885, and eight warriors were hanged in Canada's largest mass hanging.

1887—Walbank Survey

When some Kahnawà:ke residents, concerned with the encroachment of settlers on their land, asked Canadian authorities to conduct a survey to determine the exact boundaries of their territory, the Department of Indian Affairs took advantage of the situation to launch a thorough survey of land parcels, not only around but also inside Kahnawà:ke. Paralleling the infamous Dawes Act, which was passed in the United States that same year to allow the government to break up Indigenous lands, the idea was to associate lands with individual owners to circumvent traditional Mohawk land tenure policies. In September 1887, Walbank's surveying work was interrupted by a group of Mohawks, including Thiretha Peter Diome, who obstructed the work, destroying survey markers and pickets. Such movements of resistance help us to understand why today more than 50 percent of Kahnawà:ke's territory still has multiple owners in defiance of Western notions of individual land ownership.

1890—Wounded Knee

On December 29, 1890, nearly three hundred Lakota people were massacred by the US Army in Wounded Knee. As the buffalo population on which the Indigenous people of the prairie survived were decimated during the second half of the nineteenth century, Paiute prophet Wovoka began having visions of the upcoming departure of the white invaders and the restoration of the precolonial landscape, replete with its formerly abundant wild animal population, believing the Ghost Dance was the way to bring on this prophetic vision. As news spread, the Ghost Dance became immensely popular among the Lakota people. Incapable of circumventing the propagation of the Ghost Dance prophecy and its attendant rituals, the US government soon started to massacre its practitioners.

1899—Police Raid on Akwesasne

In 1894, 1,200 people gathered in Akwesasne for a grand council of the Six Nations Confederacy. The council formally rejected the Indian Act and announced that it would restore its traditional governance structure. Supporters of the traditional government successfully blocked band council elections twice in 1898 and 1899. Yet on May 1, 1899, federal Indian agents lured Akwesasne traditional chiefs, called *Rotinonkwiseres*, or *longhairs*, into attending a meeting where they were supposed to discuss the construction of a bridge. When Chief Ohnehtotako Jake Fire entered the room and saw the Dominion police officers accompanying the Indian Agents, he protested, and the shouts heard outside quickly alerted the community that something was wrong. Ohnehtotako's brother Saiowisakeron Jake Ice rushed in, and Dominion police Lieutenant-Colonel Percy Sherwood shot him twice, killing Saiowisakeron on the spot. Seven chiefs were imprisoned, five of whom remained in prison for more than a year. Following this raid, representatives from the Canadian government formed the first Mohawk band council, with Mohawk individuals which they had selected.

1911—Society of American Indians

Established in 1911, the Society of American Indians was among the first pan-Indigenous organizations, gathering Native rights activists and professionals from various fields, including lawyers, anthropologists, physicians and politicians. Among its founders was Oneida writer and activist Laura Cornelius Kellogg (1880–1947), known for reclaiming lands in New York State as part of her "Lolomi Plan", which envisioned building new Indigenous villages where utopian urban planning inspired by the garden city movement would coexist with traditional government structures and a cooperative economic system. After winning the inauguration of an "American Indian Day" to acknowledge Indigenous contributions to modern America in 1915, the Society of American Indians dissolved in 1923.

1914—Thunderwater Movement

The Council of the Tribes was a fraternal organization dedicated to developing mutual political, legal and economic aid among aboriginal peoples, notably through organizing resistance to land sales and by promoting autonomous agriculture and education. Tuscarora-born Oghema Niagara (1865–1950), better known as Chief Thunderwater, was a prominent, if not all-powerful, figure in this organization. Following a model similar to the Rotinonhsión:ni Confederacy, the Council of Tribes used secret passwords and gestures, its own calendar (which started in 1492) and advocated for the creation of an independent Indian nation the size of Texas. Thunderwater's group ended in turmoil, as the Canadian government accused him of stealing the money of his members and fraudulently presenting himself as Indigenous while being African American.

1916—First Published Version of the Kaianerehkó:wa

Having been raised as a Seneca, where the Handsome Lake Code prevailed, anthropologist Arthur C. Parker, the great-nephew of Ely S. Parker, did not think that Kaianerehkó:wa followers still thrived in Six Nations of the Grand River when he met Seth Newhouse, of Onondaga and Mohawk descent. Using the information gathered by Newhouse on the original provisions of the Kaianerehkó:wa, Parker published the first complete account of the 117 articles of the Constitution of the Five Nations in 1916. As only Dekanawida's epic and specific rites, such as the condolence ceremony had previously been published, Parker's work was bound to elicit criticism. The Six Nations council refused to endorse Newhouse's version of the Kaianerehkó:wa, which gave a prominent place to the Mohawks and gave women the power to depose erring chiefs with the help of the warriors. A Committee of Confederacy Chiefs, thus, worked on their own version of the Kaianerehkó:wa, and Seneca knowledge keeper John Arthur Gibson was commissioned to deliver an oral account in the Onondaga language. Despite the differences between these various attempts, they all sought to document the existence of the Rotinonhsión:ni's sovereign governance structure at a time when Canadian authorities were forcefully imposing the band council system on Rotinonhsión:ni communities. In 1993, Louis Karoniaktajeh Hall, Kahentinetha and Ganyetahawi would publish a new and revised version of the Kaianerehkó:wa in the Mohawk language.

1923—Deskaheh Travels to Switzerland

In 1923, the Royal Canadian Mounted Police (RCMP) built new barracks on Rotinonhsión:ni territory in Ohswé:ken (Six Nations of the Grand River) and were increasingly harassing Natives by conducting searches in their homes and prohibiting them from cutting wood. Cayuga chief Deskaheh traveled to Switzerland, using a passport issued by the Rotinonhsión:ni Confederacy, to raise awareness at the League of Nations about Canada's violation of Indigenous people's rights and about European countries' responsibility to enforce the Two Row Wampum. His eloquent speeches resulted in several countries supporting his plea for Rotinonhsión:ni autonomy, notably Ireland, Persia, Japan and Panama.

1924—Raid on Ohswé:ken

On October 7, 1924, RCMP officers stormed the old 1864 council house in Ohswé:ken, declared that the Rotinonhsión:ni traditional government was hereby dissolved and called for elections to appoint band council members in accordance with the provisions previously laid forth in the 1876 Indian Act. The police also seized legal documents and wampum belts proving the sovereignty of the traditional government. The culmination of a series of attempts by Duncan Campbell Scott, the minister of Indian affairs, to impose the Indian Act on the Rotinonhsión:ni, this 1924 RCMP raid resulted in band council elections which were largely boycotted by the community. Chief David Hill Sr. claimed that only twenty-six individuals had voted, some of them several times. The first act of the band council was to swear allegiance to the king. The Rotinonhsión:ni traditional government never recognized the band council, and both continued to exist as parallel governments.

1924—Indian Citizenship Act

Also known as the Snyder Act, the Indian Citizenship Act stated that Indigenous peoples living in the United States should be considered normal citizens. Although the act was partly meant to acknowledge the participation of Native Americans in the World War I, many Indigenous peoples refused to become American citizens, as they would then lose the birthrights guaranteed by previous treaties.

1928—Border Crossing Victory

In the aftermath of the 1924 Indian Citizenship Act, Indigenous people who refused to become American citizens experienced trouble crossing the US-Canada border. After a Six Nations Cayuga Roiá:ner was denied re-entry into Canada in 1925, Tuscarora chief Clinton Rickard decided to create the Indian Defense League of America to fight the colonial imposition of an artificial border on Native land. Mohawk ironworker Paul

Kanento Diabo, who had been threatened deportation to Canada from Philadelphia, where he often traveled as an ironworker, also launched a major court case to secure Indigenous people's right to cross the border freely. In 1928, President Coolidge finally signed a bill stating that the border restrictions would not be applied to First Nations, reasserting the validity of the 1794 Jay Treaty. To celebrate this victory, the first Free Border Crossing from Ontario to New York State was staged in Niagara on July 14, 1928, becoming an annual tradition still followed today.

1928—Kahnawà:ke Longhouse

Kahnawà:ke's first modern-age longhouse was built by Agnès Kawisaienton Beauvais and her husband John Kanatasa Beauvais at the intersection of Saint-Isidore road and the Old Malone Highway in 1928. The event that provoked the construction of the longhouse was the Jesuits' refusal to let confederacy representatives use their church hall for a meeting to discuss the case of Paul Kanento Diabo. In 1936, longhouse member Agnès Beauvais wrote a letter to the king of England requesting lands to use as burial grounds for longhouse people, separate from Christians. Other prominent figures from this longhouse included chiefs Frank Karionwakeron Diabo and Dominic Onenhariio Two-Axe, the father of Mary Two-Axe Earley, who became famous contesting the Indian Act's patriarchal bias. Most Mohawk longhouse revivalists from the 1920s sustained themselves by working as farmers in the summer and ironworkers in the winter.

1949—Akwesasne Elections at Gunpoint

When the community of Akwesasne decided in a referendum that the authority of traditional Rotiianérshon selected by clan mothers super-seded that of band and tribal council chiefs, the latter wrote a letter acknowledging that they did not have any authority over their people. New York State authorities sent a police detachment that tried to storm the longhouse, but clan mothers inserted themselves and kept them from entering the building. Band council elections were, thus, held outside the territory of the reservation, in the town of Hogansburg, monitored by heavily armed police officers.

1957—Mohawk River Valley Re-establishment

In 1957, a group of Kanien'kehá:ka from Kahnawà:ke and Akwesasne decided to move back to their original homeland in the Mohawk River

Valley. With Louis Diabo as a guide and Standing Arrow as an English-speaking spokesperson, they established themselves near Fonda, New York, along the Schoharie River. Unwilling to file a land claim using colonial laws and lacking funding, they were finally evicted from the homes, farms and the longhouse they had built, in spite of the good relations they had established with their neighbours.

1959—Raid on Ohswé:ken

On March 12, 1959, the RCMP forcibly put an end to an occupation of the old council house of Ohswé:ken, wounding many community members. Lasting for more than a week, this occupation had disrupted the activities of the band council and briefly succeeded in re-establishing the traditional confederacy government. The occupation had been in support of the legitimacy of the traditional Rotiianérshon Joseph and Irvin Logan, with more than one thousand community members accompanying Roiá:ner Josie Logan Sr. as he nailed his proclamation to the council house door, calling for the reinstatement of the traditional confederacy Rotiianérshon. Temporarily stopping land sales by the band council, this occupation also sparked a revival of sovereignist Rotinonhsión:ni politics. After another smaller occupation in 1970, a legal battle would lead Ontario High Court Justice Osler to acknowledge that the Rotiianérshon better represent the Rotinonhsión:ni than band council chiefs, but Osler's judgment was overturned on appeal, and the building was only officially returned to the confederacy in 2007.

1959—Saint Lawrence Seaway

Built at the cost of 470 million Canadian dollars by twenty-two thousand workers, the 2,300-mile-long Saint Lawrence Seaway was completed in 1959. Ahnionken Louis Diabo famously resisted the construction of the seaway, refusing to leave his home until almost every inch of the territory around his home was dug up and overturned to make room for the seaway's path. In compensation for the 1262 acres of prime farmland it had lost, along with its access to the river, Kahnawà:ke initially received no more than $3,000. The compensation would be changed to $1.5 million in 1973, although most of this money was earmarked for aesthetic and landscaping work that took place around the seaway. Akwesasne was also deeply affected by the seaway, which included the construction of the Moses-Saunders Power Dam over the Long Sault rapids upstream of the village. In addition to flooding fifteen thousand acres of traditional

Mohawk land, including ten islands belonging to Akwesasne, to allow large vessels to pass through the seaway, the dam also attracted a number of highly polluting factories to the area, including General Motors, Reynolds Metals and the Aluminum Company of America.

1960—Niagara Power Project

On March 7, 1960, the Supreme Court authorized the New York Power Authority (NYPA) to expropriate 550 acres of Tuscarora reservation land, which it would flood by building new power dams. Infamous urban planner Robert Moses, known for installing low bridges on New York parkways to bar poor and racialized populations from accessing state parks by public transit, designed the dams, which were installed on two creeks, both of which had previously provided the Tuscarora with freshwater. A lasting water crisis resulted for the Tuscarora, whose wells remain poisoned with lead and bacteria to this day, even though they live next to the Great Lakes, which contain one-third of the world's freshwater supply.

1965—Kinzua Dam

Completed in 1965 by the United States Corps of Engineers, the Kinzua Dam flooded ten thousand acres of fertile land belonging to the Allegany Seneca, who lost nearly one-third of their territory. Despite the delays caused by the legal measures taken by the Seneca, as well as a public campaign which garnered popular support—including Johnny Cash's song "As Long as the Grass Shall Grow"—the dam was constructed and six hundred Senecas lost their homes.

1965—Protest on Parliament Hill

On June 22, 1965, while Canadian members of Parliament were debating a bill intended to create an Indian Claims Commission, Rotinonhsión:ni protesters, including Karoniaktajeh, held a protest outside the building to remind members of Parliament of their treaty obligations under the 1763 Royal Proclamation.

1968—Akwesasne International Bridge Blockade

On December 18, 1968, in response to the Canadian government's decision to impose duties on goods crossing the US-Canada border in Akwesasne, hundreds of Rotinonhsión:ni protesters from both sides of the border proceeded to block the Seaway International Bridge that traverses

Akwesasne. They were contesting the imposition of the imaginary line between Canada and the United States onto Indigenous peoples and their land. After a long cold day of blocking traffic and skirmishes with police officers from nearby Cornwall, forty-eight protesters were arrested, including Kahentinetha and Tekarontakeh. The Canadian government was forced to grant duty-free status to Rotinonhsión:ni people the following year.

1968—Akwesasne Notes
In 1968, Rarihokwats, an ex-Indian affairs agent who changed allegiances and was adopted as a member of the Mohawk community of Akwesasne, along with Ateroniatakon and other Akwesasne traditional people, published the first issue of the journal *Akwesasne Notes*. Distributed by mail by members of the community, this publication soon became the world's most important journal on Indigenous struggles and issues, reaching a circulation of seventy-four thousand in the mid-1970s. After changing its editorial committee and publishing books, including *Basic Call to Consciousness* (1977), *Akwesasne Notes* released its last issue in 1991.

1969—White Paper
A "white paper" (government report) prepared by Canadian prime minister Pierre Elliott Trudeau and the minister of Indian affairs Jean Chrétien in 1969 proposed to eliminate the Indian Act and transform Indigenous reservations into Canadian municipalities and Indigenous people into Canadian citizens. The white paper elicited widespread criticism from Indigenous communities and was finally abandoned.

1969—Chicago Indian Village
Immediately after its foundation, the Native American Committee (NAC) occupied the Chicago Bureau of Indian Affairs in December 1969. The following spring, the NAC set up an encampment behind Wrigley Field, the Chicago Indian Village (CIV), to protest against the poor housing and social services provided to Indigenous people in Chicago. It was followed by several other land occupations, notably near Fort Sheridan and Camp Logan, in Illinois.

1969—AIM Occupation of Alcatraz
When the Alcatraz maximum security federal penitentiary closed in 1963, the island in the San Francisco Bay where it had been built, nicknamed

the Rock, had already been occupied once for four hours in March 1964, by Richard McKenzie and other Sioux protesters, who had argued that the 1868 Treaty of Fort Laramie between the US and the Sioux provided for the return of all federal lands if they were abandoned and out of use. On November 9, 1969, activists from the Indians of All Tribes (IAT), including Mohawk Richard Oakes, Cherokee Jim Vaughn and Inuit Joe Bill, attempted another occupation. They approached the island by boat, swam to the shore and claimed the island, before being removed the same day by Coast Guards. However, on November 20, hundreds of other activists, including actor Benjamin Bratt, returned to the island, avoiding a Coast Guard blockade. Even after the government tried to drive out the protesters by cutting the island's electricity, water and telephone lines, the occupation continued, only to finally be dislodged by a massive police operation that removed the last occupants on June 11, 1971.

1970—Akwesasne Islands Reoccupied

On May 9, 1970, a group of Akwesasne Mohawks landed in a barge on Stanley Island, planting signs stating that the island was Mohawk territory, setting up tents on the lawns of wealthy homeowners and starting to plant gardens. Three weeks later, they followed this by taking over Loon Island. The Mohawks of Akwesasne have a claim on forty-two islands in the Saint Lawrence River.

1970—High School Protest

In March 1970, Mohawk students staged a sit-in at and walk-out from the Howard S. Billings Regional High School in Châteauguay, near Kahnawà:ke, to protest the absence of any instruction on their own culture and language in the school curriculum. The protests resulted in the creation of an Indian Studies program run by an Indigenous staff. Eight years later, in 1978, the same high school experienced another round of protests from its Mohawk students, this time to oppose the passage of Bill 101 in Québec, which required Mohawk parents to apply for certificates to have their children use a language other than French in school. The Kahnawà:ke community decided in a referendum that they would establish their own high school on their territory. On September 6, 1978, around three hundred Mohawk students walked out of the Châteauguay high school and solemnly marched towards the new school that was opened for them in Kahnawà:ke, the Kahnawà:ke Survival School (KSS), which still exists today.

1971—Highway 81 Protest

In 1971, Onondaga warriors and community members resisted the expansion of Highway 81 across their territory, with hundreds of protesters occupying the construction site for several weeks. Celebrities like John Lennon, Yoko Ono, Phil Spector and Allen Ginsberg visited and voiced their support for the encampment. Highway 81's planned third lane was finally abandoned.

1972—Indian Affairs Occupations in Washington and Ottawa

On November 3, 1972, as the Canadian Minister of Indian Affairs' offices in Ottawa were being occupied by Mohawk warriors, the American Bureau of Indian Affairs (BIA) in Washington, DC, was simultaneously taken over by around five hundred Indigenous activists. Washington, DC, was the end point of the Trail of Broken Treaties, which had departed from the West Coast in October to raise awareness about the discrimination and inequalities faced by Native Americans, the theft of 110 million acres of their land and the past and ongoing violations of treaty agreements. The occupation of the BIA lasted for seven days before the lack of provisions convinced the protesters to leave the building, which was considerably damaged. As he was trying to get re-elected when the occupation was going on, Richard Nixon adopted a surprisingly favourable attitude towards Indigenous people's right to self-governance.

1972—Protest against Highway in Kahnawà:ke

On February 15, 1972, Tekarontakeh accompanied three Rotiianérshon—Louis Karoniaktajeh Hall, Joey Phillips and Mitchell Woodrow—to Ottawa to protest against the construction of a six-lane highway in Kahnawà:ke. In an interview, Louis Karoniaktajeh Hall warned that if the Mohawks' demands were not respected, "we can no longer control our younger people like we used to".

1973—Wounded Knee

On February 27, 1973, two hundred Oglala Sioux and activists affiliated with the American Indian Movement (AIM) occupied the site of Wounded Knee, on the Pine Ridge Indian Reservation, in South Dakota. They were protesting against Pine Ridge tribal council chief Dick Wilson's reign of terror and his violent persecution of his political opponents, including many traditionals. In response, within a few hours, more than two thousand

FBI agents, United States Marshals and other police forces, equipped with military-grade weapons, tanks and helicopters, besieged the town. The siege lasted until May 8, with two Indigenous activists killed by police gunfire. Yet the bloodiest phase of this battle would happen after the police left, as an estimated sixty Native activists were killed in the aftermath of the occupation, allegedly assassinated by Dick Wilson's personal paramilitary forces, the so-called GOON (Guardians of the Oglala Nation) squad. Previously, on December 29, 1890, Wounded Knee had also been the site of one of the largest massacres in American history, when nearly three hundred Lakota people had been murdered by soldiers of the US Army.

1973—Kahnawà:ke Evictions

In September 1973, following a resolution from the longhouse, the Rotihsken'rakéhte' asked that non-Indigenous people living in Kahnawà:ke without familial ties with the community to move out of the territory. As housing was in short supply in Kahnawà:ke, many Mohawks could not stay in their community and had to live in nearby settler towns. White residents were given two weeks to leave, although delays were granted when justified. Unhappy that the warriors were taking up too much space in the community, Chief Ron Kirby and the band council of Kahnawà:ke decided to propose their own eviction orders, issuing their own deadlines and arresting six warriors, including Tekarontakeh and Louis Karoniaktajeh Hall. Contesting the jurisdiction of Québec's provincial court in addressing events that took place on Rotinonhsión:ni land, Karoniaktajeh delivered the following statement before the jury:

> The defendants hereby declare the events [in question] to have occurred on land under the title of the Six Nations Confederacy, and as such the provincial court does not have the jurisdiction to try the case. The Six Nations Confederacy never gave up its nationhood and has treaties with both England and the United States guaranteeing such status. Therefore, they have the right to try cases in their own courts and this right has been exercised by the Kahnawà:ke branch of the Six Nations Confederacy. Anyone wishing to start legal action against a member of the confederacy must appeal to the confederacy court.

In October, only one white family still refused to leave Kahnawà:ke. Thus, the warriors intervened to force them to leave and occupied their house. Québec police, the Sûreté du Québec (SQ), arrived at the scene, and a fight broke out. The house was burnt down during the fight, and many warriors were arrested. In response, hundreds of Kahnawà:ke residents surrounded the police station, and a riot erupted, with three police cruisers being overturned. The warriors, armed with rifles, then took refuge in the longhouse, where they were besieged by 150 SQ police for a week, before the police agreed to withdraw, provided that the "agitators" from the American Indian Movement, who had come in numbers to support the Mohawk warriors in Kahnawà:ke, promised to go home.

1974—Ganienkeh

In May 1974, a 612-acre resort camp in Moss Lake, New York, was occupied by a group of several hundred traditional Mohawks. Similar armed reoccupations of Native lands happened the same year in Cache Creek, British Columbia, and Anicinabe Park, Ontario.

1974—Native People's Caravan

Organized by members of the Toronto Warrior Society, the Ojibwa Warrior Society of Kenora, the Regina Warrior Society and Cree activists Vernon Harper and Pauline Shirt, the Native People's Caravan traversed Canada from coast to coast to raise awareness about the mistreatment of Indigenous peoples and the necessity of respecting treaty rights. Starting in Vancouver, the caravan gradually gathered two hundred protesters, before it ended on Parliament Hill, in Ottawa, on September 30, 1974. Some protesters occupied an abandoned warehouse nearby, on Victoria Island, and stayed there until 1975.

1976—Grand Council Dehorning

The Onondaga grand council's constitution was put to a test when an Iakoiá:ner, exasperated by the behavior of a Roiá:ner who had called the band council police on young longhouse people, proceeded to apply Wampum 59 of the Kaianerehkó:wa to have him deposed. According to this article, the women's fire can depose erring chiefs by asking the Rotihsken'rakéhte' to physically remove him in the longhouse if he refuses to change. This procedure, called "dehorning", as the Rotiianérshon's traditional horn headdress is removed, led the Rotihsken'rakéhte' to usher the indicted Roiá:ner out of the Onondaga longhouse during a grand council session. The divorce between the Rotihsken'rakéhte' and the grand council in Onondaga became an accomplished fact after this event.

1977—United Nations Conference

On September 20, 1977, a group of traditional Mohawk people partici-
pated in the first annual meeting of the International NGO Conference on
Discrimination Against Indigenous Populations in the Americas, in Geneva,
Switzerland. The Mohawk delegation notably distributed the book *Basic
Call to Consciousness*, edited by Akwesasne Notes.

1977—Ganienkeh Moves to Miner Lake

In the spring of 1977, negotiations with the secretary of New York State,
Mario Cuomo, authorized Ganienkeh to move to a new 5700-acre site
near Miner Lake, in Altona, New York. State senator James H. Donovan
reacted by saying that "Cuomo's so-called negotiation with a small group
of Canadian renegades that took over the state's $800,000 Moss Lake
property consisted of giving them everything they wanted to get them
out". Ganienkeh's spokesperson, Kakwirakeron, said, "We think that the
state's objective was to have our community move away from the controversial Moss Lake site. Their main stumbling block was that they wanted
to relocate us somewhere, anywhere, in a legal sort of way". Mario Cuomo,
on the other hand, declared, "We disengaged them from a hostile situation, we ceased the continuous flaunting of our laws and we reduced the
possibility of violence. And what were the alternatives? I don't believe the
Indians should have been killed". Ganienkeh completed the move to Miner
Lake on August 2, 1978.

1978—Kahnawà:ke Survival School

Thanks to the efforts of Mohawk teachers and activists, many of whom
worked on a volunteer basis, the Kahnawà:ke Survival School opened
its doors on September 7, 1978. The previous day, approximately three
hundred Mohawk students had marched from Châteauguay to Kahnawà:ke,
where they would now receive their education in the Mohawk language
from grade 7 to grade 11.

1979—David Cross Killing

On October 20, 1979, twenty-eight-year-old Kahnawà:ke Mohawk David
Cross, father of two children, was chased by an SQ police cruiser on the
Mercier Bridge. Cross managed to get home, and later came out with a
pool cue. Officer Robert Lessard responded by firing three shots at Cross,
killing him on the spot. The SQ were subsequently barred from entering

Kahnawà:ke, and the reserve essentially became a police no-go zone, with the local Peacekeepers becoming the only police force on the territory.

1979—Fort Kanasaraken

On May 22, 1979, Kanasaraken and his friend Joe Swamp caught a group of people cutting trees on his Akwesasne property at Raquette Point and proceeded to confiscate their equipment. Kanasaraken discovered that they were part of the federally funded Young Adult Conservation Corps, and that their work was part of a larger project to build a fence around Akwesasne and delineate its boundaries, as land claims were under discussion. Shortly thereafter, the Akwesasne police and the New York State Police attempted to arrest Kanasaraken on a larceny warrant. Given the threat to its sovereignty with the arrest of Kanasaraken, a condoled Roiá:ner, the Rotinonhsión:ni grand council called an emergency meeting in Akwesasne and decided to use Kanasaraken's property as a headquarters for the traditionals. On May 29, several hundred unarmed traditionals took to the streets to protest the Akwesasne police's submission to the laws of New York State, and then occupied the tribal council's offices, while five longhouse chiefs officially requested the disarming of the tribal council's police force. The ensuing negotiations with the federal government failed, as county district attorney Joseph J. Ryan refused to drop the charges held against Kanasaraken, calling the Mohawk people "a bunch of animals". Meanwhile, Kanasaraken and Joe Swamp missed their arraignment, refusing to submit to the foreign laws of New York State. In response, Ryan pushed charges against an estimated twenty-one other community members, using sealed indictments, which forced many of the indicted to take refuge in the defensive encampment erected around Kanasaraken's house, for fear that they would be arrested if they left. Tribal council chief Rudy Hart threatened to arm his own militia and enter the encampment forcibly to execute the warrants if the state police did not do so immediately. On August 27, New York state troopers supported by airplanes and SWAT teams surrounded "Fort Kanasaraken", bringing the situation to the brink of a Wounded Knee–type shootout. They entered Joe Swamp's home and dragged his wife around the house in her nightgown, trying to get her to deliver her husband. Following a public outreach campaign using telephones and telegraphs, the state police finally withdrew from Akwesasne the same evening, bringing three arrested warriors with them. However, the situation would remain tense for another year, as the police sealed off all roads around Fort Kanasaraken, and armed pro–tribal council vigilantes manned the barricade half a mile away from the defensive camp, where seventy "traditionals" remained entrenched.

1981—Raid on Listuguj

On June 11, 1981, no less than five hundred SQ officers stormed the Mi'kmaq community of Listuguj to stop community members from fishing salmon in the Restigouche River, injuring and arresting dozens of community members. This brutal rejection of Aboriginal fishing rights by the Québec government, then controlled by the separatist Parti Québécois, did not keep Mi'kmaq fishermen from putting their nets back in the river once the police left the area. The SQ came back on June 20, using rubber bullets to try to force their way through Mi'kmaq residents who had formed a human shield. The police were incapable of entering Listuguj, and the Québec government lost their wager, as they were forced to acknowledge Mi'kmaq fishing rights the following year. Listuguj adopted its own fishing law in 1993. During the standoff in Restigouche in 1981, Kahnawà:ke warriors slowed down traffic on the Mercier Bridge in solidarity with the Mi'kmaq, and children impeded police helicopters from landing nearby by occupying potential landing sites.

1985—Bill C-31

Rejecting the matrilineal structure of Rotinonhsión:ni kinship, the Indian Act resulted in Indigenous women who married outside their community losing their Indian status, their right to live on reservation territory and even their right to be buried there. In 1981, Wolastoqiyik (Maliseet) lawyer Sandra Lovelace won her case against the Canadian government before the United Nations Human Rights Committee, which found Canada guilty of violating the 1976 International Covenant on Civil and Political Rights. As a result, the Canadian Parliament adopted Bill C-31 in 1985, granting Indian status to Native women who had married non-Native men. In the wake of Bill C-31, many Mohawks who had been raised outside of Rotinonhsión:ni territories then reintegrated themselves into the reservations, changing the cultural landscape of the territories. Bill C-31 left to local band councils the responsibility of determining their reservations' criteria for membership, provided that the criteria did not include gender-based discrimination. Kahnawà:ke in particular has been at the center of debates on tribal membership, as the band council adopted a moratorium on mixed marriages and adoption of non-Natives, on May 22, 1981. The moratorium determined that a 50 percent Mohawk blood quantum was required to live in Kahnawà:ke and stated that Mohawks who married non-Natives would have to leave the community. Even though Kaianerehkó:wa traditionals and the Mohawk Warrior Society had famously evicted non-Native people living in Kahnawà:ke in 1973, they were among the strongest opponents to the band council's ban on mixed marriages. In 2017, Tekarontakeh's expert witness testimony notably helped Waneek Horn-Miller, Kahentinetha's daughter, win a court case before the Superior Court of Quebec, allowing her to live in Kahnawà:ke even though she had married a non-Native.

1988—RCMP Raid on Kahnawà:ke
In the spring of 1988, nearly two hundred RCMP officers and SWAT team agents cracked down on Kahnawà:ke cigarette dealers, arresting five people. Mohawk warriors replied by blocking two provincial highways running through the reserve, thereby closing the Mercier Bridge leading to Montréal.

1989—Akwesasne Casino
After a 1988 referendum organized by the tribal council rejected the proposed construction of a $2.7 million high-stakes casino on the reservation, a group of Akwesasne warriors blocked roads entering the reservation on July 20, 1989. This was followed by a ten-day armed stand-off with police forces. A local anti-casino faction was formed to oppose the Rotihsken'rakéhte', leading to shots being fired in the streets and several buildings being burnt down.

1990—Turmoil in Ganienkeh
In March 1990, a helicopter was shot down over Ganienkeh, wounding Dr. James Van Kirk. Both New York State police and Mohawk warriors set up roadblocks to control traffic after the incident.

1990—Oka Crisis
Disputing the extension of a golf course over an ancestral cemetery in the pines of Kanehsatà:ke, Mohawk community members decided to occupy the pines to make sure they would not be destroyed. The SQ set out to remove them on July 11, 1990, provoking an exchange of fire which left police corporal Marcel Lemay dead; it was never established who had

fired the first shot. The SQ retreated, leaving several police vehicles behind, which warriors then used to build barricades on the highway. In solidarity, Kahnawà:ke warriors seized and blockaded the Mercier Bridge, a vital route into Montréal. The stand-off would last seventy-eight days, with more than 2,000 police officers and 4,500 Canadian soldiers being deployed, equipped with tanks, armored personnel carriers and helicopters. It was the largest military operation ever initiated by the Canadian government on its alleged soil. The Mohawk resistance at Kanehsatà:ke sparked solidarity actions across Canada, and thousands of supporters swarmed the area, setting up solidarity camps. Frustrated by the Mercier Bridge blockade increasing their commute time, white residents of towns around Kahnawà:ke grew increasingly violent towards their Mohawk neighbours, with numerous cases of white vigilantes beating up Indigenous people and rioting around burning effigies of Mohawk warriors. On August 28, 1990, seventy-five families trying to leave Kahnawà:ke, now surrounded by the army, were attacked by white gangs who threw rocks at them as they traversed the narrow passage of Whiskey Point. SQ officers stood by, not reacting, and after the event a Mohawk elder died from a heart attack provoked by the trauma. On September 18, 1990, SQ officers and Canadian soldiers landed on Tekakwitha Island, attempting to move into Kahnawà:ke, but hundreds of Mohawks blocked their way. The soldiers ended up having to be airlifted out by helicopter after a seven-hour fight that left twenty-two soldiers and seventy-five Mohawks wounded. On September 26, 1990, Mohawk defenders decided to move out of the Kanehsatà:ke Treatment Center, which was besieged by the army. Canadian soldiers attacked Mohawk warriors, women and children as they tried to make their way out, bayoneting fourteen-year-old Waneek Horn-Miller, Kahentinetha's daughter, as she was exiting the camp with her four-year-old sister Kaniehtiio. The Oka Crisis left a substantial legacy, which resulted in the Royal Commission on Aboriginal People being launched in 1991, in an attempt to understand the underlying causes of the conflict, in the hope of avoiding similar outbreaks of violence in the future. This process eventually led to the formation of the Truth and Reconciliation Commission of Canada in 2008.

1991—Visit to Libya

On June 11, 1991, a group of Mohawk traditionals, including Ateronhiatakon, traveled to Tripoli, Libya, to receive a $250,000 award from Colonel Muammar al-Qaddafi.

1993—Ipperwash

In 1993, protesters from the Stony Point First Nation near Sarnia, Ontario, set up an encampment on a military base from which their elders had previously been evicted in 1942 and forced to live in harsh conditions in the nearby territory of the Kettle Point First Nation. The reoccupation of the military base followed an eviction notice which the Stony Point First Nation had sent to the Department of National Defense, reminding the federal government of its original promise to return the land to its Indigenous owners. Two years later, the reoccupation was extended into a portion of the Ipperwash Provincial Park where the community had an ancestral cemetery. On September 6, 1995, heavily armed riot police forces intervened. Sixteen-year old Nicholas Cotrelle drove a school bus in their direction as they approached, and RCMP forces fired thousands of rounds of ammunition in Cotrelle's direction wounding him and killing his dog. In the ensuing firefight, Ojibwa land defender Dudley George was killed by the police. After a commission determined that the government was responsible for the tragedy, the Stony Point community continued living on the southwestern Ontario military base, where they remain until this day.

1994—Operations Campus and Scorpion-Saxon

Alleging that the Mohawk Warrior Society possessed heavy weaponry, making it "the biggest extremist Aboriginal group and potentially the most violent in Canada", and estimating that the warriors funneled $3.6 billion worth of tobacco products from the United States to Canada through Akwesasne's porous border, Canadian authorities prepared to launch massive raids on several Mohawk communities. As a result, Operation Scorpion-Saxon trained 1,500 Canadian soldiers, 2,000 RCMP and 2,000 provincial police officers for an invasion of Mohawk territories, conducting combined arms exercises at Petawawa, Valcartier and Gagetown Canadian Forces bases. Yet the actual invasion, Operation Campus, was called off eight days before its scheduled start, when CSIS (Canadian Security Intelligence Service) agents warned the government that the invasion might cause a nationwide Indigenous uprising and result in many deaths.

1995—Gustafsen Lake

Lasting from August 18 to September 17, 1995, the Gustafsen Lake standoff started as a conflict between Secwépemc traditionals, who at time were performing their Sun Dance ceremonies, and the alleged owner of a cattle ranch. The landowner's eviction notice against the Sun Dancers provoked what became the largest domestic operation in the history of the RCMP, with more than 350 police and military officers armed with M-16 assault rifles, machine guns and armoured personnel carriers besieging eighteen Indigenous land defenders in the Sun Dance camp, including Mohawk allies, such as AIM member John Dacajeweiah Hill, "Splitting the Sky". On September 11, two Ts'Peten land defenders driving around the area to get water stumbled on a powerful explosive device that had been planted by the RCMP, who then opened fire on them. They managed to escape by jumping in a lake. While an armed personnel carrier was disabled by Secwepemc elder Wolverine, the RCMP shot a total seventy-seven thousand rounds of ammunition at the encampment. On September 17, after the police shut off all media communication coming out of Gustafsen Lake and launched what would later be revealed as an avowed "smear campaign", presenting the land defenders as terrorists, the Indigenous land defenders decided to burn their weapons and walk out of their camp. Fifteen of them received jail sentences, including a five-year sentence for Wolverine. Their lawyer Bruce Clarke was charged with criminal contempt of court, arrested in the courtroom and put in jail after he invoked both the Royal Proclamation of 1763 and Section 35 of the Constitution Act of 1982 to argue that traditional Indigenous laws still held sovereign status on unceded territories.

1997—Onondaga Beating

On May 18, 1997, two hundred New York state troopers raided a Rotinonhsión:ni ceremonial gathering taking place next to Highway 81, near Onondaga, to oppose New York State's attempts to collect taxes from Indigenous businesses. Under the pretense that they were blocking the highway, the protesters, children included, were violently clubbed by the police, and a baby was thrown out of his stroller. Two years later, Ronald Jones Sr., one of the organizers of the gathering and the father of the owner of the land where people had gathered was brutally murdered under mysterious circumstances, with his hands severed and his house burnt down. Even though all charges were dropped against the twenty-six Rotinonhsión:ni traditionals arrested in 1997, the victims of the police beating never obtained justice for the violence they experienced. However, the state did revoke its plan to collect taxes from Indigenous businesses.

1999—Burnt Church

In 1999, non-Native fishermen destroyed thousands of Mi'kmaq lobster traps to contest a September 17 Canada Supreme Court ruling recognizing Aboriginal people's right to harvest lobster out of season. Mi'kmaq warriors responded by setting up an encampment in Burnt Church, New Brunswick. The reaction from the part of non-Natives was particularly violent, with six hundred armed fishermen blocking the Yarmouth Harbor in Nova Scotia to keep Native ships out of the waters, sinking one of them. Three Mi'kmaq men were wounded by a truck driven by a non-Native, and a sacred Burnt Church ceremonial arbor was set on fire. The conflict continued in 2000 and 2001, with several standoffs between the RCMP and Mi'kmaq fishermen, costing the federal government over $15 million.

2004—James Gabriel's Police Raid

On January 14, 2004, based on a 2003 agreement with Canadian authorities, Kanehsatà:ke band council chief James Gabriel ordered sixty-seven police officers from outside the community to crack down on businesses linked to the Warrior Society. On April 12, after swarming James Gabriel's office, Kanehsatà:ke community members surrounded the police station and confiscated police weapons, stating that the community would be patrolled by its own residents and setting up barricades in case they were attacked. James Gabriel's house was burnt to the ground. On May 3, 2004, the band councilor ordered a new raid against the warriors, who managed to repel his sixty policemen. The date was symbolic given that it was five years after the death of Mohawk warrior Joe David, who died from injuries sustained when he was shot by James Gabriel's police officers in 1999. Accused of mismanaging the crisis, Québec's minister of public security Jacques Chagnon was forced to resign.

2006—Kanonhstá:ton

On February 28, 2006, a group of community members from Ohswé:ken erected tents and a wooden house on the site of a projected housing project, Douglas Creek Estates, in what settlers consider to be the town of Caledonia. The site was renamed *Kanonhstá:ton*, meaning *a land to defend*. Stating that the territory belongs to the Rotinonhsión:ni by virtue of the 1784 Haldimand Proclamation, the land defenders burnt the injunction ordering them off the land. In the early morning of April 20, 2006, heavily armed Ontario Provincial Police (OPP) took over the site, arresting sixteen people. The same day, several hundred land defenders returned to the site forcing the police to retreat. Tire bonfires were lit on Highway 6 in protest, and a wooden bridge over a railway was burnt. In solidarity with the protesters, the Mercier Bridge in Kahnawà:ke was blocked for close to an hour, while railroad tracks were shut down in Tyendinaga. Later, on May 22, a truck crashed through the gates of a hydro substation next to Kanonhstá:ton, causing a blackout in the region for close to a week, pushing authorities to declare a state of emergency. After numerous clashes with settler residents and an incident involving a US Border Patrol vehicle being seized by protesters, on June 9, Ontario Premier Dalton McGuinty called off the ongoing negotiations. However, on August 27, the Ontario Court of Appeal ruled that the protesters could remain on the site. Rotinonhsión:ni traditionals are still at Kanonhstá:ton to this day, with it serving as a base for a new reoccupation which began nearby in February 2020, which protesters have dubbed the 1492 Land Back Lane.

2009—Protests against Armed Border Guards

In the spring of 2009, hundreds of Akwesasne Mohawks protested the decision that Canadian border guards would be allowed to carry 9-mm Beretta handguns, given the risk that these weapons could be used against Indigenous people, who experienced difficulties with border agents on a daily basis. A protest camp was set up next to the office of the Canada Border Services Agency (CBSA) on Cornwall Island, in Akwesasne, pushing the guards to leave the premises and shut down the bridge and the border crossing on May 31, 2009. This made it impossible for Akwesasne community members to circulate through their own territory for six weeks. The CBSA office on Cornwall Island was abandoned, and its staff moved to new buildings built closer to the settler town of Cornwall. It is estimated that Akwesasne community members constitute 70 percent of daily traffic across the border.

2012—Idle No More

Following Attawapiskat chief Theresa Spence's hunger strike to oppose conservative Canadian prime minister Stephen Harper's omnibus Bill C-45, which facilitated environmentally destructive infrastructure projects without the permission of traditional Indigenous caretakers of the land and allowed a single band council vote to trigger the "absolute surrender" of their land, the Idle No More movement quickly spread throughout

Canada. In addition to numerous flash mobs in Canada and beyond, Akwesasne's International Bridge crossing was blocked on January 5, 2013, an action that was coordinated with other blockades of border crossings on Indigenous territories, in Sarnia, Ontario, Fort Erie, Ontario, and Surrey, British Columbia.

2012—Three Feathers Casino Raided
The Three Feathers Casino, operating independent of the tribal council in a fifty-five-thousand-square-foot building in Akwesasne since the summer of 2011, was raided by US federal marshals, Border Patrol agents and Mohawk Tribal Police officers in December 2012. The federal court trial saw all charges dropped against the four members of the Kaianerehkó:wa longhouse who were suspected of operating the casino.

2013—Elsipogtog
In June 2013, Texas-based Southwestern Energy (SWN Resources) started preliminary tests for fracking shale gas in the Mi'kmaq territory of Elsipogtog, near Moncton, New-Brunswick. Outraged by the project starting without their permission, Elsipogtog community members obstructed Highway 126 and staged several demonstrations in the following weeks, with some protesters being arrested. Hundreds of supporters soon swarmed to Elsipogtog, setting up encampments and blocking several highways in the area. The Mi'kmaq stressed that their sovereignty had been recognized by the 1760 and 1761 Peace and Friendship Treaties, and that no project could be undertaken on their land without their permission. On October 17, 2013, several hundred heavily militarized RCMP officers raided their camp on Highway 134, wounding a Mi'kmaq warrior with a rubber bullet and arresting and beating forty land and water defenders. SWN Resources reported that it was losing $60,000 daily because of the roadblocks and the destruction of its equipment and quietly abandoned the shale gas fracking project.

2016—Standing Rock
Opposing the construction of the Dakota Access Pipeline on lands recognized as Sioux territory by the 1851 Fort Laramie Treaty, Indigenous activists started gathering near the Standing Rock Reservation in North Dakota in the spring of 2016. By the fall, more than seven thousand supporters from three hundred different Indigenous nations had

joined three different camps blocking construction work for the pipeline, making it the largest gathering of North American Native peoples in modern history. Hundreds of militarized police officers from several police departments, including the National Guard, attacked the "Treaty Camp" on October 27, 2016, and would soon use water cannons against the protesters in the freezing November weather. Despite this, hundreds of protesters remained in the area until the end of February 2017. The pipeline was completed in April 2017. Although a district court judge subsequently ordered the Army Corps of Engineers to shut down the pipeline temporarily to conduct an environmental impact review in July 2020, the decision was overturned on appeal in August 2020, and the pipeline resumed its operations.

2018—Cannabis Dispensaries

With the legalization of cannabis in Canada, several independent dispensaries opened in Tyendinaga and Kanehsatà:ke, where they soon outnumbered Québec-owned cannabis shops. While the mayor of Oka, the settler town next to Kanehsatà:ke, pressed the police to shut down Mohawk dispensaries to no avail, tribal and band councils also attempted to curtail this emergent business in other Mohawk territories. After a raid in Tyendinaga in February 2019, the Mohawk Council of Akwesasne ordered police raids on two unlicensed cannabis dispensaries on the Canadian portion of the reservation. As tensions were already high with the band council, which had recently supported the Dundee settlement relinquishing the Mohawk Nation's claim of over twenty thousand acres of its traditional territory, the police officers found themselves surrounded by warriors while conducting a second raid, and a police cruiser was subsequently burnt.

2020—Railway Blockades in Support of the Wet'suwet'en

In the early morning of February 6, 2020, thirty-six RCMP police vehicles, along with their dogs, assault rifles, bulldozers, excavators, drones and infrared sensors, crossed the barricade where West Coast Wet'suwet'en land defenders had written "reconciliation" to guard the entrance to their territory. The RCMP were serving an injunction which Coastal GasLink had obtained from the Supreme Court of British Columbia to allow their employees to build a $6.6 billion pipeline on unceded Wet'suwet'en territory, despite the opposition of the nation's hereditary chiefs. Following the February 2020 raid, a large solidarity movement rose in support of the Wet'suwet'en, spearheaded by the railway blockades organized by Mohawk warriors in Tyendinaga and Kahnawà:ke, which in turn caused virtually all freight and passenger train traffic to grind to a halt for several weeks throughout the country. On February 24, despite the ongoing negotiations with Canadian minister of Indigenous services Marc Miller, Ontario Provincial Police officers raided the Tyendinaga blockade, arresting ten warriors. The police refused, however, to raid the Kahnawà:ke blockade, fearing that its defenders had military-grade guns. In the wake of the movement, land reoccupations also took place in Akwesasne and Ohswé:ken, where a camp called 1492 Land Back was set up against a housing development project bordering the town of Caledonia. The struggle was interrupted by the COVID-19 pandemic but came back to the forefront in November 2021, when the RCMP conducted another violent raid in Wet'suwet'en territory, violently arresting more than thirty land and water defenders, following the Wet'suwet'en hereditary chiefs' decision to close the road to the pipeline workers' camp, given their refusal to leave the area.

Skakwatakwen—Concept Glossary[*]

Aión:wes—*Keeper of the house*. This official title is often understood as the Kanien'kehá:ka war chief, but the role of the Aión:wes is just as important in times of peace. *Aión:wes* literally means *long winding river/creek*, as his responsibility as a keeper of the longhouse involves offering counsel and assistance to all families, bringing him to zigzag in all directions. Although he normally comes from the Turtle Clan, the Aión:wes is said to lose his clan when he takes on his new responsibilities; he must work for everyone and never take sides. The women's fire customarily appoints him to bring their matters to the council and can ask him to give them the floor. It is also his role in peacetime to ensure that the council always operates in accordance with the Kaianerehkó:wa. In wartime, the Aión:wes leads the Rotihsken'rakéhte' on the warpath, while women take charge of the administration of civil life. The word *A'share'kó:wa*, meaning *big knife*, is sometimes used for *war chief*, but it is a more recent word that many traditionalists consider to be incorrect. The Aión:wes is also often compared to the sun and referred to as the *Rosken'rhakehte'kó:wa*, or *the great warrior*. The war chiefs of the other Rotinonhsión:ni nations are the *Kahonwatí:ron* (Oneida), *Raién:tes* (Onondaga), *Wén:nen's* (Cayuga) and *Kanenó:ton* (Seneca). When the issue concerns the Rotinonhsión:ni Confederacy as a whole, the Seneca Kanenó:ton is supposed to take the lead.

A'nowarà:ke—*Turtle Island*, literally *on top of the turtle*. According to the Rotinonhsión:ni creation story, the world as we know it was created when the "Skywoman" Aatensic was thrown down a hole underneath a tree in the

---

[*] Audio recordings of these words read by Kaniehtiio Horn are available at http://www.ruedorion.ca/mohawk

Skyworld by her husband. Water birds, specifically loons, alleviated her fall, and because the world was then submerged in water, the animals convened to decide how to welcome her. Several animals, including a beaver, perished trying to plunge to the bottom of the sea and bring back soil to the surface, before a muskrat (in other versions, an otter) succeeded in bringing back some soil and putting it on the turtle. Aatensic landed on the turtle, which grew bigger and bigger until it became the North American continent.

Atónhnhets—*Life*, with a meaning that encompasses both the *breath* that animates the soul (similar in that sense to the ancient Greek word for *soul*, *pneuma*) and *livelihood* in the sense of what sustains us and keeps us alive.

Atón:wa—Thanksgiving words used to encourage or to express gratitude for someone's generosity, for the naming of a newborn child, for the adoption of a new family member, for condolences when a Roiá:ner passes away or for choosing a new one. The Atón:wa is used in the first part of the Midwinter and the Harvest Festivals. It literally means *to enjoy and appreciate life* and invites people to celebrate peace and happiness.

Enskerihwakwatá:ko'—As Iroquoian languages contain no word for *I'm sorry*, the *Enskerihwakwatá:ko'* is used to say *I will make it right*. This word suggests a commitment and a responsibility to repair whatever wrongs one has committed. *Enskerihwakwatá:ko'* can be contrasted with its Christianized version, *Sakatathré:wahte'*, which means *to repent* or *to confess*, and literally translates as *I hurt myself* or *I punished myself*, in reference to self-mortification. Although nowadays the word *Sakatatehriwá:sten* is sometimes also used to express regrets for wrongdoings, the meaning of the original Mohawk term *Enskerihwakwatá:ko'* goes farther by committing to repair them, as it is habitually opposed to *Iakonó:wen*, a liar, literally meaning hiding, bending over or arching one's back so that the truth cannot be seen.

Iah tehotiianerenhserá:ien—This term is used to designate white people and means both *they have no rights* and *they have no path*. This notion can be understood in relation to the Teiohá:te (Two Row Wampum), which states that European peoples must keep their language and culture on their own ship. They are, thus, expected to remain in their ship and on the water, kept at bay, so as to leave no trace, because they have no path of their own on a land which is not their mother. Iah Tehotiianerenhserá:ien, thus, suggests that non-Indigenous people have no birthright in North America, as the word derives from the negation (*Iah te*) of *Kaianerénhsera*, a word that means *law* or *right*, but without the legalistic, state-oriented connotation that it has in European languages. A literal way to say *they have no path* would be *Iah tehotiháhaien*, from *Oháha*, meaning *path*, *road* or *row*.

Iakoiá:ner—*Clan mother*, who is selected by her matrilineal kin on the basis of her qualities of care, knowledge and judgment. The Iakoiá:ner has a central role in representing the consensual positions of her matrilineal kin, who are responsible for selecting the Rotiianérshon by virtue of the Women's Nomination Belt.

Iethi'nisténha tsi ionhontsá:te'—*Mother Earth*. All plants that grow out of her are also understood to be female, while men are associated with the sun and the stars. (Alternate variations are *Iethi'nisténha tsi ionhwentsá:te'* and *Ionkhi'nisténha tsi ionhontsá:te'/ionhwentsá:te'*).

Kahrhákta—*At the edge of the woods*, from *Káhrha*, meaning *forest*. This welcoming protocol states that when someone arrives near a village, he must make a fire at the edge of the woods to announce his arrival. The villagers come to him and determine if it is safe to bring him in. In times of strife and disorganization, the men are required to "lay on their bellies at the edge of the woods" to let the women restore the original clan structure that existed before the fighting.

Kahwá:tsire'—*Family*, literally the *gathering of all embers*, in reference to the family's hearth in the longhouse. The family is a fire created when each person, *Ó:tsire'*, or *ember*, gathers with his relatives to create a flame and intensify the heat. Families do not only include biological relatives, as clans cross the borders of nations in such a way that Mohawk members of the Wolf Clan are considered to be members of the same family as Wolf Clan members from other Rotinonhsión:ni nations, and even from beyond the Iroquoian language group. When the Kahwá:tsire' of all clans reunite in the grand council of the Rotinonhsión:ni Confederacy, it creates a *Katsenhowá:nen*, or *big fire*. The idea of fire is also related to how decisions are arrived at in councils. Even though it may look like a fire is out, meaning that a decision has been arrived at, it is necessary to "stir the ashes" to make sure all the coals are burnt out. The coals that are still burning represent those who still did not voice their opinion, and whose insight may still be necessary to ensure a full consensus.

Kaianerehkó:wa—The constitution of the Rotinonhsión:ni Confederacy that was brought by Dekanawida, Hiawatha and Jigonhsasee to resolve conflicts between and among nations. The Kaianerehkó:wa comprises 117 articles and wampums, defining protocols for consensual decision-making in the longhouse. The *Kaianerehkó:wa* is often translated as the *Great Law*, the *Great Law of Peace* or the *Great Binding Law*, but it has little to do with law in the Western, coercive sense of the word. More accurate translations would include the *Great Peace*, the *Great Goodness* (given that *Kaiáneren* is the nominal form of *ioiánere*, meaning *it is good*, and that the suffix *kó:wa* means *great*) and the *Great Path*, or the *Footprints to the Great Good* (as *kaiana* means a *path* or *footprints*).

Kaientowá:nen—*Peach stone/bowl game*, a game similar to dice played with peach seeds which have been darkened on one side, and which are thrown into a bowl. At the Midwinter Festival, the peach stone/bowl game opposes clans (Wolves and Turtles play against the Bears and other clans, including adoptees), but at the Harvest Festival, it has men and women playing against each other ("the house is divided"). The winners receive prizes prepared by the families, including crafts such as baskets and water drums, but they also win the responsibility of planning work in the garden and ceremonies for the coming year: they will be "taking care of the house". The side that did not win will sit back and watch, preparing to do better the next year. More than a game, it is a social event that brings the families together to remind themselves of what makes their community strong.

Kaión:ni—A wampum, or, rather, the message enclosed in it. The root *ión:ni* means something that had been *made*, while *Kaión:wa* refers to *wampum belts*. This suggests that *Kaión:ni* literally means that a *message*, *pledge* or *agreement* has materialized into the Onekò:rha, the purple and white quahog shells of which wampums are made, which provide shelter for the words. The words must be reinstated in the wampums and the dust removed from them every year, a task whose responsibility among the Kanien'kehá:ka belongs to the Hiawatha, or Ayonwentha, family, as *Ayonwentha* means *removing the dust*.

Kanenhó:ron—*Seed Festival*, from *Ká:nen*, meaning *seeds*, and *Ka'rhó:ron*, meaning *it is covered*. This festival contains a drum dance and a thanksgiving address in honor of the elements of creation that provide models for human life.

Kanien'kehá:ka—*People of the land of flint*, also known as *Mohawks*.

Ka'nisténhsera'—*Life-givers*, meaning the *women* and the *mothers*. *O'nísta* refers to the point where the umbilical cord is attached to the mother. In this sense, the connection between the women and Mother Earth is similar to the stem that connects the apple to the tree. In this manner, Ka'nisténhsera' have a power, a Ka'shatsténhsera', that is rooted in the Earth. Wampum 44 of the Kaianerehkó:wa states that the women are "the progenitors of the soil" and its caretakers for the *Tahatikonhsontóntie*, the *children yet to come*, or the *future generations*.

Kanonhsionni'ón:we—*One real/original house*. The entire territory of the Rotinonhsión:ni Confederacy is understood to be one big longhouse, whose eastern door is guarded by the Kanien'kehá:ka, while the Senecas guard its western door. Yet the real/original house extends even beyond these borders to all Turtle Island, as the sky is understood as its ceiling, Mother Earth as its floor and the people as its walls. The analogy between Rotinonhsión:ni society and a house is also present in the word *Wahatinastó:ton*, which means *to rebuild the community by bending and binding the poles together to hold up the roof*.

Kanonhstá:ton—*Land to defend*. This word shares roots with Kanien'kehá:ka words *Enhsenónhstate'*, meaning *territory*, which literally means *you will protect and respect it*, and *Ó:nenhste'*, meaning *corn*, which literally means *it supports us/we will protect it*. Kanonhstá:ton suggests that one should do whatever is necessary to preserve the goodness of the land that supports life. It is often used in struggles to protect the land for future generations and was specifically used as a name for the land near Ohswé:ken that was reoccupied in 2006.

Kanoronhkwáhtshera'—This word refers to *love* in the sense of taking the best of yourself to embrace another person with your goodness.

Kanoronhkwáhtshera' is a lovingfulness (for one another, for the land and for creation) that acts as a medicine by giving strength to someone. It means to have the ability to show and to share the love that you have for your life experiences, the people that you know, the language that you speak and the Earth where you are. The adjective *Kanó:ron* suggests a love that is all the more valuable and cherished, because it is rare and should not be taken for granted. Instead of presenting it as a passion or emotion, the Kanien'kehá:ka idea of love conveys a sense of responsibility and action, as it is so precious that one has to give the best of oneself to protect it. This word is very present in condolence ceremonies, based on the "small condolence", which consists of clearing the eyes, the ears, the throat and the stomach to overcome grief.

Karihwí:io—Often translated as *righteousness*, this word means something closer to *that which is real*, as *Orihwí:io* means *something that is definite and unquestionable*. Karihwí:io is the way in which things are real. Today, the word is used in reference to the Handsome Lake Code, but Kaianerehkó:wa people consider the "longhouse religion" of Handsome Lake to be a *Karihwiiohstónhtshera'*, a *man-made reality*, that only exists in the mind, as it was created by men, like all religions. Along with *Skén:nen*, meaning *peace*, and *Ka'shatsténhsera'*, meaning *power*, Karihwí:io is one of the three pillars of the Kaianerehkó:wa, which are bound together, because it is necessary to work with the natural reality to gain strength and acquire peace.

Ka'shatsténhsera'—*Power*. One of the three pillars of the Kaianerehkó:wa, Ka'shatsténhsera' refers to the inner power carried by every living creature to make life continue. As for human beings, their power is to be grateful for everything that sustains their lives. Ka'shatsténhsera' is a willful desire to persevere by sharing our strength with all our relations. Creation here must be understood as a power that is not of a personal nature, in contrast with the human-like entity which the Handsome Lake Code calls the *Creator*, or *Shonkwaia'tíson*, literally *he who made our bodies*.

Katsenhowá:nen—*Rotinonhsión:ni grand council gathering*, literally *big fire*. It comes from the words *Otsénha'*, meaning *fireplace*, *hearth* or *council fire*, and *Kowá:nen*, meaning *big*.

Kontihontsakwe'ní:io—*Women's fire.* It literally means *they are the main ones of Earth*, in the sense that the women and the Earth share the same power as givers of life. Another variation of this word is *Konnonhwentsakwe'ní:io.*

Ohén:ton tsi karihwatéhkwen—Thanksgiving address to the natural elements. It literally means the *words that come before everything else*, as thanksgiving words serve to introduce and close not only Rotinonhsión:ni ceremonies and festivals but also political and social events. Giving thanks to the natural elements that sustain life constitutes the basis of Rotinonhsión:ni spirituality, in contrast to "religions" based on the rejection of the natural world, which rely on authority, law, guilt and repentance.

Oien'kwèn:ton—*Tobacco hangers*, in reference to the tobacco hung on the rafters of the longhouse so that it would always be available when needed. *Oien'kwèn:ton* designates special forces within the Rotihsken'rakéhte', who are always ready to intervene. They used to cover themselves with the oil of fermented chestnuts to blend in with the shadows in the forest. The Oien'kwèn:ton are accountable to the Aión:wes and to the council. After some warnings, they deliver the Black Wampum as a last offer of peace, launching a battle if the opposite party lets it drop on the floor. From then on, the Kaianerehkó:wa states that the war must continue until it is won completely. It is also said that the Oien'kwèn:ton used to carry pouches of tobacco on them when they went to war.

O'nikòn:ra'—*Mind*, or literally *it takes care of you, it protects you* or *it watches over you*. The mind is connected to all the elements of creation through all its senses and emotions. If it is taken care of, it will reciprocally provide the answers that will allow life to endure.

Onkwehón:we—*Native, original* or *real people*. This word literally means *people who will always be part of creation, the original way, the way of forever* or *the way of creation*, as *ón:kwe* means *human* and *ón:we* means *forever*. *Onkwehón:we:néha* refers to the language, customs and ways of the original, or Native, people, while *Onkwehón:wè:keh* refers to their land.

Orén:na'—*Life substance* pervading all living beings. This word is also often written *Orén:ta* or *Orenda*. Its broader meaning is *energy that* *invigorates one.* More specifically, it means a *power* or *skill* (hunting skills, for example) that humans share with non-human living beings. Tuscarora anthropologist J.N.B. Hewitt recounted that all the animals were understood to have their own Orén:na', which they sang to communicate with the other elements of creation. Today, this word is mostly associated with singing and music, while Christians have adopted it to refer to *prayer.*

Ostowa'kó:wa—*Binding Festival*, which features the Feather Dance. Dekanawida brought this festival to complete the Kaianerehkó:wa. This word may have been adopted into the Mohawk language from the other sister confederate nations. Equivalent Kanien'kehá:ka words would be *Osto'sera'kó:wa,* meaning *great feather*, or *Oron'onhkwa'kó:wa,* meaning *great feather cluster.*

Roiá:ner—*Chief*, or *sachem*, although Roiá:ner does not imply any coercive power. This word literally means *they who have a clear path/footprints to walk on*, a path following the footsteps of their predecessors. The plural form *Rotiianérshon* includes both *Roiá:ner* men and *Iakoiá:ner* women. The forty-nine Rotiianérshon forming the Rotinonhsión:ni Confederacy lose their name when they receive their title and duties and pass their title on through the condolence and requickening ceremonies when they pass away.

Rotihsken'rakéhte'—*Men's council fire*. It was translated into *Warrior Society* when the fire was rekindled in the 1970s, but the Rotihsken'rakéhte' traditionally includes all male adults. While women make the real decisions, given their connection to the Earth, men are associated with the sun and stars, which provide light, warmth and energy. According to Tekarontakeh, *Rotihsken'rakéhte'* comes from the root *o'kén:ra*, meaning *soil* and, thus, means *carriers of the Earth*, referring to the pouch containing a man's umbilical cord, totem and natal soil. Other translations have been proposed as well. For instance, Tuscarora ethnologist J.N.B. Hewitt suggested that *Rotihsken'rakéhte'* means *they carry mats on their back*—referring to the hemp (*Óhskare'*) mattresses that warriors used to bring on their expeditions, on which they would sleep and sit. For his part, Kahnawà:ke Bear Clan Roiá:ner Frank Natawe suggested that the root word *oskèn:rha'* means *rust, mold* or *corrosion*, and that in past times this word was also used for *war*, which was seen as corrosion. Alternatively, it may have described

Europeans wearing metal armor, which would rust. Some elders suggest that it rather refers to *bones* or *skeletons*, as warriors carry the legacy of their ancestors on their back. Etymological debates concerning the meaning of *Rotihsken'rakéhte'* are not a new phenomenon, as French Jesuit Jean-François Lafitau remarked in 1724 that the Iroquois could not agree on its meaning, and all suggested that it was a very old word.

Rotinonhsión:ni—*Iroquois or Five/Six Nations Confederacy*. This word literally means *they who make the house*, as the Rotinonhsión:ni longhouse extends over all of Turtle Island.

Sha'oié:ra—*Way of creation forever* or *direction of reality*. Used in every-day language to refer to *nature* or *natural*, in the sense of *part of the order of things*, the root *oie:ra*, meaning *direction*, suggesting a continuous temporality whereby nature never ceases to become itself. Its relation to creation can be contrasted with the Christian-influenced *Creator*, or *Shonkwaia'tíson*. *Sha'oié:ra*, instead, refers to creation and nature as a self-generative process that is not directed by a human-like conscious-ness. It refers to how the sun rises, the winds blow and the plants and animals—the natural family of the universe, all that which support life—grow continuously together in harmony to ensure the continuity of life.

Sha'tetionkwátte'—*We are equal in height*. This word suggests that nobody's voice is above any other, as every person has a mind. The Circle Wampum, Teiotiohkwahnhákton, suggests that the forty-nine Rotinonhsión:ni families have made a pact that they will treat each other equally in the longhouse, no matter their numbers or their strength. All their voices are equal. This idea can be associated with *Tewatatewenní:io*, meaning *we are all free*.

Tahatikonhsontóntie—*Children yet to come*, who will come forward to become the future generations. This word literally means *those whose faces are still in the ground*. As they still dwell within Mother Earth, the babies are considered to be the true "owners" of the land, whose caretakers are the *Ka'nisténhsera'*, the women *life-givers*.

Teiohá:te—Literally meaning *two paths*, this word refers to the Two Row Wampum exchanged with the Dutch in the early seventeenth century. This wampum belt displays two purple rows on a white background, symbolizing a river where the original people's canoe and the settlers' ship are said to sail side by side, ready to help one another if their vessel should ever capsize but always making sure to keep their culture and ways of life within their own boat. As an alliance belt, it suggests that parties can only move in the same direction in the river of life if they remain parallel and refrain from crossing each other's path. Sometimes the word *Kaswénhta* is also used for this wampum, although its meaning is unclear. *Kaswénhta* might be related to the word *Teka'swénhtha*, meaning *it shuts all the fires out*, or it could have been adopted from the pidgin Lenape word *Sewant*, which means *it is scattered about*, and which was used at the time to refer to wampum shells.

Teiotiohkwahnhákton—*Circle Wampum*, comprising all Rotinonhsión:ni families, along with their names, ways, traditions, birthrights, etc. The Teiotiohkwahnhákton implies that if someone leaves the circle, he is left naked and has alienated himself (*Tehonatonkóhton*) from the Kaianerehkó:wa. Alternate forms of this word are *Teiokiohkwahákton* and *Teyotyohkwahnhákton*.

Tewatatewenní:io—*We are all free/sovereign* or *we all carry ourselves*. Given that the prefix *tewa* encompasses everyone without exception, *Tewatatewenní:io* means that freedom is a universal condition inscribed in nature. According to Tekarontakeh, *Tewatatewenní:io* contains the word *Tsi ní:io(ht)*, which means *the way it is*, in the sense of *the way it arrived/ got here*. It would also seem that *Tewatatewenní:io* also contains the word which Iroquois Christians have adopted for *God*, *Rawenní:io*. Consequently, for Christians *Tewatatewenní:io* would suggest the sacrilegious idea that *everyone is a god*. However, *Rawenní:io* may itself be derived from the old Wendat word for the *thunder*, *Ratiwenní:io*, which means *they have big voices*.

Thadodáho/Atotáhrho—Literally the *entangled*. This was the name of the snake-haired Onondaga chief who waged war against all other Rotinonhsión:ni nations before Dekanawida and Hiawatha convinced him to join the alliance. Thadodáho then became the grand chief of the confederacy, who welcomes grand councils in Onondaga. He is also entangled, because having no clan mother, he belongs to all the families, and everyone is connected to his title.

Tionerahtase'kó:wa—*Great White Pine* or *Tree of Peace*. This word literally means the *great forever renewing tree*. Dekanawida first erected this tree in Onondaga and buried the weapons of war underneath it, but Trees of Peace were often planted symbolically and physically throughout history to mark alliances. The branches of the Tionerahtase'kó:wa are said to cover the territories of all Rotinonhsión:ni nations and their allies, extending over all Turtle Island. Falling needles represent those who have passed away and returned to the soil, yet new needles always appear, representing the coming faces emerging from the ground. The Tionerahtase'kó:wa lives forever, symbolizing how Rotinonhsión:ni ways of living remain intact. To ensure this continuity, the *Ronterontanónhnha, they watch the log*, are instructed to climb up the tree to see incoming threats. The Ronterontanónhnha are often called *Pine Tree Chiefs*, but traditional people consider all individuals as responsible for monitoring incoming threats. In times of strife, war or disease, Article 61 of the Kaianerehkó:wa suggests that the Rotinonhsión:ni should leave the Pine Tree and retreat under the *Great Swamp Elm*, the *Onerahté:sons*, meaning *long leaves*—a protocol which explains how traditional people often had to practice their traditions underground. Alternate forms of the word *Tionerahtase'kó:wa* are *Tsonerahtase'kó:wa* and *Onerahtase'kó:wa*.

Tionitiohtià:kon—*Montréal*. This word is better known in its short- ened version, *Tiohtià:ke*, which means nothing by itself. *Tionitiohtià:kon* means *where the people broke up*. Montréal used to be a gathering place where the Anishinaabe peoples north of the Saint Lawrence River and the Rotinonhsión:ni peoples from the south met. The people broke up when such meetings were no longer possible after the colonizers had settled there.

Wahsá:se'—*War song*, from *á:se*, meaning *new*. *Wahsá:se'* is a traditional song used to greet and acknowledge the grandfather thunders who wake up the hibernating animals and plants and replenish Mother Earth, who has been resting under her *winter blanket*, or *Akohserà:ke*.

Traditional Festivities

Wáhta—Maple Festival, middle of February

Ratiwè:ras—Thunder Dance, first week of April

Ká:nen tánon' Onónhkwa'—Seeds and Medecine Festival, May

Ken' niiohontésha—Strawberry Festival, May

Skanekwen'tará:nen—Raspberry Festival, June

O'rhótsheri—Green Bean Festival, August

Okahserò:ta'—Green Corn Festival, August

Kaienthókwen—Harvest Festival, October

Sha'tekohséhrhen—Midwinter Festival. This festival starts five days after the new moon has reached its zenith, in January or February. First day: *Sha'tekohséhrhen*, the stirring of the ashes, the flesh of Mother Earth. Second day: *Ostowa'kó:wa*, the Great Feather Dance. Third day: *Wa'therarà:ken*, sacrifice of a white basket. Fourth day: *Atón:wa*, personal thanksgiving and naming ceremony. Fifth day: *Onehó:ron*, Water Drum Dance. Sixth day: *Kaientowá:nen*, peach stone/bowl game.

Ohkí:we—Feast for the dead

Place Names and Peoples' Names

The definitions provided in this section refer to the names featured in the map at the center of this book.

Kanien'kehá:ka Territories

Akwesasne (place of partridges), or **Ahkwesáhsne**
> Kanien'kehá:ka territory (est. 1755). Its colonial name is Saint-Regis.

Canajoharie, or **Kana'tsóhare'** (washed pail, [referring to the potholes in the riverbeds])
> Upper Kanien'kehá:ka Castle, destroyed during the American Revolutionary War.

Ganienkeh (place of flint)
> Kanien'kehá:ka territory reoccupied in 1974 in Moss Lake, New York, before it was moved further north to Miner Lake, New York, in 1977.

Kahnawà:ke (at the rapids)
> Kanien'kehá:ka territory (est. 1716). Before moving to its current location, Kahnawà:ke was situated further east, originally known as the Jesuit Catholic mission of Ken'tà:ke, in present-day La Prairie.

Kanehsatà:ke (place of sand)
> Kanien'kehá:ka territory (est. 1721). Some say Kanehsatà:ke originally referred to a *place at the bottom of the hill*, as it was originally established at the bottom of Mount Royal in 1676. After the mixed Rotinonhsión:ni and Anishinaabe Sulpician mission moved the shores of the Lac-des-Deux-Montagnes in 1721, Kanehsatà:ke most likely took the meaning of *place of the sand*, from *O'néhsa*, the word for the kind of sand that can be found its shores. Its colonial name is Sault-Saint-Louis.

Kenhtè:ke (at the grasslands/at the bay) or **Tyendinaga** (he put two pieces of wood side by side)

Kanien'kehá:ka territory (est. 1784). There are two different possibilities for the meaning of *Kenhtè:ke*. It could be a distortion of *Kahentà:ke*, meaning *at the grasslands/prairies*, most likely derived from Cayuga language. Alternately, it would come from an old Mohawk word for *bay*, *Kénhte*, as the village sits on the Bay of Quinte. As for the name Tyendinaga, it is the anglicized version of the Kanien'kehá:ka name *Thaientané:ken*, which means *he put two pieces of wood side by side* or *he put two bets side by side*, which was Joseph Brant's name. Kenhtè:ke is said to have been the birthplace of Dekanawida, back when it was a Wendat village.

Ohswé:ken (an undercurrent created by forked lips/mouth/spout) or **Six Nations of the Grand River**

Kanien'kehá:ka territory (est. 1784). The origin of the word *Ohswé:ken* for this multinational Rotinonhsión:ni village remains obscure, but it likely refers to an undercurrent created by the lips, mouth or spout in the river there. Some say it was originally pronounced *Teiohswé:ken*, meaning *the lips/spout/mouth is forked* but was shortened to *Ohswé:ken* over time.

Tionontogen or **Teionontó:ken** (between two hills)

Lower Kanien'kehá:ka Castle, destroyed during the American Revolutionary War.

Tioweró:ton (a wind that comes from underneath), or **Doncaster**

Kanien'kehá:ka territory (est. 1851). These eighteen-thousand-acre hunting grounds are currently managed by the communities of Kahnawà:ke and Kanehsatà:ke, which received it as compensation for lands lost to the construction of the Lake Saint Louis and Province Line (LSL & PL).

Wahta (Maple), or **Gibson**

Kanien'kehá:ka territory (est. 1881). Approximately fifty Kanien'kehá:ka families moved with Chief Joseph Onesakenrat to this formerly Anishinaabe territory in 1881 due to political and religious conflicts in Kanehsatà:ke.

Other Rotinonhsión:ni Territories

Allegany
Seneca territory (est. 1797).

Cattaraugus (the clay stinks [because of the sulfur there])
Seneca territory (est. 1797).

Cayuga (at the marshlands)
The Cayuga people have had no official territory since the 1799 Sullivan-Clinton expedition chased them from their land. They now mainly live in Ohswé:ken and started buying back their territory at the north end of Cayuga Lake in 2005.

Oil Springs
Seneca territory, formerly Wenro territory (before 1639).

Oneida (at the standing stone)
Traditional Oneida territory.

Oneida Nation of the Thames
Oneida territory (est. 1840), formerly Mississauga and Neutral territory.

Oneida Nation of Wisconsin
Oneida territory (est. 1820), formerly Ho-Chunk and Mamaceqtaw territory.

Onondaga (at the hills)
Onondaga territory, central fire of the confederacy.

Seneca-Cayuga Nation of Oklahoma
Seneca and Cayuga territory (est. 1831), formerly Cherokee territory. The Seneca and Cayuga inhabitants of this settlement are descendants of the Mingo Iroquois who relocated to Ohio in the second half of the eighteenth century, moving along the Sandusky River, before ending up further west, in Oklahoma, in 1831.

Tonawanda or T'ohnawanta (there are rapids there)
Seneca territory, formerly on the territory of the Neutral Nation in the seventeenth century.

Tuscarora (hemp gatherers/splitters)
Tuscarora territory, formerly Seneca and Neutral territory. Originally from North Carolina, Tuscarora people have also lived in Ohswé:ken, Buffalo, Ohio and Oklahoma since the early nineteenth century.

Colonial Settlements

Anatakariásne (place of the president)
  Washington, DC

Kanatà:ke (at/on the town)
  Green Bay, Wisconsin

Kanà:tso (pot/cauldron in the water [in reference to Chaudiere Falls])
  Ottawa, Ontario

Kanawa'tstákeras (the mud stinks)
  Massena Springs, New York

Kanón:no (place of reeds [used for pipes or splints]) or Tkaná:to (a town in
  water there) or, more recently, Kanorónsne (place of expensive things)
  New York City, New York

Kanontowá:nen (big mountain [because of the Cahokia site nearby])
  Saint Louis, Missouri

Karonhiatsi'kowáhne (at the big sky)
  Longueuil, Québec

Kawehnohkwésne (place of the long island)
  Long Island, New York

Kenhtà:ke (at the grasslands/prairies) or **Ken'tà:ke**
  La Prairie, Québec

Ken'tarà:ke (place of clay) or **Cataraqui**
  Kingston, Ontario

Nikahionhwa'kó:wa (big river)
  Watertown, New York

Nikentsà:ke (place of big fish)
  Massena, New York

Ohrón:wakon (in the ditch, ravine)
  Hamilton, Ontario

O'nionkserì:ke (place of the onion/wild garlic [in reference to the Illiniwek
  origin of the name Chicago])
  Chicago, Illinois

Oshahrhè:'on (bulrushes/cattails [*Osháhrhe*] scattered here and there)
  Châteauguay, Québec

Skahentowá:nen (across the large meadow/grassland/prairie)
  Wilkes-Barre, Pennsylvania

Skahnéhtati (on the other side of the pines [where canoes used to land to avoid the waterfall separating the Mohawk River from the Hudson River])

Albany/Schenectady, New York

Teiohswathénion (many bright things)

Pittsburgh, Pennsylvania

Teió:ken (it splits)

Buffalo, New York, and Athens, Pennsylvania

Tekahiónhake (two rivers/streams)

London, Ontario

Tekahswen'karó:rens (at the sawmill)

Hogansburg, New York

Tekanatà:ronhwe' (a town that extends over one side to the other)

Malone, New York

Tekashó:ken (a forked mouth)

Philadelphia, Pennsylvania

Thatinatón:ni (they build towns/cities there)

Guelph, Ontario

Tiaontarí:kon (where the waterway comes back together [from being previously split])

Québec City, Québec

Tiehoniokwáhtha' (lift the boat [portage])

Rome, New York

Tiohná:wate' (it is a strong current there)

Louisville, Kentucky

Tiohsahróntion (there are many mouths running along it)

Detroit, Michigan

Tionitiohtià:kon (the place where the people broke up)

Montréal, Québec

Tkarón:to' (logs in the water there [in reference to the two-thousand-year-old human-built Mnjikaning Fish Weirs in Lake Simcoe])

Toronto, Ontario

Tken'taresónsne (many long chimneys there [probably a postcolonial name])

Fredonia, New York

Tsi Ietsénhtha' (where one draws up water)

Plattsburgh, New York

Tsi Kahiatonhserón:ni (where the papers are made)
   Salaberry-de-Valleyfield, Québec
Tsi Kahionhó:kon (at that place on the [Cuyahoga] river)
   Cleveland, Ohio
Tsi Kanatáhere' (where the town is situated on [something undetermined])
   Brantford, Ontario

Natural Features
Akohserà:ke (in winter [as this region was used as a winter camp])
   Saratoga Springs region, New York
Chautauqua Lake (place where the fish have been taken out)
   New York State
Iohskóhare' (the bridge is hanging up there)
   Schoharie Creek, New York
Kahentà:ke (at the grasslands/prairies)
   origin of the name Kentucky
Kahoniókwen (portage/lift the canoe)
   Cayuga Lake, New York
Kahrhionhwa'kó:wa (great-sized river)
   the Saint Lawrence River, the Hudson River and the Ottawa River
   are all known as *great-sized rivers.* Iroquoian place names are almost
   always descriptive and should not be considered as immutable proper
   names, as in European languages.
Kanatasè:ke (place of the new town)
   Seneca Lake, New York
Kaniatarahòn:tsi (black river)
   Oswegatchie River, New York
Kaniatarakwá:ronte' (where the waterway bulges)
   Lake Champlain
Kaniatariio (main/good lake)
   origin of the name Ontario, via the Wendat word *Oniatariio*
Kaniá:taro'kte (lake end)
   Lake George, New York
Kinzua (fish on a pole [as it was an important spearfishing spot])
   Pennsylvania
Ohi:yo (a great river)
   origin of the name Ohio

Ohnawiiò:ke or **Kahnawiiò:ke** (at the gentle rapids)
   Mississippi River
Ohrhionhwí:io (the river is good/important)
   Allegany River and Ohio River
Ohsa'kentà:ke (at the bulrushes/cattails)
   Sacandaga River, New York
Oniá:kara' (neck)
   Niagara Falls
Ononhwaróhare (head up on a pole [as it was named by Dutch explorer
   Harmen Meyndertsz van den Bogaert in his 1634 voyage, in reference
   to a scalp that had been placed on a pole there])
   Oneida Lake, New York
Oròn:ia' (blue)
   Tupper Lake, New York
Skahentowanè:ke (at the big prairie)
   Delaware River
Skaniá:tares (a long lake)
   Skaneateles Lake, New York
Skanontkaraksèn:ke (the mountains are rough)
   Green Mountains, Vermont
Teiohonwahkwat' (where you lift the boat [in reference to the great Oneida
   carrying place near Fort Stanwix])
   Mohawk River, going upstream
Teió:ken (it splits)
   Mohawk River, going downstream towards the Hudson River
Tewahskóhon (bridge submerged into water there)
   Owasco Lake, New York
Tiohio'tsista'kowáhne
   Atlantic Ocean
Tkanatarákwen (a town chosen there)
   Canandaigua Lake, New York
Tkarón:to (logs in the water there [in reference to the Mnjikaning Fish
   Weirs])
   Lake Simcoe, Ontario
Tsi tiontahsehtahkhwà:ke (where they used to hide at [from the Yesañ/
   Tutelo, who joined the confederacy with the Tuscaroras])
   Appalachian Mountains

Indigenous Peoples[1]
Rotinonhsión:ni Peoples in Kanien'kehá:ka Language
Kahoniokwenhá:ka
  Cayuga Nation (people of Kahoniókwen, Cayuga Lake)
Kanien'kehá:ka
  Mohawk Nation (people of Kanièn:ke, the Mohawk River Valley)
Oneniote'á:ka
  Oneida Nation (people of Onén:iote, a town)
Ononta'kehá:ka
  Onondaga Nation (people of Onontà:ke, a town)
Thatiskarò:roks
  Tuscarora Nation (people who gather up hemp)
Tsonontowane'á:ka
  Seneca Nation (people of Tsonontó:wane, a town)

Other Indigenous Peoples
Andastoerrhonon (people of the blackened ridge pole, a name of Wendat origin), **Susquehannock** (colonial name, mixing Algonquian and Iroquoian stems referring to a river, the Susquehanna), **Minquas** (Lenape name apparently meaning *treacherous*, given their mutual hostility, and used by Dutch and Swedish settlers) or **Conestoga** (colonial name derived from the Iroquoian word, *Kanastoge, place of the upright pole)*; Iroquoian language family. After subsuming and transforming the Leni Lenape into their tributaries in the early seventeenth century, the Andastoerrhonon were included in a Covenant Chain offered by the Rotinonhsión:ni in 1679, and the majority of its people joined the Seneca and Onondaga.
Anigiduwagi (principal people), **Cherokee** (colonial name, possibly derived from a Choctaw word meaning *people of the mountains*) or **Oyata'ge'ronoñ** (*inhabitants of the cave country* [as they were called by the Rotinonhsión:ni]); Iroquoian language family. The Anigiduwagi may have originally migrated south from the Great Lakes, where most Iroquoian peoples lived. In the nineteenth century, they adopted European lifestyles and farming and began writing their language with their own calligraphy, invented by Sequoyah. In 1839, American president Andrew Jackson forcibly removed them from their lands in the new Georgia State, and sixteen thousand Anigiduwagi and

one to two thousand of their slaves marched west, four thousand of them dying on the way. This is known in America as the Trail of Tears.

Anishinaabe (original people) or **Omàmiwinini** (downriver people [used specifically in Ontario]) or **Algonquins** (colonial name); Algonquian language family. Although their alliance with the French often pitted the Anishinaabe people of the Great Lakes and Ottawa River against the Rotinonhsión:ni, they share cultural traits, such as the use of wampum and the principle of shared hunting grounds (one dish, one spoon).

Bodéwadmi (firekeepers), **Neshnabé** (original people) or **Potawatomi** (colonial name); Algonquian language family. They were the "youngest brothers" of the Three Fires Confederacy, which also included the Ojibwa and Odaawaa peoples.

Chonnonton (keepers of the deer) or **Neutral people** (colonial name, because they stayed neutral in conflicts between the Iroquois and the Wendat); Iroquoian language family. The Chonnonton were organized in a confederacy which included the Aondironon, the Ongniaahrarono and the Wenrohronon (also known as Wenros). They were dispersed in the 1650 and integrated mainly by the Senecas and the Wendat.

Eeyou (the people, used in *Eeyou Istchee*, James Bay), **Nehiyawak** (those who speak the same language, used in the Plains) or **Cree** (from the Ojibwa word *Kiristino* used to designate people living around Hudson Bay); Algonquian language family. Now the largest Indigenous group in Canada. In the seventeenth and eighteenth centuries, the Nehiyawak were part of the Iron Confederacy with the Ojibwa, the Nakoda/Assiniboine, the Métis and some Rotinonhsión:ni groups that had moved west for the fur trade.

Eriechronon (long tail [in reference to either the racoon, the cougar or the eastern panther]), **Erie** or **Nation du Chat** (French colonial name); Iroquoian language family. After losing a war against the Rotinonhsión:ni in the 1650s, most Eriechronon people were absorbed by the Seneca.

Ho-Chunk (people of the big voice), **Hoocągra** or **Winnebago** (colonial name, from the Bodéwadmi word for *people of the muddy water*, in reference to Green Bay); Siouan language family.

Illiniwek (speaking the ordinary way) or **Illinois** (colonial spelling); Algonquian language family. The Illiniwek were organized in a confederacy of thirteen tribes along the Mississippi River, including the Cahokia, Kaskaskia, Michigamea, Peoria and Tamaroa.

Innu (human being) or **Montagnais** (colonial name); Algonquian language family.

Kiikaapoa (stands here and there) or **Kickapoo** (colonial spelling); Algonquian language family. The Kiikaapoa were part of the Wabash Confederacy led by the Myaamiaki and joined the larger Northwestern Confederacy to resist colonial encroachment following the American Revolutionary War.

Leni Lenape (real people) or **Delaware** (colonial name coming from the Delaware River, which they lived along; the river in turn is named after the first Governor of Virginia, the Baron De la Warr); Algonquian language family, divided between Munsee, Unami and Unalachtigo speakers. The Leni Lenape were a tributary to the Rotinonhsión:ni Confederacy from 1676 to 1753. They now live mostly in Oklahoma, after having been removed from their lands by the United States government in the 1860s.

Mamaceqtaw (people) or **Menominee** (wild rice people [colonial name derived from the Ojibwa word *Manoominii*]); Algonquian language family.

Mascouten (treeless country/plains/fire) or **Fire Nation**; Algonquian language family. The last reference to the Mascouten was recorded in 1779, when they were living near the Wabash River.

Massachuseuck (at the great hill) or **Massachusett**; Algonquian language family.

Meskwaki (the red-earths [from the cultural hero Wisaka who created humans out of clay]) or **Fox people** (colonial name); Algonquian language family.

Misi-zaagiing (those at the great river mouth) or **Mississauga** (colonial spelling); Algonquian language family.

Mohegan (people of the wolf) or **Pequot** (colonial name, from the Anishinaabe word for *destroyers*); Algonquian language family.

Montaukett (place of observation) or **Montauk** (colonial spelling); Algonquian language family. On their Long Island homeland, the Montaukett harvested the quahog shells of which wampums were made.

Muhhekunneuw (people of the great tidal river) or **Mahican/Mohican** (colonial name); Algonquian language family. After numerous skirmishes with the neighbouring Mohawks in the 1620s, most Muhhekunneuw people joined the Oneida, who gave them twenty-two thousand acres for their use in the wake of the American Revolutionary War.

Myaamiaki (downstream people), **Mihtohseeniaki** (people) or **Miami** (colonial spelling); Algonquian language family. The Myaamiaki were a confederacy including many groups (Atchakangouen, Kilatika, Mengakonkia, Pepikokia, Peeyankihšia/Piankashaw, Wea), but the term is mostly used for the Atchakangouen today. They were forcefully displaced to the west (Oklahoma, Indiana) in the mid–nineteenth century.

Nahahiganseck (people of the small points) or **Narragansett** (colonial spelling); Algonquian language family.

Nehirowisiw (autonomous being) or **Atikamekw** (white fish); Algonquian language family.

Nentego (tidewater people) or **Nanticoke** (colonial name); Algonquian language family. They originally included the Choptank, the Assateague, the Piscataway and the Doeg peoples.

Nipamaug (people of the freshwater pond) or **Nipmuc**; Algonquian language family.

Norridgewock (people of the still water between the rapids) or **Kennebec**; Algonquian language family.

Odaawaa/Odawa (traders) or **Ottawa** (colonial name); Algonquian language family. The Odaawaa belong to the larger Anishinaabe peoples, alongside the Algonquins and Ojibwa. They were part of the Three Fire Confederacy with the Ojibwa and Bodéwadmi peoples.

Ojibwa/Ojibwe (possibly meaning *folded/wrinkled*, in reference to how moccasins are made), **Chippewa** (colonial spelling), **Saulteaux** (French colonial name in reference to the rapids in Sault Ste. Marie/Michilimakinac); Algonquian language family. The Ojibwa were both part of the Iron Confederacy and the Three Fires Confederacy.

Othâkîwa (people from the water) or **Sauk** (French colonial name from the Anishinaabe word *Ozaagii, those at the outlet*); Algonquian language family. They were displaced from their homelands in Wisconsin, where they were rivals with the Illiniwek, and now live in Iowa, Oklahoma and Kansas.

Peeyankihšia (splitting off) or **Piankashaw** (colonial spelling); Algonquian language family. The Peeyankihšia were part of the Myaamiaki but lived separately. However, they joined the Myaamiaki and other Great

Lakes Indigenous peoples in the Northwestern Confederacy following the American War of Independence.

Penawapskewi (people of where the white rocks extend out) or **Penobscot** (colonial spelling); Algonquian language family. They are part of the Wabanaki Confederacy with the Wôbanakiak (Wabanaki), Mi'kmaq, Wolastoqey (Maliseet) and Peskotomahkati (Passamaquoddy) peoples.

Pennacook (at the bottom of the hill); Algonquian language family. The Pennacook, who lived in a network of villages, were close to the Wabanaki Confederacy, without officially being part of it.

Piscataway (long river with a fork) or **Conoy** (colonial name); Algonquian language family.

Powathan (at the waterfalls); Algonquian language family. The Powathan Confederacy regrouped thirty tribes within the territory of Tsenacommacah (densely inhabited land) at the end of the sixteenth century. This was after the first English colony, Jonestown, was established on their territory in 1607, causing many Powathan people to die from infectious diseases, before the English outright enslaved them in 1676.

Shaawanwaki (people from the warm south) or **Shawnee** (colonial name); Algonquian language family. In the seventeenth century, the Shaawanwaki engaged in a dispute over the Shenandoah Valley with the Rotinonhsión:ni. During the Northwest Indian War (1785–1795), their leader Tecumseh led a large Indigenous confederation to fight the encroachment of American settlers in Ohio. In the nineteenth century, they were forcibly removed to Oklahoma.

Shinnecock (people of the stony shore); Algonquian language family, closely related to the Montaukett dialect. The Shinnecock were wampum makers.

Tionontati (people among the hills), **Khionontateronons** (where the mountain stands) or **Petun** (colonial name, after an Iroquoian word for tobacco); Iroquoian language family. The Tionontati were very close to the Wendat (Huron) people, whom they joined after being defeated by the Rotinonhsión:ni in the mid–seventeenth century, becoming the Huron-Petun people, also known as the Wyandot.

Wangunk (the people at the bend in the river) or **Mattabesset** (colonial name, after the name of a village); Algonquian language family.

Wappinger (unknown origin); Algonquian language family.

Wendat (island dwellers, in reference to a peninsula in the Georgian Bay of Lake Huron), **Wyandot** (once they were joined by the Tionontati) or **Huron** (French colonial name, possibly in reference to hairstyles resembling a boar's head); Iroquoian language family. The Wyandot formed a confederacy comprising five nations: the Attignawantan (people of the bear), the Attigneenongnahac (people of the cord), the Arendarhonon (people of the rock), the Tahontaenrat (people of the deer) and the Ataronchronon (people of the marshes, who may have been a division of the Attignawantan rather than a distinct nation). Many of its members were absorbed by the Rotinonhsión:ni after the Beaver Wars and the epidemics in the mid–seventeenth century, while others resettled in Wendake, near Québec City, or westwards in Ohio, Oklahoma, Michigan and Kansas, where they are known as the Wyandot.

Wenrohronon (people of the place of the floating film) or **Wenro**; Iroquoian language family. Living near Niagara Falls, the Wenrohronon were conquered and absorbed by the Rotinonhsión:ni in 1643.

Wôbanakiak (people of the land of dawn), **Wabanaki** or **Abenaki**; Algonquian language family. The Wôbanakiak are part of the Wabanaki Confederacy.

Wôpanâak (people of the dawn, from Lenape language) or **Wampanoag**; Algonquian language family. With their leader Metacom and allies, such as the Nipamaug, the Wôpanâak fought against New England colonists in the 1670s, during King Philip's War.

Yesañ (people) or **Tutelo** (colonial name, from the Algonquin variant of the Iroquois name for Virginia Siouan speakers, Toderochrone); Siouan language family. After allegedly having been forced to leave Kentucky for Virginia because of Rotinonhsión:ni attacks, the Yesañ were adopted by the Cayuga in 1753 and moved with them to Canada after the American War of Independence.

Note

1   This list is not exhaustive, as it does not include denominations for smaller Indigenous groups or peoples outside the territories displayed on the map. When possible, it uses endonyms, i.e., names that Indigenous peoples use for themselves.

Pronunciation Guide[*]

Vowels	English example
A, a	Father
E, e	Red
I, i	Eve
O, o	Open
En, en	Entrée
On, on	Noon

The "o" sound is similar to the Spanish pronunciation of "o"
The "en" and "on" are nasal sounds, sounded out through the nose

Vowels can also have diacritic marks.
á / é / í / ó / én / ón
—an accent acute means you quickly stress on that part of the word.

á: /é: / í: / ó: / én: / ón:
—an accent acute plus a colon means you stress and hold the vowel sound.

à: / è: / ì: / ò: / èn: / òn:
—a grave accent plus a colon means you stress, hold and bring down the vowel sound.

---

[*] Audio recordings of Kanien'kehá:ka words read by Kaniehtiio Horn are available at http://www.ruedorion.ca/mohawk

Consonants	English example
H, h	Hat
I, i	Yes
K, k	Girl, Kite (sounds between "k" and "g")
N, n	No
R, r	Rojo (similar to the Spanish "r", but without the rolling)
S, s	Zen, Sea
T, t	Day, Ten (sounds between "t" and "d")
W, w	Wind
'	Patent (glottal stop)

About the Contributors

An Introduction to Sovereignty and Survival
> Kahentinetha Rotiskarewake, Philippe Blouin, Malek Rasamny and Matt Peterson

Tekarontakeh Interview
> compiled and edited by Philippe Blouin and Malek Rasamny, revised by Alma Marie Diabo

Kakwirakeron Interview
> compiled and edited by Matt Peterson and Malek Rasamny

Kanasaraken Interview
> compiled and edited by Matt Peterson and Malek Rasamny

Ateronhiatakon Interview
> compiled and edited by Matt Peterson, Malek Rasamny and Philippe Blouin, including materials collected by Kanenhariyo Seth Lefort for Real People's Media

Basic Principles of the Kaianerehkó:wa
> Kahentinetha Rotiskarewake

The Iroquoian Use of Wampum
> Ateronhiatakon

I Am a Warrior
> Karhiio

Who Was Karoniaktajeh?
> Kahentinetha Rotiskarewake

Karoniaktajeh Remembered
> compiled by Kahentinetha Rotiskarewake

Ganienkeh Manifesto, Warrior's Handbook, Rebuilding the Iroquois Confederacy
> Karoniaktajeh

Mohawk Warrior History Timeline
> written by Philippe Blouin, revised by Eric Pouliot-Thisdale

Skakwatakwen—Concept Glossary
> definitions by Tekarontakeh, compiled and written by Philippe Blouin, spelling by Karonhiio Delaronde and Akwiratékha'

Place Names and Peoples' Names
> written and compiled by Karonhiio Delaronde, Rebekah Ingram and Philippe Blouin, graphic design by Mathieu Delhorbe, revised by Kahentinetha, Karennatha and Akwiratékha'

Pronunciation Guide
> Karonhiio Delaronde
> written in collaboration with the Louis Karonhiaktakeh Hall Foundation

Louis Karoniaktajeh Hall (1918–1993) was a prolific Kanien'kehá:ka painter and writer from Kahnawà:ke, whose work continues to inspire generations of Indigenous people today. A man of all trades, Karoniaktajeh worked as a butcher, a carpenter and a mason. Initially groomed for a life in the priesthood, *Karoniaktajeh*, meaning *on the edge of the sky*, began his life as a devout Christian, before later turning against what he saw as the fallacies of European religion and deciding to reintegrate himself into the traditional longhouse and to help revive "the old ways". Appointed as the secretary of the Ganienkeh Council Fire, he became a prominent defender of Indigenous sovereignty and was instrumental in the reconstitution of the Rotihsken'rakéhte' (Mohawk Warrior Society). His distinctive artwork includes the iconic Unity flag, which still symbolizes Indigenous pride across Turtle Island (North America). His legacy as a reviver and innovator of traditional Mohawk culture includes his works *The Warrior's Handbook* (1979) and *Rebuilding the Iroquois Confederacy* (1980). Both of these texts, which served during their time as a political and cultural call to arms for Indigenous communities across Turtle Island, were initially printed by hand and distributed in secret.

Kahentinetha Rotiskarewake is a Kanien'kehá:ka from the Bear Clan in Kahnawà:ke. Initially working in the fashion industry, Kahentinetha went on to play a key role as speaker and writer in the Indigenous resistance, a role which she has fulfilled consistently for the last six decades. During this time, she witnessed and took part in numerous struggles, including the blockade of the Akwesasne border crossing in 1968. She has published several books, including *Mohawk Warrior Three: The Trial of Lasagna, Noriega & 20–20* (Owera Books, 1994), and has been in charge of running the Mohawk Nation News service since the Oka Crisis in 1990. She now cares for her twenty children, grandchildren and great-grandchildren. *Kahentinetha* means *she who is always at the forefront*.

Philippe Blouin writes, translates and studies political anthropology and philosophy in Tionitiohtià:kon (Montréal). His current PhD research at McGill University seeks to understand and share the teachings of the Teiohá:te (Two Row Wampum) to build decolonial alliances. His work has been published in *Liaisons*, *Stasis* and *PoLAR*. He also wrote an afterword to George Sorel's *Reflections on Violence*.

Matt Peterson is an organizer at Woodbine, an experimental space in New York City. He is the co-director of The Native and the Refugee, a multimedia documentary project on American Indian reservations and Palestinian refugee camps.

Malek Rasamny co-directed the research project The Native and the Refugee and the feature film *Spaces of Exception*. He is currently a doctoral candidate in the department of Social Anthropology and Ethnology at the Ecole des hautes études en sciences sociales (EHESS) in Paris.

Index

"Passim" (literally "scattered") indicates intermittent discussion of a topic over a cluster of pages.

ABOUT PM PRESS

PM Press is an independent, radical publisher of books and media to educate, entertain, and inspire. Founded in 2007 by a small group of people with decades of publishing, media, and organizing experience, PM Press amplifies the voices of radical authors, artists, and activists. Our aim is to deliver bold political ideas and vital stories to all walks of life and arm the dreamers to demand the impossible. We have sold millions of copies of our books, most often one at a time, face to face. We're old enough to know what we're doing and young enough to know what's at stake. Join us to create a better world.

PM Press
PO Box 23912
Oakland, CA 94623
www.pmpress.org

PM Press in Europe
europe@pmpress.org
www.pmpress.org.uk

FRIENDS OF PM PRESS

These are indisputably momentous times—the financial system is melting down globally and the Empire is stumbling. Now more than ever there is a vital need for radical ideas.

In the many years since its founding—and on a mere shoestring—PM Press has risen to the formidable challenge of publishing and distributing knowledge and entertainment for the struggles ahead. With hundreds of releases to date, we have published an impressive and stimulating array of literature, art, music, politics, and culture. Using every available medium, we've succeeded in connecting those hungry for ideas and information to those putting them into practice.

Friends of PM allows you to directly help impact, amplify, and revitalize the discourse and actions of radical writers, filmmakers, and artists. It provides us with a stable foundation from which we can build upon our early successes and provides a much-needed subsidy for the materials that can't necessarily pay their own way. You can help make that happen—and receive every new title automatically delivered to your door once a month—by joining as a Friend of PM Press. And, we'll throw in a free T-shirt when you sign up.

Here are your options:

- **$30 a month** Get all books and pamphlets plus 50% discount on all webstore purchases

- **$40 a month** Get all PM Press releases (including CDs and DVDs) plus 50% discount on all webstore purchases

- **$100 a month** Superstar—Everything plus PM merchandise, free downloads, and 50% discount on all webstore purchases

For those who can't afford $30 or more a month, we have **Sustainer Rates** at $15, $10, and $5. Sustainers get a free PM Press T-shirt and a 50% discount on all purchases from our website.

Your Visa or Mastercard will be billed once a month, until you tell us to stop. Or until our efforts succeed in bringing the revolution around. Or the financial meltdown of Capital makes plastic redundant. Whichever comes first.

500 Years of Indigenous Resistance

Gord Hill

ISBN: 978-1-60486-106-8
$12.00   96 pages

The history of the colonization of the Americas by
Europeans is often portrayed as a mutually beneficial
process, in which "civilization" was brought to the Natives,
who in return shared their land and cultures. A more
critical history might present it as a genocide in which
Indigenous peoples were helpless victims, overwhelmed and awed by European
military power. In reality, neither of these views is correct.

500 Years of Indigenous Resistance is more than a history of European colonization
of the Americas. In this slim volume, Gord Hill chronicles the resistance by
Indigenous peoples, which limited and shaped the forms and extent of colonialism.
This history encompasses North and South America, the development of nation-
states, and the resurgence of Indigenous resistance in the post-WW2 era.

*Gord Hill is a member of the Kwakwaka'wakw nation on the Northwest Coast. Writer,
artist, and militant, he has been involved in Indigenous resistance, anti-colonial and
anti-capitalist movements for many years, often using the pseudonym Zig Zag.*

Red Nation Rising: From Bordertown Violence to Native Liberation

Nick Estes, Melanie K. Yazzie, Jennifer Nez Denetdale, and David Correia with a Foreword by Radmilla Cody and Brandon Benallie

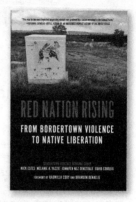

ISBN: 978-1-62963-831-7 (paperback)
      978-1-629639-062 (hardcover)
$17.95/$39.95   176 pages

Red Nation Rising is the first book ever to investigate and explain the violent dynamics of bordertowns. Bordertowns are white-dominated towns and cities that operate according to the same political and spatial logics as all other American towns and cities. The difference is that these settlements get their name from their location at the borders of current-day reservation boundaries, which separate the territory of sovereign Native nations from lands claimed by the United States.

Bordertowns came into existence when the first US military forts and trading posts were strategically placed along expanding imperial frontiers to extinguish indigenous resistance and incorporate captured indigenous territories into the burgeoning nation-state. To this day, the US settler state continues to wage violence on Native life and land in these spaces out of desperation to eliminate the threat of Native presence and complete its vision of national consolidation "from sea to shining sea." This explains why some of the most important Native-led rebellions in US history originated in bordertowns and why they are zones of ongoing confrontation between Native nations and their colonial occupier, the United States.

Despite this rich and important history of political and material struggle, little has been written about bordertowns. *Red Nation Rising* marks the first effort to tell these entangled histories and inspire a new generation of Native freedom fighters to return to bordertowns as key front lines in the long struggle for Native liberation from US colonial control. This book is a manual for navigating the extreme violence that Native people experience in reservation bordertowns and a manifesto for indigenous liberation that builds on long traditions of Native resistance to bordertown violence.

"The borders racking our world are in constant motion and, like the explosive grinding of tectonic plates, the violence of this movement and resistance to it emerges most sharply at the edges. This essential volume brings together militant intellectuals to provide an accessible introduction to the violent encirclement of indigenous communities, and to provide crucial concept-weapons to deepen ongoing collective resistance."
—George Ciccariello-Maher, author of *Decolonizing Dialectics*

Wielding Words like Weapons: Selected Essays in Indigenism, 1995–2005

Ward Churchill
with a Foreword by Barbara Alice Mann

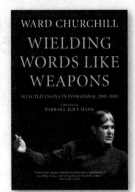

ISBN: 978-1-62963-101-1
$27.95   616 pages

Wielding Words like Weapons is a collection of acclaimed American Indian Movement activist-intellectual
Ward Churchill's essays in indigenism, selected from material written during the decade 1995–2005. It includes a range of formats, from sharply framed book reviews and equally pointed polemics and op-eds to more formal essays designed to reach both scholarly and popular audiences. The selection also represents the broad range of topics addressed in Churchill's scholarship, including the fallacies of archeological and anthropological orthodoxy such as the insistence of "cannibalogists" that American Indians were traditionally maneaters, Hollywood's cinematic degradations of native people, questions of American Indian identity, the historical and ongoing genocide of North America's native peoples and the systematic distortion of the political and legal history of U.S.-Indian relations.

Less typical of Churchill's oeuvre are the essays commemorating Cherokee anthropologist Robert K. Thomas and Yankton Sioux legal scholar and theologian Vine Deloria Jr. More unusual still is his profoundly personal effort to come to grips with the life and death of his late wife, Leah Renae Kelly, thereby illuminating in very human terms the grim and lasting effects of Canada's residential schools upon the country's indigenous peoples.

A foreword by Seneca historian Barbara Alice Mann describes the sustained efforts by police and intelligence agencies as well as university administrators and other academic adversaries to discredit or otherwise "neutralize" both the man and his work. Also included are both the initial "stream-of-consciousness" version of Churchill's famous—or notorious—"little Eichmanns" opinion piece analyzing the causes of the attacks on 9/11, as well as the counterpart essay in which his argument was fully developed.

"Compellingly original, with the powerful eloquence and breadth of knowledge we have come to expect from Churchill's writing."
—Howard Zinn

"This is insurgent intellectual work—breaking new ground, forging new paths, engaging us in critical resistance."
—bell hooks

Liberating Sápmi: Indigenous Resistance in Europe's Far North

Gabriel Kuhn

ISBN: 978-1-62963-712-9
$17.00   220 pages

The Sámi, who have inhabited Europe's far north for thousands of years, are often referred to as the continent's "forgotten people." With Sápmi, their traditional homeland, divided between four nation-states—Norway, Sweden, Finland, and Russia—the Sámi have experienced the profound oppression and discrimination that characterize the fate of indigenous people worldwide: their lands have been confiscated, their beliefs and values attacked, their communities and families torn apart. Yet the Sámi have shown incredible resilience, defending their identity and their territories and retaining an important social and ecological voice—even if many, progressives and leftists included, refuse to listen.

Liberating Sápmi is a stunning journey through Sápmi and includes in-depth interviews with Sámi artists, activists, and scholars boldly standing up for the rights of their people. In this beautifully illustrated work, Gabriel Kuhn, author of over a dozen books and our most fascinating interpreter of global social justice movements, aims to raise awareness of the ongoing fight of the Sámi for justice and self-determination. The first accessible English-language introduction to the history of the Sámi people and the first account that focuses on their political resistance, this provocative work gives irrefutable evidence of the important role the Sámi play in the resistance of indigenous people against an economic and political system whose power to destroy all life on earth has reached a scale unprecedented in the history of humanity.

The book contains interviews with Mari Boine, Harald Gaski, Ann-Kristin Håkansson, Aslak Holmberg, Maxida Märak, Stefan Mikaelsson, May-Britt Öhman, Synnøve Persen, Øyvind Ravna, Niillas Somby, Anders Sunna, and Suvi West.

"I'm highly recommending Gabriel Kuhn's book Liberating Sápmi *to anyone seeking to understand the world of today through indigenous eyes. Kuhn concisely and dramatically opens our eyes to little-known Sápmi history, then in the perfect follow-up brings us up to date with a unique collection of interviews with a dozen of today's most brilliant contemporary Sámi voices. Bravo."*
—Buffy Sainte-Marie, Cree, singer-songwriter

Pacifism as Pathology: Reflections on the Role of Armed Struggle in North America Third Edition

Ward Churchill and Michael Ryan with a Preface by Ed Mead and Foreword by Dylan Rodríguez

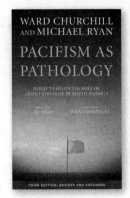

ISBN: 978-1-62963-224-7
$15.95   192 pages

Pacifism as Pathology has long since emerged as a dissident classic. Originally written during the mid-1980s, the seminal essay "Pacifism as Pathology" was prompted by veteran activist Ward Churchill's frustration with what he diagnosed as a growing—and deliberately self-neutralizing—"hegemony of nonviolence" on the North American left. The essay's publication unleashed a raging debate among activists in both the U.S. and Canada, a significant result of which was Michael Ryan's penning of a follow-up essay reinforcing Churchill's premise that nonviolence, at least as the term is popularly employed by white "progressives," is inherently counterrevolutionary, adding up to little more than a manifestation of its proponents' desire to maintain their relatively high degrees of socioeconomic privilege and thereby serving to stabilize rather than transform the prevailing relations of power.

This short book challenges the pacifist movement's heralded victories—Gandhi in India, 1960s antiwar activists, even Martin Luther King Jr.'s civil rights movement—suggesting that their success was in spite of, rather than because of, their nonviolent tactics. Churchill also examines the Jewish Holocaust, pointing out that the overwhelming response of Jews was nonviolent, but that when they did use violence they succeeded in inflicting significant damage to the nazi war machine and saving countless lives.

As relevant today as when they first appeared, Churchill's and Ryan's trailblazing efforts were first published together in book form in 1998. Now, along with the preface to that volume by former participant in armed struggle/political prisoner Ed Mead, new essays by both Churchill and Ryan, and a powerful new foreword by leading oppositionist intellectual Dylan Rodríguez, these vitally important essays are being released in a fresh edition.

"Although Churchill couches his psychological analysis in much more polite terms than I would, he believes that some white upper-middle-class activists are deeply conflicted about whether they really want to dismantle capitalism and give up their position of privilege."
—*Greanville Post*

The Art of Freedom: A Brief History of the Kurdish Liberation Struggle

Havin Guneser with an
Introduction by Andrej Grubačić and
Interview by Sasha Lilley

ISBN: 978-1-62963-781-5 (paperback)
        978-1-62963-907-9
$15.95/$39.95   192 pages

The Revolution in Rojava captured the imagination of the Left sparking a worldwide interest in the Kurdish Freedom Movement. *The Art of Freedom* demonstrates that this explosive movement is firmly rooted in several decades of organized struggle.

In 2018, one of the most important spokespersons for the struggle of Kurdish Freedom, Havin Guneser, held three groundbreaking seminars on the historical background and guiding ideology of the movement. Much to the chagrin of career academics, the theoretical foundation of the Kurdish Freedom Movement is far too fluid and dynamic to be neatly stuffed into an ivory-tower filing cabinet. A vital introduction to the Kurdish struggle, *The Art of Freedom* is the first English-language book to deliver a distillation of the ideas and sensibilities that gave rise to the most important political event of the twenty-first century.

The book is broken into three sections: "Critique and Self-Critique: The rise of the Kurdish freedom movement from the rubbles of two world wars" provides an accessible explanation of the origins and theoretical foundation of the movement. "The Rebellion of the Oldest Colony: Jineology—the Science of Women" describes the undercurrents and nuance of the Kurdish women's movement and how they have managed to create the most vibrant and successful feminist movement in the Middle East. "Democratic Confederalism and Democratic Nation: Defense of Society Against Societycide" deals with the attacks on the fabric of society and new concepts beyond national liberation to counter it. Centering on notions of "a shared homeland" and "a nation made up of nations," these rousing ideas find deep international resonation.

Havin Guneser has provided an expansive definition of freedom and democracy and a road map to help usher in a new era of struggle against capitalism, imperialism, and the State.

"Havin Guneser is not just the world's leading authority on the thought of Abdullah Öcalan; she is a profound, sensitive, and challenging revolutionary thinker with a message the world desperately needs to hear."
—David Graeber author of *Debt: The First 500 Years* and *Bullshit Jobs: A Theory*

Building Free Life: Dialogues with Öcalan

Edited by International Initiative

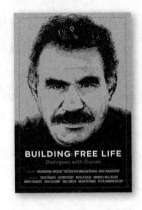

ISBN: 978-1-62963-704-4 (paperback)
       978-1-62963-764-8 (hardcover)
$20.00/$49.95   256 pages

From Socrates to Antonio Gramsci, imprisoned philosophers have marked the history of thought and changed how we view power and politics. From his solitary jail cell, Abdullah Öcalan has penned daringly innovative works that give profuse evidence of his position as one of the most significant thinkers of our day. His prison writings have mobilized tens of thousands of people and inspired a revolution in the making in Rojava, northern Syria, while also penetrating the insular walls of academia and triggering debate and reflection among countless scholars.

So how do you engage in a meaningful dialogue with Abdullah Öcalan when he has been held in total isolation since April 2015? You compile a book of essays written by a globally diverse cast of the most imaginative luminaries of our time, send it to Öcalan's jailers, and hope that they deliver it to him.

Featured in this extraordinary volume are over a dozen writers, activists, dreamers, and scholars whose ideas have been investigated in Öcalan's own writings. Now these same people have the unique opportunity to enter into a dialogue with his ideas. Building Free Life is a rich and wholly original exploration of the most critical issues facing humanity today. In the broad sweep of this one-of-a-kind dialogue, the contributors explore topics ranging from democratic confederalism to women's revolution, from the philosophy of history to the crisis of the capitalist system, from religion to Marxism and anarchism, all in an effort to better understand the liberatory social forms that are boldly confronting capitalism and the state.

Contributors include: Shannon Brincat, Radha D'Souza, Mechthild Exo, Damian Gerber, Barry K. Gills, Muriel González Athenas, David Graeber, Andrej Grubačić, John Holloway, Patrick Huff, Donald H. Matthews, Thomas Jeffrey Miley, Antonio Negri, Norman Paech, Ekkehard Sauermann, Fabian Scheidler, Nazan Üstündağ, Immanuel Wallerstein, Peter Lamborn Wilson, and Raúl Zibechi.

There can be no boundaries or restrictions for the development of thought. Thus, in the midst of different realities—from closed prisons to open-air prisons— the human mind will find a way to seek the truth. Building Free Life stands as a monument of radical thought, a testament of resilience, and a searchlight illuminating the impulse for freedom.

Zapatista Stories for Dreaming Another World

Subcomandante Marcos
Edited and translated by Colectivo
Relámpago/Lightning Collective with a
Foreword by JoAnn Wypijewski

ISBN: 978-1-62963-970-3
$16.95   160 pages

In this gorgeous collection of allegorical stories,
Subcomandante Marcos, idiosyncratic spokesperson of the Zapatistas, has
provided "an accidental archive" of a revolutionary group's struggle against
neoliberalism. For thirty years, the Zapatistas have influenced and inspired
movements worldwide, showing that another world is possible. They have infused
left politics with a distinct imaginary—and an imaginative, literary, or poetic
dimension—organizing horizontally, outside and against the state, and with a
profound respect for difference as a source of political insight, not division. With
commentaries that illuminate their historical, political, and literary contexts and an
introduction by the translators, this timeless, elegiac volume is perfect for lovers of
literature and lovers of revolution.

*"From the beating heart of Mesoamerica the old gods speak to Old Antonio, a glasses-
wearing, pipe-smoking beetle who studies neoliberalism, and both tell their tales
to Subcomandante Marcos who passes them on to us: the stories of the Zapatistas'
revolutionary struggles from below and to the left. The Colectivo Relámpago (Lightning
Collective), based in Amherst, Massachusetts, translates and comments with bolts of
illumination zigzagging across cultures and nations, bringing bursts of laughter and
sudden charges of hot-wired political energy. It seems like child's play, yet it's almost
divine!"*
—Peter Linebaugh, author of *Red Round Globe Hot Burning*

*"This is a beautiful, inspired project. In a joyful Zapatista gesture readers will welcome,
this volume invites us to play, to walk on different, and even contrary paths through
smooth and crystalline translations that bring these 'other stories' to life. The
translators' commentaries preserve a delicate balance of expertise and autonomy as
they illuminate the historical, political, and cultural forces that provoked the stories'
creation. Among these forces are Zapatista women, whom the translators rightly
dignify in their meticulous and provocative introduction. This volume is a gift to so
many of us as we (attempt to) bring the Zapatista imagination to our students and
organizing communities."*
—Michelle Joffroy, associate professor of Spanish and Latin American & Latino
Studies, Smith College and co-director of Domestic Workers Make History